CONTEMPORARY ADULTHOOD

JEFFREY S. TURNER

DONALD B. HELMS

Mitchell College

1979

W. B. SAUNDERS COMPANY *Philadelphia* • *London* • *Toronto*

W. B. Saunders Company: West Washington Square
Philadelphia, PA 19105

1 St. Anne's Road
Eastbourne, East Sussex BN21 3UN, England

1 Goldthorne Avenue
Toronto, Ontario M8Z 5T9, Canada

Library of Congress Cataloging in Publication Data

Turner, Jeffrey S

Contemporary adulthood.

1. Young adults.   2. Adulthood.   3. Retirement.   I.
Helms, Donald B., joint author.   II. Title.

HQ799.5.T87   301.43′4   77-11356

ISBN 0-7216-8935-3

Contemporary Adulthood   ISBN   0-7216-8935-3

Last digit is the print number: 9   8   7   6   5   4   3   2   1

Dedicated to our wives, who have made adulthood a beautifully shared experience.

Nancy G. Turner

Molly A. Helms

PREFACE

To know how to grow old is the master-work of wisdom and one of the most difficult chapters in the great art of living.

Amiel, *Journal,* 1874

Aging is a lifelong process that everyone experiences. Learning how to age successfully and adapting to the developmental tasks which mark the path of adult life are challenges that are formidable in scope. This book is an attempt to explain the dynamics behind growing old and the nature of adulthood as it exists in contemporary society.

For the most part, adult psychology is a newly emerging discipline, and only recently have academic institutions offered courses focusing on the later portions of the life cycle. We have attempted to assemble and organize ideas, theories, experimental data, and even folklore from many diverse sources into a meaningful body of knowledge. One of our primary objectives was to produce a readable, comprehensive, and interesting text that would become a classroom companion for both the professor and the student.

As an introductory-level text, *Contemporary Adulthood* is organized so that uniform coverage is given to the stages of early, middle, and late adulthood as well as death, the final stage of the life cycle. As such, *Contemporary Adulthood* can be used as a supplement to any childhood and adolescence text to offer complete coverage of the life span or as the primary text for those courses focusing strictly on adulthood and aging.

The major sections of this book are divided into relatively small, compact units rather than longer, more unwieldy chapters. Because of the structure of these units, professors can select a topic (e.g., Personality and Social Learning) and analyze it via a chronological approach, a topical approach, or a combination of both. Whatever approach is used, it is our hope that readers will gain knowledge about adulthood and aging and, in the process, acquire more insight into their own adult lives.

Many individuals have contributed to the overall development of this book. To our reviewers we extend our deepest appreciation, since their ideas, suggestions, and insight provided us with direction from the very beginning. In particular we would like to acknowledge the contributions of Dr. James Booth of Philadelphia Community College, Dr. Merv Dissinger of Rider College, Dr. Therese Howe of the University of Missouri at St. Louis, Dr. Robert Pasen of William

Rainey Harpur College, Dr. Bernard S. Sadowski of the University of Washington, and Dr. Dennis Thompson of Georgia State University.

We are especially indebted to the staff of the W.B. Saunders Company. We owe special thanks to Baxter Venable, Psychology Editor, who played an instrumental role in the conception, development, and eventual publication of *Contemporary Adulthood*. His insight, creativity, and limitless enthusiasm—but most of all his support—were sources of continual inspiration. The dedicated and impeccable work of Mrs. Teddy Dunbar, Assistant to the Psychology Editor, proved to be indispensable as the book gradually evolved. Special acknowledgment is also extended to Lillian Rodberg, copy editor, Lorraine Battista of the Design Department, Tom O'Connor and Frank Polizzano of the Production Department, and Donna Cutler, who prepared the index.

Our appreciation and special acknowledgment is also given to Molly Helms, who typed the final manuscript and painstakingly proofread the entire book. Her ability to meet deadlines faithfully, decipher frequently illegible handwriting, and offer constructive observations along the way were of irreplaceable value.

Finally, to our families and loved ones go our most heartfelt thanks. While publishing a book reaps its share of rewards, the long hours associated with researching and writing frequently represent a lonely pursuit. Without the love and understanding that come from our wives, children, relatives, and friends, this project could never have been nurtured. For their gentle patience and continual encouragement, we are indebted.

JEFFREY S. TURNER

DONALD B. HELMS

New London, Connecticut

CONTENTS

UNIT 1

THE SCOPE OF ADULT PSYCHOLOGY

1

Introduction

Adult psychology is a relatively new, emerging extension of developmental psychology. As a systematic field of study, it attempts to examine the physical, intellectual, social, and personal characteristics of human beings during the adult years.

In the past few decades, considerable time, money, and research emphasis have been spent on studying child development. Less emphasis has been placed on studying adolescent behavior and, with the possible exception of the field of gerontology, still less attention has been given to the study of adulthood. This emphasis upon childhood is somewhat paradoxical, since adulthood is the longest and most significant portion of the life cycle (Bischof, 1976). However, a growing number of developmental psychologists maintain that adulthood is the most critical phase of the life span. At the very least, adulthood is a period of active and systematic change (Gould, 1975).

Birren (1964) suggests that the key events in adult life, such as marriage, childbirth, change of occupation, and retirement, are without any directly equivalent events in childhood and consequently need separate attention and investigation. More and more social scientists are devoting their time and energy to the study of adult development. Consequently, revised theories of personality and theories of psychological adaptation are emerging. Simultaneously, we are increasing our knowledge of the various processes of social accommodation that take place during adulthood (Neugarten, 1968).

This book is primarily intended to explain the nature of adulthood and aging in contemporary society. Before we turn our attention to some developmental stages of adulthood, namely the early, middle, and retirement years, let us examine some of the issues involved and the underlying dynamics of adulthood in general.

THE NECESSITY FOR EXPLORING ADULT DEVELOPMENT

There appear to be at least five trends in contemporary society that increase the need for exploring the nature of adulthood. Each will require careful examination from nearly all segments of society, particularly in the years to come. These trends include:

1. A lengthened life span, which has resulted in a growing number and proportion of older people;
2. More leisure time for adults, further increased in many cases by early retirement;
3. Better health and health care, and higher educational level of adults;
4. More emphasis on the quality of life in a society that is becoming more service-oriented; and
5. Greater tolerance of a variety of life styles for persons of all ages.

(Kimmel, 1976, p. 103)

STUDYING THE ADULT POPULATION

Studying adults presents more than its share of problems. As Bischof (1969) so aptly states, "[the researcher] cannot peek at them through one-way mirrors; they are most intelligent in ferreting out hidden meanings, and they demand explanations at times for problems and questions which psychologists themselves are not quite sure about." (p. 19) To be sure, investigators face a formidable challenge in their efforts to collect meaningful data.

In surveying past literature, one finds that some ideas regarding adult behavior were developed without the support of empirical evidence. In reference to the dangers inherent in such preconceptions, Deese (1972) warns:

> The trouble with theoretical preconceptions in developmental studies is the assumption that a point of view is correct simply because it makes a sensible story. This is the problem of myth versus science. Even some highly developed and rigorous theories of developmental psychology require more data than they explain. A given theory may make a good story about how things got to be the way they are, but if it has little empirical content, it does not provide a plausible basis for action.
>
> (pp. 84–85)

Besides preconceptions, cultural and societal myths regarding adults have been passed down from generation to generation. For example, some social groups believe that at a certain age (e.g., age 65) a person is "over the hill" and should be "put out to pasture."

Figure 1–1. Developmental psychologists study the complete life span.

Ralph Guillumette
Pictures. Photograph
by Hella Hamid.

Attitudes such as these impelled members of the older generation to form organizations such as the Gray Panthers to challenge the myth that the elderly should be kept out of the way to play bingo and shuffleboard. They advocate a life-style of independence and action. This is but one example of how society must continually reexamine its perceptions of the various phases of the life cycle. Adult psychology must separate the wheat from the chaff, the facts from the societal myths and preconceptions.

There appear to be other significant problems in studying adults. *Experimenter problems* exist when research analysts get caught up in their own aging processes. There is sometimes a gap between younger analysts, who desire to observe the "old folks", and older researchers, who may like to discover what others are like and perhaps match their findings with their own unique experiences. Although the research design is usually not affected by this age bias, some conclusions and summaries presented by younger analysts display negative overtones, whereas older analysts seem more sympathetic (Bischof, 1976).

Subject survival has always created some distortion of findings, but the adult population specialist may encounter greater difficulty. Because weaker subjects may die and the stronger may survive, it is not possible to equate samples of young and old subjects. As Bischof (1976) suggests, we have some effect of the "survival of the fittest":

> We may not be measuring the developmental changes in human lives. Not all of the original population is available to measure. Many of the characteristics of adults may be correlated with longevity rather than with what we think we are measuring. Though the good may or may not die young, if they do die young, they certainly die too soon to be subjects for adult studies.
>
> (pp. 45–46)

Bischof believes that survivors in life-span psychology research projects represent an elite group of individuals.

Two other research biases have to do with *sex* and *cultural-economic differences* (Bischof, 1976). In the past, particularly in the area of female sexual behavior, research was largely carried out by men. Although the findings presented were valuable, they may have reflected interviewer bias. Today, more and more women are becoming involved in psychological theory and research. Similarly, a researcher may be unsympathetic to poor people. Because many psychologists come from middle-class families, their backgrounds may not have prepared them to understand the dynamics of lower socioeconomic groups. Investigating extremely wealthy individuals also poses its share of obstacles. Consequently, many studies focus on middle-class people, who seem to be more cooperative and less resentful of the researcher than the poor or the wealthy.

METHODS OF STUDYING THE ADULT POPULATION

There are two basic approaches to studying the adult population, the *longitudinal method* and the *cross-sectional method*.

When using the *longitudinal method,* the analyst collects data on the *same group* of individuals at intervals over a considerable period (years and sometimes even decades). Let's suppose someone wanted to collect data concerning various facets of early adult development. The researcher employing the longitudinal method might begin studying a particular group at age 20. Follow-up studies would be made at fairly regular intervals until the subjects reached age 40. At each follow-up session, relevant data would be recorded, to be applied to the final research analysis.

Researchers using the *cross-sectional method* obtain comparative data from different groups of subjects more or less simultaneously. In studying adult development, then, the analyst would select a number of groups of subjects, aged (for example) 20, 25, 30, 35, and 40, and record the differences among the various age groups. The differences would then be analyzed.

Each method has its own advantages and disadvantages. For example, the cross-sectional approach is relatively inexpensive, easier to execute, and not overly time-consuming, but it sometimes overlooks individual changes, and it is contaminated with generational differences. The longitudinal method probably provides a fairly accurate picture of developmental changes within an individual, but this approach takes a long time, is generally expensive, and frequently suffers from subject attrition. Whichever method is used, the data are only as good as the measurement techniques used to obtain them, the premises behind their collection, and their interpretation.

STAGES IN ADULTHOOD

At what point in the life span does early adulthood end and middle age begin? When does one reach old age? To investigate developmental psychology, it is helpful to have systems of age classification. These systems, which psychologists have arranged and rearranged to fit their particular needs, are constructed primarily to help clarify and organize data.

Birren (1964) proposes that the stages of the human life cycle may be interpreted in various ways, and that classification systems use varying criteria. Thus, the same person might be classified as developing, mature, or senescent, depending on whether anatomical, physiological, psychological, or social criteria were being employed. Table 1–1 shows arbitrary stages of development proposed by Birren to reflect societal demands as well as psychological capacities.

TABLE 1–1   DEVELOPMENTAL PHASES OF HUMAN LIFE SPAN ACCORDING TO BIRREN (1964)

Period	Age
Infancy	2
Preschool years	2 to 5
Childhood	5 to 12
Adolescence	12 to 17
Early maturity	17 to 25
Maturity	25 to 50
Later maturity	50 to 75
Old age	75 and over

Perhaps the most complex interpretation of the phases of the life span was the classification system developed by Bromley (1966). This approach has 16 stages, including three preceding birth and an additional five prior to late adolescence (Table 1–2). Exactly half (eight) of the stages cover the first 15 years of life, while the other half describe the remaining 55 years (the average life expectancy). It is probable that more stages of early life have been recognized because, in the past, study of human development has concentrated on childhood and adolescence.

TABLE 1–2   DEVELOPMENTAL PHASES OF HUMAN LIFE SPAN ACCORDING TO BROMLEY (1966)

Period	Approximate Age
1. Zygote	conception
2. Embryo	up to 7 weeks
3. Fetus	7 weeks to birth
4. Birth	38 weeks
5. Infancy	birth to 18 months
6. Preschool	18 months to 5 years
7. Elementary	5 to 11 or 13 years
8. Puberty and senior high school	11 to 16
9. Late adolescence	16 to 21
10. Early adulthood	21 to 25
11. Middle adulthood	25 to 40
12. Late adulthood	40 to 60
13. Preretirement	60 to 65
14. Retirement	65 and over
15. Old age	70 and over
16. Senescence	terminal illness and death

A classification system stressing the importance of mastering developmental tasks appropriate to given age levels has been proposed by Havighurst (1972), who believes that certain developmental tasks "constitute healthy and satisfactory growth in our society." (p. 2) For example, infants and young children must learn to walk and talk, to distinguish right from wrong, and so forth. Adults, too, have developmental tasks appropriate to various stages of their personal and social growth. Havighurst suggests six developmental periods (Table 1–3).

TABLE 1–3   DEVELOPMENTAL PHASES OF HUMAN LIFE SPAN ACCORDING TO HAVIGHURST (1972)

Period	Age
Early childhood	birth to 5 or 6
Middle childhood	5 or 6 to 12 or 13
Adolescence	12 or 13 to 18
Early adulthood	18 to 35
Middle adulthood	35 to 60
Later maturity	60 and over

Erik Erikson (1963) classifies the life cycle into eight specific bipolar stages and, like Havighurst, feels that individuals must face new challenges as they progress through life. For Erikson, the key to harmonious personality development is being able to resolve toward the positive pole the psychosocial crisis inherent in each stage. Erikson's life stages are summarized in Table 1–4.

TABLE 1–4   DEVELOPMENTAL PHASES OF HUMAN LIFE SPAN ACCORDING TO ERIKSON (1963)

Crises	Approximate Age
Basic trust vs. mistrust	1
Autonomy vs. shame, doubt	2
Initiative vs. guilt	3 to 5
Industry vs. inferiority	6 to puberty
Identity vs. role confusion	adolescence
Intimacy vs. isolation	young adulthood
Generativity vs. stagnation	adulthood
Ego integrity vs. despair	maturity

Peanuts   By Schultz

Figure 1–2.   © 1976 United Features Syndicate, Inc.

STAGES OF ADULT DEVELOPMENT: A CONTEMPORARY ANALYSIS

Gail Sheehy (1976) and Roger Gould (1975) have also attempted to define the stages of adulthood. Although their theories are somewhat similar, it is interesting to compare the ideas they present. Sheehy, in her best-selling book, *Passages: Predictable Crises of Adult Life,* studied subjects ranging in age from 18 to 45 and combined her observations with the findings of other researchers in the field. She offers the analysis of adult development presented in Table 1–5.

Gould's five-year study of 524 adult men and women reveals that adults are far from being fully forged by adolescence. On the contrary, he proposes seven stages of growth and development during adulthood (Table 1–6).

TABLE 1–5   SHEEHY'S DEVELOPMENTAL STAGES

Stage	Approximate Age	Development(s)
1	18 to 22	Emancipation from parents; further identity formation.
2	22 to 28	Career and family involvement; accepting responsibilities of adult world.
3	28 to 32	Questioning of life-style chosen earlier; transitory period may prompt one to change careers, seek a divorce, remarry, etc.
4	32 to 39	"Settling down stage." Rational planning, i.e., buying a home, raising a family.
5	39 to 43	Midlife transition or crisis. Realistic analysis of idealistic goals and actual attainment. Need for reassessment of aspirations in life.
6	43 to 47	Reestablishing and renewing self-worth; satisfaction with one's life-style.

TABLE 1-6   GOULD'S DEVELOPMENTAL STAGES

Stage	Approximate Age	Development(s)
1	16 to 18	Desire to escape from parental dominance.
2	18 to 22	Leaving the family; general openness about the world; peer-group orientation.
3	22 to 28	Development of independence; commitment to children and career.
4	29 to 34	Questioning of self; role confusion. Marriages and careers vulnerable to dissatisfaction.
5	35 to 43	Period of urgency to attain life's goals; awareness of limited number of years left to reach earlier aspirations; goal realignment.
6	43 to 53	Settling down stage; acceptance of one's fate in life; greater appreciation of one's children as unique individuals.
7	53 to 60	More tolerant acceptance of past failures; less negativism toward family and friends; general mellowing.

There are numerous other developmental classification systems, each of which is both like and unlike those described here. Most of them share the same general interpretation of the period from infancy through adolescence, the major dispute centering on the age at which adolescence ends and adulthood begins. Most authors seem to believe that young adulthood begins at or near age 20.

Researchers also differ regarding both the dynamics of behavior and the age limits of "middle age". Some place the beginning of middle age as early as age 25; others, at age 30; still others, at age 35. In the past, many theorists have chosen age 40 as the commencement of middle age. (Historically, this has been the cultural standard if we are to judge by book titles—e.g., *Life Begins at Forty*—or popular consensus.)

The differences of opinion concerning age limits for developmental periods suggest that age classification systems are not without their share of limitations. Age alone is not an adequate criterion for stage classification, as one may easily observe by examining actuarial tables for life expectancy across cultures (see Table 1-7). What may be considered a youthful age in one culture may be viewed as middle age in another and quite elderly in a third. Differences in life expectancy at various historical periods also must be taken into consideration. In analyzing Figure 1-3, imagine the difficulty we would have in attempting to adapt our present-day age classification systems to life expectancies of the past.

Semantic problems also interfere when we try to translate age classifications from a historical standpoint. Consider the problems we face when attempting to understand the developmental period known as *childhood* as it existed in past centuries. In many cultures, right up through medieval times, there was no one word to capture this critical developmental stage, largely because the period of childhood as we know it today simply did not exist. In most cases,

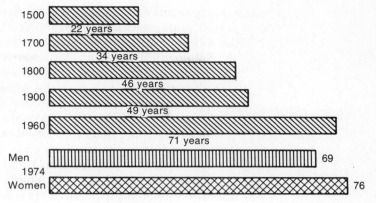

Figure 1–3. Changes in life expectancy. (Data from Irving Fisher, U. S. Public Health Service, and U. S. Department of Commerce, Bureau of the Census.)

TABLE 1–7   LIFE EXPECTANCY AT BIRTH FOR SELECTED COUNTRIES (1970 TO 1975)

37.3	Upper Volta (Africa)	62.0	Peru
39.7	Mali (Africa)	63.1	Brazil
40.5	Afghanistan	63.6	Chile
41.0	Chad	64.6	Mexico
41.0	Ethiopia	65.9	Yugoslavia
41.0	Nigeria	66.4	Venezuela
41.0	Somalia	66.9	Panama
43.5	Congo	68.2	Argentina
43.5	Liberia	69.0	Portugal
43.5	Ivory Coast	69.0	Finland
43.5	Niger	69.0	Cuba
44.3	Tanzania	70.2	Singapore
45.3	Saudia Arabia	70.2	Taiwan
46.8	Bolivia	70.2	Jamaica
47.5	Haiti	70.6	Belgium
48.1	Indonesia	70.6	United States
48.5	Ghana	70.9	Russia
50.0	Kenya	71.2	East Germany
50.0	Uganda	71.3	West Germany
50.5	Laos	71.3	Austria
50.6	Sudan	71.4	Switzerland
51.4	South Africa	71.4	Czechoslovakia
52.6	Nicaragua	71.6	Greece
52.9	Egypt	71.8	Hong Kong
53.0	China	72.1	Poland
53.0	Iran	72.2	Bulgaria
53.0	Viet Nam	72.2	Canada
53.5	Morocco	72.4	Great Britain
53.6	Algeria	72.4	Australia
53.9	Rhodesia	72.5	Puerto Rico
54.1	Guatemala	72.8	Italy
54.6	Iraq	72.9	Denmark
55.1	Libya	72.9	Japan
55.8	Syria	73.0	Ireland
59.1	Philippines	73.0	Israel
59.7	Ecuador	73.5	France
60.6	Mongolia	73.5	Norway
60.6	Korea (North and South)	75.3	Sweden
60.9	Colombia		

Adapted from *United Nations Monthly Bulletin of Statistics,* April 1971.

infancy was the term applied to the first six years of life. During this period, youngsters were kept at home in their mother's care to learn the folkways and mores of their culture.

Somewhere between the ages of six and nine, children for all intents and purposes entered *adulthood*. They either were sent directly forth to enter the workaday world or were given an apprenticeship to train them for a particular vocation (Aries, 1962). Remarkably, the developmental periods classified as middle childhood and part of adolescence were omitted, as the child began taking on adult responsibilities early in life.

We are further told by Aries (1962) that the term *youth* generally signified *the prime of one's life*. Youth, during the Middle Ages, was followed immediately by the stage referred to as *old age!* Moreover, at 20, an age when most young adults in modern society are still preparing for a career, William the Conquerer had already been victorious in the Battle of Normandy. William III (William of Orange) had led his troops in an invasion of the Netherlands when he was but 22. Charlemagne had recorded numerous victories in battles before he was crowned King of the Franks at age 26. There are young adults today who make significant and sometimes truly great contributions to society, but few, if any, are capable of shaping history as these individuals did. In contemporary western societies, it is far more likely that such feats will be accomplished by "older" adults.

As civilizations changed and technology progressed, the lives of humans changed also. With the advent of more complex divisions of labor, additional training and education were needed for job preparation, a factor that extended the developmental periods we refer to today as childhood and adolescence. Adulthood began to assume a new identity. Still later, with better medical care and more balanced nutrition, the life span itself lengthened. With this change in life expectancy, our view of the various "stages" of life began to alter considerably.

THE PROSPECTS FOR LIVING EVEN LONGER

The biology of aging is no better understood today than was the circulation of the blood before William Harvey. "We probably age because we run out of evolutionary program," according to Dr. Alexander Comfort, director of the Medical Research Council Group on Aging at University College, London. "In this we resemble a space probe that has been 'designed' by selection to pass Mars, but that has no further built-in instructions once it has done so, and no components specifically produced to last longer than that. It will travel on, but the failure rate in its guidance and control mechanisms will steadily increase—and this failure of homeostasis, or self-righting, is exactly what we see in the aging organism."

Until recently, Dr. Comfort doubted that these built-in instructions could soon be al-

tered, or the components made to last longer. Because of advances in genetics and molecular biology, however, he now believes that some method to reduce the rate of aging and to extend vigorous life by at least 15 years will be discovered within the next two decades. This extension would be in addition to the roughly five-to-seven-year increase in average life expectancy that will take place when medicine conquers cancer and vascular diseases.

More than 20 different highly speculative theories of aging are now being tested in scientific laboratories round the world. The method or methods by which the human life-span will be extended depend on which of these theories turns out to be correct. Some of them have to do with genetic engineering—attempts to alter the program of the cell by changing the coding on the DNA molecule. But nongenetic theories will probably pay off sooner. One current favorite holds that aging occurs because certain giant molecules in human cells eventually get bound together. These immobile aggregations clog the cells, reduce their efficiency, and eventually cause them to die. In Wisconsin, Dr. Johan Bjorksten is trying to find suitable enzymes, most likely from soil bacteria, that will reduce these massed molecules to small fragments that could be excreted from the cells. Such enzymes would probably be injected daily into the body with a hypodermic syringe; if the injections were begun early enough, the result might increase a man's life-span by 30 years.

The "free radical" theory of aging, if proved correct, would probably lead to a simpler method of rejuvenation. Free radicals are fragments of molecules with a high electrical charge—which by their oxidizing properties can cause changes in the body such as hardening of the arteries. An antioxidant, which can be produced cheaply and taken in pills, is supposed to deactivate the free radicals, thereby retarding the aging process. One such antioxidant, BHT, has already dramatically increased the life-span of mice by 50 per cent.

Even today the population over 75 in the U.S. is increasing at two and a half times the rate of the general population. If the average life-span is significantly further increased,

the population would indeed become aged, a trend which would be accelerated by a drop in the birth rate. As to vigor, when the breakthrough comes in aging research, people in their seventies and eighties should have the energy of those in their fifties and sixties today. Ideally this would produce a greater number of selfless, highly educated wisemen who could undertake complex new projects for the benefit of mankind. But few believe that it would work this way. Most observers suggest that increased longevity would only magnify today's ambiguities and uncertainties in defining the role of the elderly.

Would vigorous octogenarians keep the reins of politics, business and family finances, frustrating the powerless younger generations? Or would they be pushed out of power and wander around, bitter and disgruntled, unable even to talk the same language as their juniors, like Swift's awful immortals, the struldbrugs? Would conflict between generations supersede hostility between classes and races? How could insurance and pension plans continue payments for decades longer? Will aging control become as vital an issue as birth control? In short, the changes resulting from a drastic extension of the life-span, or even from a series of life-extending bonuses, may eventually exceed those brought about by splitting the atom or man's voyages to the moon.

Time, August 3, 1970, p. 52. Reprinted by permission from TIME, The Weekly Newsmagazine; Copyright Time, Inc., 1970.

PROCESSES AND THEORIES OF AGING

There are three different types of aging processes, *biological, psychological*, and *social* (Birren, 1964). The biological theory is perhaps the most obvious; it defines aging in terms of the individual's physiological functioning over time. Biological theories may focus on changes in vital (breathing) capacity, tissue structure, skeletal composition, (ossification), glucose metabolism, sensory capacity, or heart rate. A central concern of the biological aging theory is how long the organism will live. An example of a biological theory is the "wear and tear" interpretation of aging. Quite simply, it is stated that the organism, like a machine, will "wear out" over the duration of the life cycle. Aging, then, is the result of organ tissue deterioration.

Psychological aging involves a combination of factors including self-awareness, the individual's own perception of age, and the

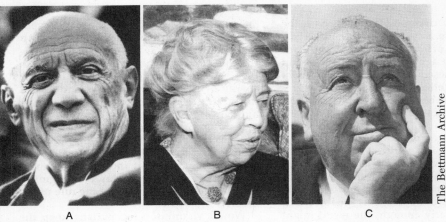

The Bettmann Archive

A   B   C

Figure 1–4. Aging is truly an individual affair. While some people lose their vitality in their fifties and sixties, others continue to enjoy an active and fulfilling life into their seventies and eighties, and beyond. *A*, Pablo Picasso. *B*, Eleanor Roosevelt. *C*, Alfred Hitchcock.

ability to adapt to age and social change. *Social* age refers to the individual's relation to society and to those in his or her immediate sphere.

As Birren (1964) describes it,

> Age is an important factor in determining how individuals behave in relation to one another, and within societies there are often elaborate age-status systems. The age grading of expected behavior is a long-evolving process in society, and it is only partly related to the biological and psychological characteristics of individuals at a given age.
>
> (p. 10)

SOCIAL AGE CLOCKS

A thought-provoking theory reflecting the social viewpoint of aging has been offered by Bernice Neugarten (1968). She suggests that each of us has a "social age clock" that is a reflection of his or her society. Society defines expectations concerning how people should behave at given ages or phases. For example, we generally expect an older couple at a rock music concert to react differently from adolescents attending the same event. We also expect such events as marriage and child-rearing to take place at certain ages.

Other factors affect the "social age clock", particularly socioeconomic backgrounds and the type of vocation one selects. Members of the blue-collar class seem to reach both middle and old age much sooner than white-collar workers. We may perceive one whose livelihood depends on intense physical labor as being "old" by age 30, whereas a professional person who is hired "to think" may appear to be still relatively youthful at age 65. This is one sense in which we find age not being the only criterion for developmental classification.

In formulating theories concerning the aging process, some researchers (Timiras, 1972) have emphasized the biological or genetic factors involved in aging, whereas others (Buhler, 1972) have chosen to stress psychological issues. Still others, such as Cowgill and Holmes (1972), are sociological in their analysis of aging. Some prefer to be eclectic in their theories, combining bits and pieces from each school of thought.

When theories of aging are discussed, the persistent question of whether adult characteristics are a continuation of earlier developmental stages or are separate, unique growth processes frequently arouses controversy. Those who consider adult characteristics to be unique to adult life may perceive them as being the accumulated effects of more or less random events (Birren, 1964). Advocates of the "continuing development" view are likely to hold a stage-theory concept of development, maintaining that the individual passes through a series of definite stages that are considered invariable and universal (Lerner, 1976).

The *developmental* or *stage* approach assumes that the end product is the result of past history (DiCaprio, 1974). The acquisitions of the past continue to exert an influence on the present. Such an analysis of growth is evident in writings of a number of developmental theorists, including Freud's Psychosexual Stage Theory and Piaget's Theory of Cognitive Development.

At variance with the stage approach is the *continuous growth* theory. According to DiCaprio (1974) this view holds that adult characteristics evolve through progressive differentiation and integration. Because of maturational growth and learning, there is continuing change. Slowly, new functions develop and are integrated within the existing structure through processes of steady transformation. Existing functions are usually transformed or superseded by new ones if development proceeds in a normal fashion. Adults then are not perceived as grown-up children but rather as distinctly different beings, requiring different concepts and principles from those that distinguished their earlier lives.

Summary

Adult psychology is a fairly recent division of developmental psychology. Presently, its primary focus is to examine critically the biological, personal, and social forces affecting the individual during the years of adulthood. A growing number of developmental psychologists believe that adulthood represents the most critical phase of the life span.

Studying the adult population poses numerous problems. It is necessary to avoid preconceptions and to challenge societal myths in order to obtain accurate data. Other difficulties include experimenter, survival, sex, and cultural-economic bias. Two popular methods used to obtain data from adults are the longitudinal and cross-sectional approaches. Each has advantages as well as disadvantages.

Numerous attempts have been made to chart the stages of adulthood. Psychologists such as Birren, Bromley, Havighurst, and Erikson have classified stages throughout the entire life cycle. Sheehy and Gould have proposed two of the more contemporary stage theories of adulthood.

Fundamental to any classification system is the life expectancy and life-style of a culture or social group. What may be defined as "old age" in one culture may be "middle age" in another. Neugarten's concept of "social age clocks" illustrates how people may behave as a function of age expectations.

Three aging processes have been fairly well identified. The *biological* approach focuses on the organism's physiological change with age. The *psychological* approach concerns itself with a number of the behavioral reactions of the individual, including self-awareness and adaptation to age and social change. The primary emphasis of the *social* approach is the individual's social relationships during the aging process.

A persistent question among theorists is whether or not adult characteristics are developmental in nature or separate and unique growth processes. Considerable controversy surrounds this issue.

Suggested Readings

1. Birren, J. E.: *The Psychology of Aging.* Englewood Cliffs, New Jersey: Prentice-Hall, 1964.

   Chapter 1 of this frequently cited text deals in great detail with the questions and problems involved in studying life-span psychology.

2. Bischof, L. J.: *Adult Psychology* (2nd ed.). New York: Harper and Row, 1976.

   In this revised and updated edition, Bischof offers the reader a historical overview of adult psychology and provides insight into the current issues of this discipline.

3. Botwinick, J.: *Aging and Behavior. A Comprehensive Integration of Research Findings.* New York: Springer, 1973.

   A clear writing style blends with an excellent summary of literature related to adult development and aging.

4. Lerner, R. M.: *Concepts and Theories of Human Development.* Reading, Massachusetts: Addison-Wesley, 1976.

   A sophisticated book recommended not only for those who wish to pursue the issues presented in this chapter but also for those who desire an in-depth look into deeper philosophical issues in developmental psychology.

5. Neugarten, B. L., (Ed.): *Middle Age and Aging.* Chicago: The University of Chicago Press, 1968.

   A fine collection of readings designed to acquaint the student with various phases of the life cycle. Of particular interest are sections related to social-psychological theories of aging, family relationships, and aging in other societies.

Section A Young Adulthood

Lawrence Lukin

UNIT 2
PHYSICAL AND INTELLECTUAL DEVELOPMENT

Introduction

During late adolescence and early adulthood, almost all physical growth and maturation has been completed. Very young adults (20 to 30 years of age) generally give the appearance of youth and vitality, especially if they take care of themselves. Some, of course, gain excessive weight or display some premature gray hairs, but most people in early adulthood have developed pleasant body proportions, having outgrown the more gangly appearance of oversized limbs and adolescent facial characteristics that often marks the teenage years. Thus, for most, early adulthood is characterized by vim, vigor, freshness, and the general physical attractiveness of youth.

PHYSICAL DEVELOPMENT

By age 17, muscle growth is complete, but the potential for increases in strength remains until about age 30 (Troll, 1975). Even though peak strength is reached, however (few actually realize their potential), it must be remembered that in any phase of life, the maximal is not maintained very long. Thus, for a few, gradual physical deterioration begins in young adulthood. For those who lead a sedentary life, it may begin as early as adolescence. For those who choose to pursue excellence in physical activities (professionals or serious amateurs), early adulthood represents less a time of preparing for the future than the peak of their careers. We tend blithely to assume that old age is a "relative" concept, but the ephemeral nature of the physical peak was brought to light when 14-year-old gymnast Nadia Comaneci, after winning seven gold medals at the 1976 Montreal Olympic Games, was asked whether this represented the pinnacle of her career. Or when Olga Korbut, who at 17 was the darling of the 1972 Olympics, was said to be looking "very old" at the age of 21 in the 1976 games.

Most people choose careers other than sports and usually do not achieve a professional level of athletic prowess, but they often pursue physical activity as a hobby. Some may join bowling leagues, some are lone joggers, some work out at the local "Y", join city baseball or basketball leagues, play golf or tennis, or go skiing on weekends. Most people who pursue these activities are combining recreation with escape from the pressures and routines of daily life.

Regular exercise and proper nutrition undoubtedly help to keep the individual healthy and fit. In support of this, DeCarlo (1974) reports a significant relationship between physical recreation and successful aging. Troll (1975) writes that exercise can improve the strength and circulatory capacity of cardiac muscles and reduce the severity of arteriosclerotic lesions. Exercise of the leg muscles appears to facilitate the flow of blood to the heart and thus indirectly to maintain bodily functioning in all areas, including the brain. Troll adds that proper nutrition in the form of balanced diets may affect not only the levels of peaks reached (i.e., height) but also the rate of decline thereafter (e.g., how long a person will remain at peak height). It is also fairly well understood that excessive smoking and

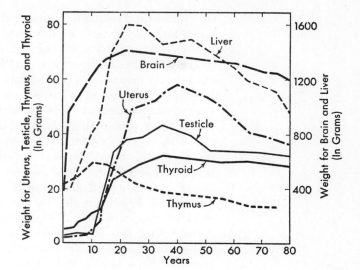

Figure 2–1. Weight changes of various organs with age. (*From* Stieglitz, E. J.: *Geriatric Medicine: Diagnosis and Management of Disease in the Aging and in the Aged.* Philadelphia: W. B. Saunders Company, 1949.)

the abusive use of alcohol and drugs are detrimental to the adult body (Timiras, 1972).

The body reaches its maximum physical potential between the ages of 19 and 26, at least as far as the muscles and internal organs are concerned. Figure 2–1 illustrates how the weight of various organs changes with age. By young adulthood, the body begins slow, imperceptible changes. The accordion-like vertebrae and spinal disks begin to settle, causing a slight decrease in height. For some, an increase in weight begins; even for those who maintain a consistent weight, there is an increase in fatty tissue with a corresponding decrease in muscle tissue. Bischof (1976) estimates there is about a ten per cent loss in muscle strength between the ages of 30 and 60, although wide individual differences exist. Reaction times, which improve from childhood until age 19 or 20 and remain constant until approximately age 26, begin a gradual decline (Hodgkins, 1962).

The sense modalities exhibit little change in young adult life. A slight difference in hearing ability exists between the two sexes in that men are less able than women to detect high tones (Timiras, 1972). The lens of the eye loses some of its elasticity and becomes less able to change shape and to focus on near objects. Figure 2–2

Figure 2–2. (*a*) Visual accommodation in relation to age from age 10 to age 70. The heavy line represents the mean and the lighter lines represent maximal and minimal values. (*b*) Decline in mean visual acuity from age 40 (when appreciable decline begins), as shown in three investigations. (*From* McFarland, R. A.: *Human Factors in Air Transportation.* New York: McGraw-Hill Company, 1953. Data of Duane and Friedenwald.)

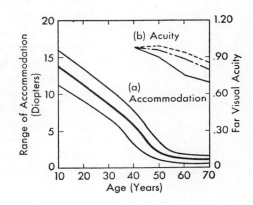

illustrates the gradual decrease in the range of accommodation of the lens. This represents a continuation of a hardening process that probably began at age 10 and is an example of aging beginning early in life. By age 30, however, the changes are seldom sufficient to cause a significant effect on the function of the eyes. Any slight loss of functional efficiency in the sensory mechanism of young adults is more than compensated for by the fact that they learn to make fuller use of their senses than they did as children (Marshall, 1973).

The nervous system has been gradually developing and maturing since the organism was an embryo. Many people mistakenly believe that a young child is neurologically mature. This is not so, since the brain will continue to grow into adolescence or young adulthood. Brain weight, for example, will reach a maximum between the ages of 20 and 30 and then will diminish (Bischof, 1976). Interpreting the electroencephalograph (EEG) waves of adults, Zubek and Solberg (1954) note that mature patterns of brain wave activity do not appear until 19 or 20 years of age, and for some, the period of maturation continues to age 30.

Birren (1964) explains that in sports such as boxing, baseball, basketball, and skiing, the speed, strength, and quick reactions of young adulthood are needed if one is to be competitive. Sports such as golf or bowling or even tennis can be played fairly well through the use of concentration and planning and can therefore be played throughout the life span, especially by those who do not become obese, smoke heavily, or live a dissipated life style. Given good health, a person can participate in skiing or tennis or bowling for decades. However, what does occur during young adulthood is loss of the vim and vigor that are characteristic of the adolescent years.

INTELLECTUAL DEVELOPMENT

There is some disagreement among psychologists as to whether intellectual function remains constant, exhibits a slight decline, or shows a slight increase with age, but most authorities agree that the ability to acquire and utilize knowledge reaches a mature state by young adulthood. It is known that advancements at this time are both *quantitative* and *qualitative*. In a quantitative sense, intelligence tests reveal that mental abilities have become highly differentiated and specialized by young adulthood. Qualitatively, changes in mental processes enable the young adult to deal with a variety of problem-solving situations, particularly those of an abstract nature (Bloom, 1964; Elkind, 1971).

Baltes and Schaie (1974) maintain that young adults are capable of improving four dimensions of intelligence in comparison with their earlier abilities. *Crystallized intelligence* includes those skills acquired through education and acculturation, such as verbal comprehension, numerical skills, and inductive reasoning. *Cognitive flexibility* encompasses the individual's "ability to shift from one way of thinking to another, within the context of familiar intellectual operations, as when one must provide either an antonym or synonym to a word, depending on whether the word appears in capital or lower case letters" (p. 35). *Visuomotor flexibility* is the capacity to shift from familiar to unfamiliar patterns in tasks dictating coordination between visual and motor abilities. Finally, *visualization* consists of the "ability to organize and process visual materials, and involves tasks such as finding a simple figure contained in a complex one or identifying a picture that is incomplete" (p. 36). Baltes and Schaie (1974) contend that in some instances each of these capacities, with the exception of visuomotor flexibility, can be improved upon further as the individual gets older. This concurs with the findings of Botwinick (1967), who stated that adults with above-average intelligence can improve, or at the very least maintain, their abilities until later adulthood, whereas those of average intelligence experience a decline of some capacities.

Parry (1973) has provided an interesting commentary concerning the development of aptitudes during young adulthood. Believing aptitude development will reach a peak between the ages of 18 and 30, he states that this means most people will be able to assimilate information, make comparisons and deductions, and learn new skills more quickly and surely at this age than at any other point in their lives. However, he states that

> Success depends on the individual's powers of selecting appropriate objectives and of pursuing them with patience, courage and persistence. The emergence and development of the latter qualities, closely related to what has become known as need achievement, cannot be plotted with the same assurance as those of the aptitudes, which so far as they are genetically endowed, tend to unfold spontaneously and at a more or less predictable tempo.
>
> (p. 75)

The rate at which intelligence matures during early adulthood is depicted in Figure 2–3. This curve is the result of a *longitudinal* study, a research design by which one collects data from the *same* individuals at different points in their lives. This interpretation of the growth of intelligence appears to be the most widely

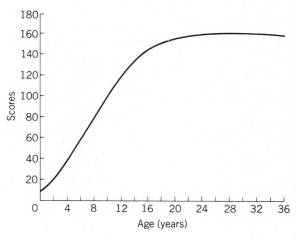

Figure 2–3. The growth of intelligence, based on data obtained from a longitudinal study. The scores represent units of growth derived from a method of absolute scaling. (*From* Bayley, N.: "Development of mental abilities." *In* Mussen, P. H. [Ed.]: *Carmichael's Manual of Child Psychology,* 3rd ed., vol. 1. New York: John Wiley and Sons, 1970.)

accepted today. Note particularly how intelligence scores increase until age 26, then remain fairly constant through the age of 36 (Bayley, 1970).

Still other research studies have indicated that intelligence reaches a peak by the early twenties and declines steadily. However, the majority of these studies were *cross-sectional*, i.e., based on comparison of groups who differ in age at a given time. The so-called decline in intelligence may be due to preexisting differences among the age groups that composed the standardized sample rather than to age per se. Difference in educational background among the age groups sampled was a key factor. Older adults, i.e., those 60 years of age and older, have a mean/median level of education that is lower than that of their younger counterparts. The education variable, when factored out of the test scores, partially explains the steady decline of scores in these cross-sectional investigations (Kimble and Garmezy, 1968).

It is important to remember that whether a particular type of mental ability is maintained or declines throughout the course of adulthood depends upon both the intellectual capacity *and* the person. As Elkind (1977) states:

> One cannot really generalize about the course of mental growth. Tests that require speed, close attention, and concentration seem to show decreasing scores earliest (in the mid twenties or even earlier). Abilities such as deductive reasoning—abilities that appear relatively later in life—decline more rapidly than tests of abilities such as language, vocabulary, and rote memory, which show little decline with age. The rate of decline of specific abilities is influenced by the individual's occupation. Scientists and logicians would probably show little deterioration in deductive reasoning, although this function ordinarily declines relatively early. On the average, bright people and those in more intellectually demanding occupations do not decline in mental ability as early as others do. Teachers, writers, artists, and scientists maintain their productivity, if not their creativity, into their later years with little apparent loss of acumen. Persons of lesser ability are likely to lose some of their mental alacrity earlier. Physical health is also a factor; among old men, those in optimal health show relatively little deterioration in intellectual test scores, while those with chronic ailments decline significantly.
>
> (p. 310)

Adding to this, Bischof (1976) suggests that certain factors may affect adult learning performances. These include: the motivation of the subject in the learning situation; levels of anxiety, rigidity, or fatigue; overall cautiousness in making responses; speed of performance (older adults value accuracy more than speed in performance); test relevance; and the amount of experience the subject is bringing into the testing situation. Two other factors, health and morale, also deserve some consideration. Birren (1964) goes a step further by saying that the tests used in the assessment of adult mental abilities frequently do not elicit the adult's interest for serious effort and are often trivial. The use of time limits in measuring the performance of older adults has also frequently been questioned. Tests of mental ability have also been criticized as being

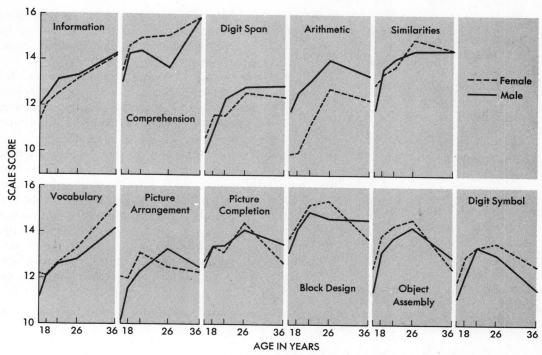

Figure 2–4. Curves of mean scores for young adults for the eleven Wechsler Subtests, Berkeley Growth Study. (*From* Bayley, N.: "Learning in adulthood: the role of intelligence." *In* Klausmeier, J. J., and Harris, C. W.: [Eds.]: *Analyses of Concept Learning.* New York: Academic Press, Inc., 1966.)

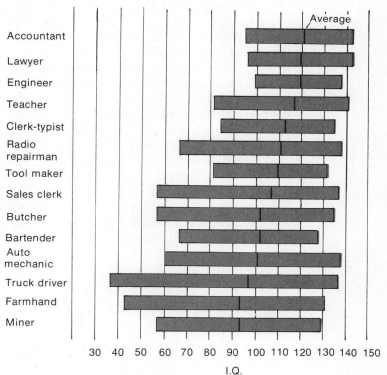

Figure 2–5. Intelligence and occupations. The bars indicate the range of IQs for men in various jobs in the United States as well as the average IQ for each occupation. (*From* Harrell, T. W., and Harrell, M. S., Army general classification test scores for civilian occupations. *Educational and Psychological Measurement,* 1945, *5,* 229–239.)

inappropriate for use with older adults since a great deal of their content was devised for younger segments of the population. In later developmental units, we will focus on these issues more closely.

Figure 2–4 illustrates how specific capacities (based on data for all eleven subtests of the Wechsler Scales) improve or decline during the years of young adulthood. Figure 2–5 depicts the more intellectually demanding occupations and the range of IQs found for men employed in these jobs.

The belief that people lose their accumulated knowledge as they grow older is incorrect. Although intelligence test scores may show a decline, many adults continue to acquire more information and interests, and even wisdom. What the older adult has acquired from diverse experiences frequently compensates for the diminished speed and efficiency of intellectual operations. Utilizing these life experiences, the older adult may be more competent in day-to-day living than the young adult, who is generally more alert and adaptable and consequently tends to perform more efficiently in intelligence tests (Elkind, 1973).

Summary

By the young adult years, physical growth and development has been virtually completed. Generally speaking, height decreases slowly while fatty tissue begins to increase. Reaction times remain fairly constant until approximately the age of 26, at which time they begin a gradual decline. Changes occur in the sense of hearing (men are less able than women to detect high tones) and the sense of sight (the lens becomes less able to change shape and to focus on near objects), while the other senses exhibit little overall change.

Intellectual capacities reach a high degree of maturity that is both *quantitative* and *qualitative*. Four aspects of intelligence can be improved upon at this time, including *crystallized intelligence, cognitive flexibility, visuomotor flexibility,* and *visualization*. Of these, it has been proposed that only visuomotor flexibility seldom exhibits further improvement during adulthood. The fact that the other areas of intelligence do improve has led some researchers to believe that intelligence does *not* decline with age, but improves or remains at the same level. However, it is important to note that whether a particular type of mental ability is maintained throughout the course of adulthood depends on both intellectual function and individual idiosyncrasies.

Suggested Readings

1. Baltes, P. B., and Schaie, K. W.: "Aging and I.Q.: The myth of the twilight years." *Psychology Today*, 7:35–40, 1974.

The authors examine the various components of intelligence and denounce the argument that intelligence declines with age.

2. Birren, J. E.: *The Psychology of Aging*. Englewood Cliffs, New Jersey: Prentice-Hall, 1964.

   This sophisticated text offers the reader excellent chapters on biological influences of aging on perception, psychomotor skills, and speed and timing.

3. Botwinick, J.: *Cognitive Processes in Maturity and Old Age*. New York: Springer, 1967.

   Excellent treatment of the nature of cognitive processes throughout the course of adult life.

4. Kimmel, D.: *Adulthood and Aging*. New York: John Wiley & Sons, Inc., 1974.

   Chapter 8 of this text offers a detailed analysis of the biological and intellectual aspects of aging.

5. Troll, L. E.: *Early and Middle Adulthood*. Monterey, California: Brooks/Cole Publishing Co., Inc., 1975.

   Troll provides a fairly comprehensive examination of physical and intellectual development in chapters two and three of this soft-cover book.

Armstrong-Roberts

UNIT 3
PERSONALITY AND SOCIAL DEVELOPMENT

Introduction

Young adulthood is characterized by numerous developmental tasks. It is a time for further value clarification, important decision-making, and careful life planning. It is also a period when young individuals attain greater insight into society's demands and expectations.

Rayner (1971) takes the position that young adulthood provides an opportunity for the individual to test activities that are satisfying to the inner self and to others in his or her environment. When a personal patterning of roles is coupled with inner satisfaction, the individual usually experiences a sense of wholeness and well-being. This state of integration is referred to as adult identity and is unique to each person.

Self-growth is further shaped, according to Sheehy (1976), when individuals are confronted with the issue of "how to take hold in the adult world." As she puts it, the adolescent's concerns of "Who am I?" or "What is truth?" shift to the young adult's emphasis on such questions as "How do I put my aspirations into effect?" "What is the best way to start?" or "Where do I go?" Sheehy stresses that although the tasks that loom ahead are enormous, they can be exhilarating as well. To shape a dream and prepare for a lifework is a project that will generate energy, aliveness, and hope.

DEVELOPMENTAL TASKS OF YOUNG ADULTHOOD

1. Courting and selecting a mate for marriage.
2. Learning to adjust to, and living harmoniously with, a marriage partner.
3. Beginning a family and assimilating the new role of parent.
4. Rearing children and meeting their individual needs.
5. Learning to manage a home and assuming household responsibilities.
6. Embarking on a career and/or continuing one's education.
7. Assuming some type of civic responsibility.
8. Searching for a congenial social group.

(Adapted from Havighurst, 1972)

MATURITY IN YOUNG ADULTHOOD

To meet the challenges of adulthood adequately requires a considerable degree of *maturity*. Generally speaking, *"maturity" refers to a state that promotes physical and psychological well-being.* In most instances, the mature person possesses a well-developed value system, an accurate self-concept, stable emotional behavior, satisfying social relationships, and intellectual insight. Coping with the demands of adulthood, a mature individual is realistic in the assessment of future goals and ideals. As White (1966) suggests, maturity implies the ability to cope more successfully with life's problems, increasing the effectiveness of our planning strategies, deepening our appreciation of the surroundings, and expanding our resources for happiness.

Figure 3–1.   The challenges of adulthood require considerable maturity.

Bonnie Freer
Photo Trends

Allport's Seven Dimensions of Maturity

One of the more extensive published descriptions of maturity is that of Allport (1961), who postulates that maturity is an ongoing process best characterized by a series of attainments on the part of the individual. Each period of life has its share of obstacles that must be overcome—roadblocks that require the development of goal-formulation and decision-making abilities. Methods for dealing with life's failures and frustrations—as well as accepting its triumphs and victories—have to be devised if maturity is to be nurtured. Age in itself is not a guarantee of maturity.

Allport has identified seven specific dimensions or criteria of maturity that manifest themselves during adulthood. These seven dimensions include extension of the self, relating warmly to others, emotional security, realistic perception, possession of skills and competences, knowledge of the self, and establishing a unifying philosophy of life.

EXTENSION OF THE SELF

The first criterion of maturity, *self-extension*, requires that individuals gradually extend their comprehension to encompass multiple facets of their environment. The sphere of the young child was primarily limited to the family, but over time the child becomes involved in various peer groups, in school activities, and in clubs. Eventually, strong bonds develop with members of the opposite sex, and interest toward vocational, moral, and civic responsibilities is generated. Each outlet provides the young adult with the opportunity to become involved in more meaningful personal relationships and to fulfill the need of sharing new feelings and experiences with others (Helms and Turner, 1976).

White (1966) refers to the foregoing process as the deepening of interests. In a series of case studies, he discovered most mature young adults tend to become engaged in a vocational, athletic, or academic pursuit. Each requires the extension of the self and the ability to experience involvement of some sort. Yet, like Allport, White maintains that merely being involved in something does not necessarily imply satisfaction or happiness. Maturity is measured by one's active participation in an activity. Maturity implies movement away from a state in which interests are casual, quickly dropped, and pursued only from motives that do not become identified with the advancement of the interest or activity. True self-extension is a state in which a sense of reward comes from doing something for its own sake. In other words, maturity is promoted when the activity undertaken has true significance to the self.

RELATING WARMLY TO OTHERS

Allport's second criterion of maturity is the ability to relate the self warmly to others. By this, Allport means the capacity to be intimate with as well as compassionate toward others.

How does one develop the capacity for intimacy? One of the more widely accepted interpretations of adult psychosocial growth has been provided by Erik Erikson (1963). He posited eight specific life stages and the manner in which personality continues to unfold throughout the life cycle. Mature personality development, he stressed, depends on the individual's ability to resolve the crisis inherent in each of the proposed stages.

During early adulthood, mature psychosocial development is measured by the successful resolution of the stage known as *Intimacy versus Isolation*. (Table 3–1 charts this stage in relation to the seven other stages Erikson proposed.) Prior to early adulthood, the individual was in the midst of an identity crisis, a struggle that reached its peak during adolescence. Erikson stresses the idea that as a young adult, the individual is motivated to fuse this newly established identity with that of others. In short, the young adult is ready for intimacy, which means not only committing the self to personal relationships but also nurturing the motivation to maintain them.

Although most young adults seek to gratify the need for intimacy through marriage, it is important to stress that intimate relationships other than sexual ones are possible. Individuals may develop strong bonds of intimacy in friendships that offer, among other features,

TABLE 3–1   ERIKSON'S EIGHT AGES OF MAN*

Stages (Ages are Approximate)	Psychosocial Crises	Radius of Significant Relations	Psychosocial Modalities	Favorable Outcome
I. Birth Through First Year	Trust vs. mistrust	Maternal person	To get To give in return	Drive and hope
II. Second Year	Autonomy vs. shame, doubt	Parental persons	To hold (on) To let (go)	Self-control and willpower
III. Third Year Through Fifth Year	Initiative vs. guilt	Basic family	To make (going after) To "make like" (playing)	Direction and purpose
IV. Sixth to Onset of Puberty	Industry vs. inferiority	Neighborhood; school	To make things (competing) To make things together	Method and competence
V. Adolescence	Identity and repudiation vs. identity diffusion	Peer groups and out-groups; models of leadership	To be oneself (or not to be) To share being oneself	Devotion and fidelity
VI. Early Adulthood	Intimacy and solidarity vs. isolation	Partners in friendship, sex, competition, cooperation	To lose and find oneself in another	Affiliation and love
VII. Young and Middle Adulthood	Generativity vs. self-absorption	Divided labor and shared household	To make be To take care of	Production and care
VIII. Later Adulthood	Integrity vs. despair	"Mankind" "My kind"	To be, through having been To face not being	Renunciation and wisdom

Source: Identity, Youth and Crisis by Erik H. Erikson. Copyright © 1968 by W. W. Norton & Company, Inc. *Childhood and Society,* 2nd Edition, by Erik H. Erikson. Copyright 1950, 1963 by W. W. Norton & Company, Inc. Reproduced by permission of W. W. Norton & Company, Inc.

mutuality, empathy, and reciprocity. As Moore (1969) suggests, intimate relationships may easily develop out of a capacity to share with and understand others. The socially mature adult is capable of effectively communicating with others, being sensitive to another person's needs, and, in general, exhibiting tolerance toward mankind. The growth of friendship, love, and devotion is much more prominent among highly mature people than among the more immature.

Yet not all relationships are characterized by intimacy. As Erikson explains, many of us are prepared to isolate and, if necessary, destroy those forces and people who seem dangerous to us, or whose "territory" appears to encroach upon our intimate relationships. "The danger of this stage," Erikson warns, "is that intimate, competitive, and combative relations are experienced with and against the self-same people. But as the areas of adult duty are delineated, and as the competitive encounter and the sexual embrace are differentiated, they eventually become subject to that *ethical sense* which is the mark of the adult." (p. 264)

EMOTIONAL SECURITY

Although numerous dimensions of maturity can be grouped under this third category, Allport maintains that four qualities in particular are important: self-acceptance, emotional acceptance, frustration tolerance, and confidence in self-expression.

Self-acceptance is the ability to acknowledge one's self fully, particularly in terms of one's imperfections. Mature people realize that they cannot be perfect in every respect, yet they nevertheless seek to fulfill their own potential. Total self-acceptance requires exploring and accepting one's weaknesses.

By mature *emotional acceptance,* people accept emotions as being part of the normal self. People acquiring this dimension of maturity do not allow emotions to rule their lives, yet at the same time they do not reject emotions as being alien in nature.

Frustration tolerance is the capacity to continue functioning even during times of stress. To be able to handle life's frustrations and still manage to carry on is a formidable goal. For maturity to develop, one must learn how to best deal with life's frustrations and maintain a healthy life-style.

The final dimension of emotional maturity is *confidence in self-expression.* Maturity in this respect implies spontaneity; one is aware of one's own emotions, is not afraid of them, and has control over their expression. Immaturity, conversely, can manifest itself in a number of different ways, including timidity and shyness, emotional overreaction, or emotional underreaction.

REALISTIC PERCEPTION

Allport's fourth criterion of maturity is *realistic perception.* Quite simply, maturity in this sense means being able to keep in touch with reality, without distorting the environment to meet individual needs and purposes. Sometimes, the complexities of events and situations combined with the ego defenses of the individual may produce an inaccurate interpretation of the environment. The mature mind is able to perceive the surroundings accurately.

Allport is not implying that the mature person does not use any type of defense or coping mechanism. On the contrary, defense mechanisms become quite automatic for many of us and tend temporarily to alleviate anxiety and frustration. Allport's point is that the overuse—or misuse—of such mechanisms usually distorts one's perception of the surroundings.

POSSESSION OF SKILLS AND COMPETENCES

Possessing some type of skill or competence represents Allport's fifth dimension of maturity. Unless one possesses some basic skill, it is virtually impossible to nurture the kind of security

Figure 3–2. Competence represents a maturation of abilities.

Jim Smith
Photo Trends

necessary for maturity to develop. While the immature adolescent may argue, "I'm no good at anything," mature adults strive to develop whatever skills they feel they possess.

Furthermore, skilled individuals are driven by a need to express their competence through some type of activity. They identify with their work and display pride in the skills needed to produce the finished product. In this sense, task absorption and ego-relevant activities are important to physical and psychological well-being.

KNOWLEDGE OF THE SELF

Knowledge of the self, or self objectification, is criterion number six. Most mature people possess a great deal of self-insight, of which many immature individuals have little. According to Allport, knowledge of the self involves three capacities: knowing what one *can* do, knowing what one *cannot* do, and knowing what one *ought* to do.

White (1966) believes that knowledge and stabilization of the self is one of the most important growth trends of young adulthood. In general, White proposes that the stabilization process owes much to those enduring roles that are characteristic of adult life. More specifically, he states that as individuals modify their behavior in order to fulfill their roles as workers, marriage partners, and parents, for example, their experience begins to accumulate more and more selectively. In this sense, the stored-up sources of stability and ego identity emerge increasingly out of behavior within roles.

TABLE 3–2   ALLPORT'S CRITERIA OF MATURITY*

Criteria	Descriptions	Examples
Self-Extension	Active and passive participation Task involvement Ego involvement	A mother quits a good job to care for her family A man devotes his energies to combating the drug problem in his community
Warm Relating of Self to Others	Intimacy Compassion Tolerance Smooth sociability	A nurse spends extra time with a frightened patient A young man and woman decide to marry A man joins a Big Brother group
Emotional Security	Self-acceptance Cooperation with inevitables Control	One who does not display his moods freely One who resists affectations One who lives harmoniously with his emotions
Realistic Perceptions	Correct knowledge of people and things Perceptual soundness	One who is not driven by his inner attitudes and traits to misperceive events A man who understands the requirements of his job (knowing the rules of the game) A student who perceives that he cannot cope with college work, after having made a sincere effort to succeed
Skills and Assignments	Competencies and worthwhile tasks to perform	One who identifies with his work and profession and is proud of his skills The dedicated teacher who works beyond the call of duty The medical man who gives up a promising private practice for a research career
Self-Objectification	Insight into oneself Deriving humor from one's pretenses and mistakes	A man who can admit that he is wrong in an argument A student who can see poor test scores as the result of lack of study rather than a bad test
Unifying Philosophy of Life	Guiding goals and values Religious faith Directedness	Valuing knowledge of learning for its own sake Striving to make money Valuing beauty Working for others Striving for power Valuing religious experiences

*From: DiCaprio, N. S.: *Personality Theories: Guides to Living.* Philadelphia: W. B. Saunders Company, 1974, p. 347.

ESTABLISHING A UNIFYING PHILOSOPHY OF LIFE

The final criterion or dimension of maturity outlined by Allport is the development of a unifying philosophy of life that embodies the concepts of a guiding purpose, ideals, needs, goals, and values. Since the mature human being is goal-seeking, such a synthesis enables him or her to develop an intelligent theory of life and to work toward implementing it. Mature people tend to view goals from a balanced perspective and are able to cope with failure if these goals are not met.

To summarize: the seven dimensions proposed by Allport are important factors in the development of maturity (see Table 3–2). Because of Allport's emphasis on *individual uniqueness*, it should be mentioned that these dimensions can be expressed differently by people. Also, as DiCaprio (1974) emphasizes, these dimensions may not be possessed by everyone. On the contrary, unfavorable conditions may hinder personality growth and prevent the attainment of maturity. Some people may remain immature because they are trapped in a conflict between cultural expectations and personal requirements. Others may be prevented by forces outside their control at the very beginning of life from ever reaching personal fulfillment.

DEVELOPMENT OF SEXUAL RELATIONSHIPS

It seems that early sexual relations are encouraged in American society today. The stimulations and excitements produced by the glandular changes associated with puberty, peer pressure, and increased sophistication acquired by constant exposure to the mass media all serve to promote an early interest in dating. As a result, dating has become an institution in itself, complete with its own set of cultural expectations (Cox, 1974). With few exceptions, dating seems to have replaced all other mechanisms of mate selection in contemporary society (Saxton, 1968).

Dating is capable of serving several important functions. At the individual level, it is a process by which people can test ideas about themselves and the opposite sex, gradually learning to shape further their own sense of identity. Furthermore, dating enables young adults to experience trust, love, and mutual respect. It is the major way in which men and women express the value of equal choice in the selection of a marriage partner. In many respects dating is the logical extension of American political ideology into the realm of personal relationships, since it nurtures individualism, freedom of choice, and equality, all hallmarks of the American Dream (Pierson and D'Antonio, 1974).

Williamson (1966) suggests that for many, dating will probably reach a culmination during the early adult years. Because both partners are more mature, dating in young adulthood is likely to be more rewarding and fulfilling than adolescent patterns of court-

THE VALUES OF TODAY'S YOUNG ADULTS: HOW TRADITIONAL ARE YOU?

In order to establish a unifying philosophy of life, certain values and needs have to be clarified. Below are some traditional American values identified by Belcher (1973, p. 99). Which of them do you believe in? Which do you not believe in?

After you have made a choice for each question, consult the results of a nationwide poll conducted by *CBS* (below).

	Believe	Not Believe
1. "Hard work will always pay off."	_____	_____
2. "Everyone should save as much as he can and not have to lean on family and friends the minute he runs into financial problems."	_____	_____
3. "Depending on how much strength and character a person has, he can pretty well control what happens to him."	_____	_____
4. "Belonging to some organized religion is important in a person's life."	_____	_____
5. "Competition encourages excellence."	_____	_____
6. "The right to private property is sacred."	_____	_____
7. "Society needs some legally based authority in order to prevent chaos."	_____	_____
8. "Compromise is essential for progress."	_____	_____

The following is the way in which a representative, nationwide sample of 1340 young adults answered the questions. The figures presented are a summed average for all the items, and the results are further broken down by the respondents' political stance.

	Believe	Not Believe
Conservatives (19%)	89%	11%
Middle-of-roaders (48%)	84%	16%
Moderate reformers, liberals (23%)	73%	27%
Radical reformers (10%)	72%	28%
Revolutionaries (1%)	30%	70%

These results indicate that most young adults accept most of these traditional American values. The proportion of respondents rejecting these values increases gradually from a low of 11 per cent among conservatives to 27 to 28 per cent among the reformers. Note particularly the tremendous leap from that point to the 70 per cent rejection rate of revolutionary youth.

The young adults involved in this poll were selected from two samples of the population. One sample was composed of 723 college students from 30 different campuses. The other was composed of 617 young people of the same age group bracket who were not college students. The results also showed that noncollege youth were much more conservative politically.

(From Belcher, 1973, pp. 99–100)

ship. Indeed, Saxton (1968) emphasizes that mate selection does not evolve as a conscious purpose of dating until the early adult years. As Allport (1955) and Erikson (1963) stress, young adults are more aware of their goals in life and are more intellectually, socially, and emotionally mature than adolescents. Consequently, Williamson (1966) states, marriage becomes something other than a remote possibility for the couple.

Rayner (1971) emphasizes the importance of mature levels of expression for rewarding heterosexual relations during adulthood. He feels that when young men and women have established a fairly stable organization within themselves, especially a realistic awareness of overall capacities, then they are in a position to admire their partners realistically and to experience sharing and reciprocity in their relationships. To put it another way, before a person can give and accept true intimacy in the Eriksonian sense, he or she must have achieved a reasonable sense of personal identity (Sheehy, 1976).

If individuals fail to nurture an integrated sense of awareness, Rayner (1971) maintains, they may fall idealistically in love, later becoming prey to overwhelming envy and possible humiliation. Lacking a coherent and integrated sense of the self, the man and woman may fall in love superficially. As time progresses, other dimensions of each partner's personality will probably emerge and appear less adorable. Because of each partner's immaturity and lack of self-integration, it is unlikely that these parts of the other person will be tolerated.

Rayner suggests that these considerations make it extremely important for people to have developed a coherent sense of adult identity before committing themselves to a lifelong relationship based on being in love.

Heterosexual Attraction

Why are individuals attracted to one another? Psychologists and sociologists over the years have attempted to answer this question by proposing various theories of mate selection. While some focus on obvious environmental factors, others emphasize subtle and largely unconscious personality forces. Landis (1975) summarizes the literature by describing the primary theories of mate choice.

The *propinquity theory* is simple in scope. Although originally applied to those living in the same general neighborhood, it would now include those who go to school or work together. It states that those who are in close proximity will eventually meet by some form of daily association. In its broadest sense, the propinquity theory states the obvious—individuals must meet if they are to select one another as mates (Bell, 1975).

The *parental image theory,* Freudian in origin, emphasizes that the child nurtures a deep affection for the parent of the opposite sex. When mate selection takes place, the individual sees the image of this childhood attachment. The popular clichés "She's looking for someone with her father's qualities" or "He wants someone like his mother" are applicable in this case. This explanation places mate selection on a level below consciousness. It should be noted that this theory has not been well documented by psychologists or sociologists.

The *theory of complementary needs* assumes that individuals seek out mates to complement their own personalities. Proposed by Winch (1958), this explanation operates on the premise that the need patterns of the partners will be complementary. A mate is chosen to fill the weaknesses of one's own personality. "In these psychological needs," Landis states, "opposites tend to attract, thus complementing the self" (p. 177). This theory is a challenging one, but evidence contradicts it. Many people, it seems, choose partners to satisfy a need for similarity.

Homogamy theory suggests that mate choice is based on similar economic, racial, and religious characteristics. Generally speaking (although interracial and interfaith marriages exist in greater numbers today), it is known that "like marries like," particularly in regard to general characteristics such as education, economic background, social class, age, race, and code of ethics.

The *value theory* is a postulation of mate choice that incorporates most other theories. Quite simply, this theory states that all individuals possess value or belief systems that guide them in the process of mate selection. This explanation is quite similar to the *ideal mate theory*, which assumes that a person possesses some set of qualifications for the perfect mate.

Patterns of Courtship

At an early age, parents begin strenuous conditioning to prepare their offspring for courtship and eventual marriage (Cox, 1974; Pierson and D'Antonio, 1974). By adolescence, most young people have accepted the idea of courting members of the opposite sex. Falling in love implies being an adult, and this is most significant for adolescents trying extremely hard to "prove" how grown-up they are (Duberman, 1974).

By early adulthood, Duberman (1974) points out, the differences between men and women in the dating relationship become pronounced.

> Because marriage is a more important source of sex-role identification and status for girls than for boys, they are more concerned with love and marriage. Nevertheless, girls tend to be more realistic in terms of the future of these relationships; boys tend to be more romantic. Perhaps this is because love and marriage are of more practical concern to girls. For a female, we must bear in mind, marriage is generally her entire future; she must take care then, in her selection. It must be romantic, no doubt of that, but she is also concerned about her total lifestyle.
>
> (p. 82)

Figure 3–3. Sexual relationships during early adulthood usually suggest a sense of intimacy and solidarity. (*From* Shope, D.: *Interpersonal Sexuality.* Philadelphia: W. B. Saunders Company, 1975.)

There are specific patterns of courtship that are typical of the early adult years. Excluding engagement and marriage, Kelley (1974) has identified three types of dating patterns: *random dating, steady dating,* and *the trial arrangement.*

Although the term *random dating* suggests the haphazard choice of a partner, it is perhaps better explained as "playing the field" or deliberately selecting a partner for public or social events. This kind of dating is random in that no further commitment is involved, and either partner may choose to continue or discontinue the relationship. Young men and women may enjoy random dating because it doesn't tie them down and allows them to enjoy their partners for the most part on their own schedule and budget.

Like adolescents, young adults enjoy "doing their own thing." *Steady dating* means courting a single partner rather than being a nondater or a random dater. Young adults in this type of relationship become involved in some type of premarital understanding. There appear to be several salient features of steady daters. First, those

COMPONENTS OF LOVE IN DATING BEHAVIOR

According to Saxton (1968), love, especially in dating and mating behavior, consists of four primary components: altruism, companionship, sex, and romance. Let's briefly examine each of these.

Altruistic Love. Altruism in a love relationship implies an emphasis upon the well-being of the loved partner. When nurture of this type brings the provider some type of intrinsic satisfaction, this emotion can be labeled as altruistic love. In some cases, providing for another person may bring a person more satisfaction than providing for his or her own physical well-being. This occurs because needs exist in a hierarchy, and the need to nurture another individual may take priority over the need to provide for one's own welfare.

Companionate Love. In its broadest sense, companionate love means the enjoyment of doing things together. Saxton (1968) maintains that the relation between "liking and loving" is essentially one of degree; both are facets of the same emotion of attraction and positive need fulfillment. Most married couples, he believes, live at the more modest levels of mutual respect, companionship, and affection rather than on the exalted heights of love celebrated by poets and song writers. However, this in no way implies that idealistic cultural expectations for ecstatic marital love are never fulfilled. On the contrary, such dreams may be not only fulfilled but surpassed.

Sexual Love. The emotion experienced when the love object is also the sex object is characterized by two primary qualities. The first consists of strong feelings of tenderness, admiration, and aesthetic appreciation, whereas the second is a strong need for tactile and, usually, genital contact. Sexual participation thus becomes an extension of intimacy and communication. Most couples who experience sexual arousal and orgasm feel deep satisfaction and intense involvement with one another.

Romantic Love. The idealization of the love object is an important component of love, especially in dating. Romantic love is a very complex emotion, and authorities are not in agreement in defining its underlying dynamics. Bell (1975) suggests that romantic love in American society includes *idealization* (the placing of the love object on a pedestal), *fantasy* (the tendency to withdraw into a world of make-believe and to create images of what should be in a most perfect of all worlds with the most perfect person), *high emotion* (the desire to feel rather than think), and *exclusiveness* (a stress on the privacy and singular nature of the love experience).

who become steady partners in their early adult years are more likely to marry as a result of their pairing than adolescents. This may be attributed to the fact that women and men, particularly college students, are closer to the end of their formal schooling; their friends are getting married and women and men are beginning to comprehend some of the advantages of marriage. Second, young people in this category are allowed greater responsibility and freedom from their parents and their friends. Many want to show evidence of this freedom by choosing a partner for serious dating. "If parents or friends object to this choice, the man or woman may feel doubly bound to prove, as a measure of his or her independence, that it is the right one." (Kelley, 1974, p. 88)

Finally, steady partners possess greater insight into the relationship they have established and its portent for development in the future. Unlike adolescents, they are likely to be aware of their basic motivations and to understand social and family patterns. In essence, young adults have begun to attain the maturity described by Allport (1955).

The third pattern of courtship described by Kelley (1974) is the *trial arrangement.* Couples engaged in this type of relationship may choose to follow a variety of life-styles such as living together or entering a commune, instead of going steady, becoming engaged, or meeting some other expectation dictated by society. Although trial arrangements accelerate the pairing process in some ways, they do not necessarily lead to early marriages. On the contrary, many of these experimenting couples are not candidates for marriage in the near future; instead, they are viewed as a subculture that is registering its protest against the old order and is seeking to establish a new one.

Sexual Behavior Outside Marriage

There appear to be few issues in American society today that continue to generate as much public and private interest as the sexual attitudes and behavior of the unmarried. Once strongly taboo as a topic for general discussion, the issue of nonmarital sex is now so widely written and talked about—in the mass media, in popular literature, and informally—that such discussion is almost commonplace (Nye and Berarado, 1973).

The first extensive study of male and female sexual behavior was undertaken by Alfred Kinsey and a team of researchers (Kinsey, Pomeroy, and Martin 1948; Kinsey, Pomeroy, Martin, and Gebhard, 1953). The findings of Kinsey's research are still widely quoted, even though the results are somewhat dated. He was able to lay the foundation for the acceptance of sex research. Since then, other sex researchers have published books about their findings, the most famous being Masters and Johnson's *Human Sexual Response* (1966) and *Human Sexual Inadequacy* (1970). A multitude of other books and studies focusing on the nature of sexual attitudes and behavior have followed.

What has this vast amount of research discovered concerning nonmarital sexual behavior? In comparison with those studied by Kinsey, today's younger and older adults hold more permissive attitudes about sexual behavior outside marriage (Landis and Landis, 1963; Pierson and D'Antonio, 1974). Table 3–3 compares attitudinal changes about this topic over a four-year period. More

TABLE 3–3   PERCENTAGE OF WHITE MEN AND WOMEN IN THE UNITED STATES WHO BELIEVE THAT PREMARITAL SEXUAL RELATIONS ARE NOT WRONG, 1969 AND 1972*

	1969		1972	
Age	Men	Women	Men	Women
Under 30	48%	27%	65%	42%
30 to 44	26	13	45	29
45 and over	12	10	21	12
Total	23	14	37	23

From: Udry, 1974, p. 108.

young adults are also willing to talk more openly and freely about sexual issues than in the past (Bell, 1966).

According to Reiss (1960), Americans have four basic attitudes toward nonmarital intercourse:

1. *Abstinence:* Nonmarital intercourse is wrong for both men and women, regardless of circumstances.
2. *Permissiveness with Affection:* Nonmarital intercourse is right for both men and women under certain conditions when the couple are engaged or a stable relationship with love or strong affection is present.
3. *Permissiveness without Affection:* Nonmarital intercourse is right for both men and women regardless of the amount of affection or stability present, provided there is physical attraction.
4. *Double Standard:* Nonmarital intercourse is acceptable for men but is wrong and unacceptable for women.

(Reiss, 1960, pp. 83–84)

Reiss believes that the number of Americans who espouse abstinence or the double standard will decline noticeably as more permissive attitudes toward sex become more prevalent. Con-

THE SATURDAY EVENING POST

"How do you feel about marriage before sex?"

Figure 3–4

versely, permissiveness toward sex without affection (or person-centered coitus) and permissiveness toward sex with affection will become the dominant standards for nonmarital intercourse in American society. As far as the latter category is concerned, many of those who engage in nonmarital sex do so with only one partner to whom they feel emotionally close (Kantner and Zelnick, 1972).

An examination of some research findings is in order so that we can learn to what extent young adults engage in nonmarital sexual relations. To be sure, the question of premarital coitus is one of the most important issues confronting couples who do marry from the beginning of their casual contacts through the engagement period (Landis, 1975). Of Kinsey's original sample, he found that approximately 20 per cent of the women and 40 per cent of the men experienced sexual intercourse by the time they were 20. However, more recent evidence indicates increasing rates of premarital intercourse (Shope, 1975). In 1973, Sorenson conducted a nationwide survey concerned with the sexual behavior of young men and women between the ages of 13 and 19. He found that 59 per cent of the boys and 45 per cent of the girls had engaged in sexual intercourse at least once before they were 20. Furthermore, a substantial percentage of the respondents had experienced intercourse at surprisingly early ages. Bell and Chaskes (1970) found that premarital coital permissiveness among college students increased significantly between 1958 and 1968. In another investigation (Bell, 1971), it was found that approximately half the adolescent men surveyed and slightly less than half the women had engaged in sexual intercourse by age 21. Burr (1976) has provided a summary of the findings from a number of studies appearing between 1915 and 1972 (see Table 3–4).

What are some of the reasons behind a couple's decision to engage in nonmarital coitus? Conversely, why do some couples abstain? Kinsey (1953) suggested a partial list explaining the reasons for and against premarital intercourse:

Reasons For Premarital Intercourse

1. It may satisfy a physiological need for a sexual outlet.
2. It may become a source of immediate physical and psychological satisfaction.
3. If there is no guilt, it may increase one's ability to function more effectively in other, nonsexual fields.
4. It is more valuable than solitary sexual activity for developing one's capacity to make emotional adjustments with other persons.
5. It may develop one's capacity to make the particular sorts of emotional adjustments which are needed in marital relationships.
6. It may provide training in the sorts of physical techniques that may be involved in marital coitus.
7. It may test the capacities of two persons to make satisfactory sexual adjustments after marriage.
8. It is easier to learn to make emotional and physical adjustments at an earlier age; they are learned with greater difficulty after marriage.
9. Failure in a premarital relationship is socially less disastrous than failure after marriage.

TABLE 3–4 PERCENTAGE OF YOUNG ADULTS IN THE UNITED STATES WHO REPORTED PARTICIPATION IN PREMARITAL SEXUAL INTERCOURSE

Author	Date of Publication	Men	Women
Eastman	1972	55	49
Fujital	1971	46	31
Christensen and Gregg	1970	50	34
Robinson	1970	65	37
Luckey and Nass	1969	58	43
Peretti	1969	48	21
Katz	1968	36	23
Packard	1968	57	43
Burr, Lewis	1967	54	27
Elias	1967	72	53
Freedman	1967		22
Kaats and Davis	1967	60	41
Robinson	1965	65	29
Ehrmann	1959	65	13
Christensen and Gregg	1958	51	21
Reevy	1954		7
Burgess and Wallin	1953	68	47
Landis and Landis	1953	41	9
Gilbert	1951	56	25
Ross	1950	51	
Finger	1947	45	
Hohman and Schaffner	1947	68	
Porterfield and Salley	1946	32	9
Landis	1940		23
Bromley and Britten	1938	52	25
Peterson	1938	55	
Terman	1938	61	37
Dickinson and Beam	1934		12
Davis	1929		11
Hamilton	1929	54	35
Peck and Wells	1925	35	
Peck and Wells	1923	35	
Exner	1915	36	

From Burr, W. R.: *Successful Marriage, A Principles Approach.* Homewood, Illinois: The Dorsey Press, 1976, p. 253.

10. Heterosexual experience may prevent the development of a homosexual pattern of behavior.
11. Premarital coitus may lead to marriage.
12. In at least some social groups, an individual may acquire status by fitting into the group pattern for behavior.

Reasons Against Premarital Intercourse

1. The danger for the female of pregnancy.
2. The danger if abortion is used to terminate a pregnancy.
3. The possibility of contracting a venereal disease.
4. The undesirability of a marriage which is forced by a premarital pregnancy.
5. The traumatic effects of coitus which is had under the inadequate circumstances which are supposed to attend most premarital relations.
6. The damage done by the participant's guilt over the infringement of the moral law.
7. The guilt at the loss of virginity, and its subsequent effect on marriage.

8. The fear that males lose respect for and will not marry a female with whom they have had coitus.
9. The damage done when guilt feelings are reawakened after marriage.
10. The guilt resulting from fear of public disapproval.
11. The risk and fear of social difficulties that may follow discovery of the relationship.
12. The risk and fear of legal difficulties that may follow any discovery of the relationship.
13. The possibility that premarital coitus which is satisfactory may delay or prevent altogether the individual from marrying.
14. The possibility that the coitus may make one feel obligated to marry the sexual partner.
15. The possibility that guilt over the coitus may break up an otherwise desirable friendship with the sexual partner.
16. The overemphasis which premarital experience may place on the physical aspects of friendship and marriage.
17. The likelihood that premarital irregularites will lead to later extramarital infidelities, with consequent damage to the marriage.
18. The possibility that the female will be less capable of responding satisfactorily in her marital coitus because of the traumatic effects of premarital experience.
19. The fact that premarital coitus is morally wrong.
20. The principle that abstinence from such activities may develop one's will power.

In conclusion, available studies on sexual relations point to the fact that nonmarital coitus is more common today than it was fifty years ago (Kelley, 1974). Furthermore, it has been recognized that attitudes toward sex in general have become more tolerant. As a result, some writers contend that American society has moved from an anti-sex to a pro-sex orientation (Pierson and D'Antonio, 1974). The change that has taken place appears to be a shift along a continuum, in regard not only to the nature and extent of the sexual stimulation that is permitted but also the manner in which society perceives this sexual activity.

Summary

Young adulthood implies the need for careful life planning and sound decision-making strategies. Meeting the numerous developmental tasks that this time period encompasses requires considerable maturity, which Gordon Allport has described as consisting of seven critical components: (1) extension of the self, (2) relating warmly to others, (3) emotional security, (4) realistic perception, (5) possession of skills and competences, (6) knowledge of the self, and (7) establishing a unifying philosophy of life.

Dating, for many, will most likely culminate during the early adult years. The three patterns of courtship that appear at this time are random dating, steady dating, and the trial arrangement. Four components of love have also been identified, including altruism, companionship, sexuality, and romance.

Since Alfred Kinsey and his team of researchers published their findings, numerous other investigators have undertaken similar research. It would appear that today's young adults hold more permissive attitudes toward nonmarital sexual behavior than those of fifty years ago. Permissiveness for sex with or without affection also appears to be more dominant in contemporary American society.

Suggested Readings

1. Allport, G. W.: *Pattern and Growth in Personality*. New York: Holt, Rinehart and Winston, 1961.

   Allport describes the nature of the mature personality in Chapter 12 of this widely cited text.

2. Gagnon, J. H., and Simon, W.: *Sexual Conduct*. Chicago: Aldine Publishing Company, 1973.

   Interesting and thought-provoking analysis of the social origins of sexual development as well as other topics related to human sexuality.

3. Kelley, R. K.: *Courtship, Marriage, and the Family*. New York: Harcourt Brace Jovanovich, Inc., 1974.

   This text presents excellent discussion of the young adult living in today's society as well as various patterns of courtship. Of particular interest are sections related to premarital sexual relations, role expectations, and cultural, class, and family influences on courtship.

4. Sheehy, G.: *Passages: Predictable Crises of Adult Life*. New York: E. P. Dutton and Company, Inc., 1976.

   In Part 3 of this book, Sheehy offers a highly readable account of the turmoils, struggles, and triumphs of young adulthood. Her points are well taken and painfully real.

5. White, R. W.: *Lives in Progress*. New York: Holt, Rinehart, and Winston, 1966.

   Three lengthy case histories supplement White's coverage of adult personality development. Chapter 9 offers exclusive treatment of the various growth trends at work during young adulthood.

UNIT 4
THE FAMILY: MARRIAGE

Introduction

Perhaps no other culture in the world, past or present, has exhibited as great a social and personal concern with marriage as has the United States. Newspapers and magazines, television, radio, and movies, devote vast amounts of time and energy analyzing the subject of marriage, and much of their attention is focused on its problems: marital frustrations and unhappiness, sexual maladjustments, role confusion, and divorce. These areas, along with many others, have generated considerable interest among social scientists studying the family as an institution (Bell, 1975).

Despite the fact that interest in alternative life styles is high, it has been reported that 95 per cent of American women are married by age 54 and 94 per cent of American men by age 64 (Kelley, 1974). In 1970, for the third consecutive year, over two million marriages took place in the United States (Bell, 1975).

THE PATH TO MARRIAGE

Kelley (1974) writes that the final stage of courtship has conventionally been the engagement. Well-established social customs surrounding the engagement appear to have remained durable and appealing in spite of our rapidly changing times.

It is during the public engagement period that most couples are directly preparing for their marriage and establishing their new joint identity. The engagement period is usually one in which the couple prepare emotionally for their future together. It is the time for serious life planning concerning such issues as where the couple will live, their projected life-style, how many children they would like to have, and the personal expectations they might have for one another (McGinnis and Finnegan, 1976).

However, Kelley (1974) stresses that the engagement does not adhere to an immutable pattern, since approximately half to two thirds of all first engagements are broken, causing partners to go their separate ways to seek more suitable spouses. As Landis (1975) agrees, engagement does not constitute or imply an irrevocable commitment. The contract is oral and personal, not institutionalized.

WHY DO PEOPLE MARRY?

Although it is true that the motives for entering married life vary from couple to couple, it is possible to categorize some of the more prevalent reasons. Clayton (1975) has classified the influences that motivate couples to marry as "push" and "pull" factors. "Push" factors are those that pressure a couple to move more rapidly toward marriage. "Pull" factors are those magnetic agents that seem to neutralize the fears single people may have about married life, such as the fear of losing their freedom or being "tied down."

THE MIDDLE CLASS ENGAGEMENT: IT'S A WOMAN'S WORLD

There appear to be two symbols of engagement with a long historical heritage that still can be found in the American middle class: the engagement announcement and the engagement ring. Although historically the function of the announcement was to inform the community that a couple intended to marry, the purpose of the announcement today appears to be to give prestige to the individuals involved. The announcement is made by means of engagement parties or through announcements carried in local newspapers.

The ring, also a prestige symbol, is usually a diamond, and often the belief is "the bigger the better." The size and cost of the diamond indicate to many that the girl has succeeded not only in being chosen but also in being selected by an affluent male. Often, the cost of the ring may represent a sum of money the couple might have better used in other ways. Yet, many women will not feel truly engaged unless they have a ring, a notion frequently supported by friends or relatives. In some instances, if the man does not have money to buy his fiancée an appropriate ring, his family will buy it for her.

For most American women, the peak of personal prestige is reached during the engagement period. The engaged woman in the United States is frequently a symbol of happiness and beauty. Yet, while the engagement period is a period of high prestige for the woman, it is not equally prestigious for the man. The woman has the symbol of engagement—the ring—the man has no observable symbol. The woman is entertained at engagement parties and (along with her parents) traditionally participates in the planning of the wedding to a far greater extent than the man. Frequently, the principal duty of the man is to chauffeur his fiancée and her mother. For that matter, during the engagement and at the wedding the bride's mother may well be the second most important figure. The engaged man's role is much less significant.

(Adapted from Bell, 1975)

Push Factors

Conformity.   As we discovered earlier, nearly 95 per cent of Americans marry at one time or another. The entire socialization process emphasizes preparation for the husband-wife/father-mother roles that individuals are expected to undertake. "The American culture," Clayton (1975) states, "is so thoroughly structured to produce married couples that conformity is a primary, though not necessarily a manifest and readily recognized reason for marriage in the United States." (p. 320)

Love.   Another "push" factor that operates in American marriage is love. We consider marriage to be the "normal" way of translating a couple's emotional commitments into a more permanent and visible type of social undertaking. However, as Kephart (1977) suggests, the romantic love experienced during courtship is not the kind that lasts very long after marriage. Romantic love is an emotion, and like all emotions, it is difficult if not impossible to sustain. It is possible, however, for married love to become more rewarding and satisfying than premarital romance.

Legitimization of Sex and Children.   Traditionally, society has sanctioned sexual intercourse only among those persons who have declared a legal commitment to one another, although we noted in Unit 3 that a large proportion of men and women engage in nonmarital intercourse and that many of today's Americans have adopted a more tolerant view of nonmarital sexual relations. In many instances, regular sexual encounters will lead couples to legalize their sexual

THE LOVE SCALE

An innovative testing device designed to measure the feelings of love that couples have toward one another has been developed by Swenson (1968). The test is the result of numerous interviews with men and women about their reactions to this emotion.

Selected and adapted statements from Swenson's "Love Scale" are given below. The test is more a form of self-examination than a formal test. The more "yes" answers tallied, the more likely that love has the qualities of endurance and devotion.

Part A

(*Note:* Substitute the correct sex for each question.)

He (she) is truthful and honest with you.

He has told you things he likes about your appearance.

He listens with interest when you talk.

He tells you that he wants to live up to your expectations for him.

He tries to get you in a good mood when you are angry.

He does things for you.

He provides constructive criticism when you need it.

He tries to look attractive for you.

He tells you what behavior annoys him in you or other people.

He has taught you values and ideals in life.

He has given up his own preferences when you go out on a date to do what you want to do.

He is not overdemanding but considerate of your time and energy.

He has definite feelings about morals in regard to sex, and has expressed his views to you.

He has expressed his feelings by some physical affection.

He encourages you to try to succeed when you are discouraged about something.

He had discussed his thoughts and feelings about religion.

He consults you about major decisions (new job, schooling, purchases).

He has told you that he feels free to discuss anything with you.

He has told you what he is most ashamed of in the past.

He has told you his favorite jokes, the kind he likes to hear.

Part B

The following questions are more personal and related to your part of the love relationship:

You feel he (she) approves of you.

You feel that you get along well.

You feel that you understand each other.

You feel that you do not have to pretend you are something you are not with him.

You trust him completely.

You will do things or go places with him even though they do not particularly appeal to you.

You feel more cheerful when you are with him.

You feel free to talk about anything with him.

You feel safe with him.

You admire him.

The differences that come up between you do not spoil your love.

You respect and consider his opinions.

You have confided your strongest ambition to him.

You have a warm and happy feeling when you are with him.

You feel he is considerate and kind to you.

You have tried to live up to his ideals and expectations for you.

You consider him attractive.

You approve of his friends.

You have confided the pressures and strains of your life to him.

You have prayed for him.

Figure 4–1. The motives for marriage are many, from love to tax breaks.

acts by means of marriage. Even those who disavow any acceptance of societal norms about marriage, Clayton (1975) stresses, will usually make some kind of effort to declare their mutual commitment publicly so that their relationship will not be labeled as totally hedonistic or exploitative.

Obviously, one motive for marriage is to give children born of the relationship a legitimate identity. The stigma of illegitimacy is one that is not easily ignored.

Pull Factors

Companionship. One of the magnetic factors that "pull" partners toward the marriage commitment is the prospect of a regular companion. In one study, it was found that a significant 48 per cent of the married couples surveyed felt that the single most important feature of their marriage was the companionship it offered (Blood and Wolfe, 1960). The concept of married life not only includes sex on a fairly regular basis with the same partner but also emphasizes the importance of intimacy, an idea stressed by Erikson (1963) in his developmental theory (see Unit 3).

DEVELOPMENTAL TASKS OF THE YOUNG MARRIED COUPLE

1. Giving full expression to love and affection held for each other.
2. Developing what will hopefully become a sound system of communication between the pair.
3. Establishing a relationship with the respective in-laws, with neighbors, and with organizations in the community.
4. Locating and establishing a home.
5. Securing and maintaining an occupational pursuit that will provide for the economic necessities.
6. Developing an initial set of reciprocal role relationships that will allow individual initiative but will suggest spheres of authority.
7. Developing a procedure for organizing and allotting tasks.
8. Establishing a time schedule and routine correlated with outside work activities.
9. Developing a *modus operandi* of decision-making.
10. Establishing and developing a mutually acceptable philosophy of life and set of family goals.
11. Developing methods of maintaining morale as a couple.
12. Establishing a relationship that will allow the incorporation of children into the home.

(Atlee L. Stroup: *Marriage and Family: A Developmental Approach.* © 1966, p. 68. By permission of Prentice-Hall, Inc., Englewood Cliffs, N.J.)

Sharing.   Another magnetic force is the desire to share the same life-style, ideas, and income. Sharing, of course, also includes the routine aspects of married life, such as housecleaning chores and baby care. Those couples who actively seek to share and who handle family matters in a democratic fashion are far happier than those couples who do not (Landis and Landis, 1968).

Communication.   Many couples want to become more deeply involved in meaningful and intimate communication. Couples anticipating married life often say, "I want to really get to know her/him and communicate openly and freely." This requires a two-way exchange, and each must learn to adapt to criticisms and misunderstandings. Happily married couples are skilled in verbal and nonverbal communication and are sensitive to the needs of each other; they work hard to overcome disagreements and misunderstandings (Navran, 1967).

TYPES OF MARITAL ROLES

Several different types of marriages can be identified, each stressing different statuses and roles for the husband and wife. In each classification there are different rights and obligations for each spouse, but these are ideal types, and many features tend to overlap. Duberman (1974) offers an excellent description of some of the major types of marriages.

In the *traditional marriage,* the husband is recognized as the undisputed head of the family. In this type of marriage, deference flows from wife to husband, and although the wife has some authority in household matters and in child care, all other areas are under the husband's jurisdiction.

Companionship marriage operates on the assumption that no difference exists between female and male roles and that either

Holt, Rinehart and Winston

Figure 4–2.   Many contemporary marriages emphasize the sharing of household chores.

parent can assume the rights and fulfill the obligations of the other. This concept of marriage is growing in popularity among modern middle-class partners who emphasize such qualities as companionship, understanding, equality, affection, and democracy.

The *colleague marriage* is quite similar to the companionship marriage in that the qualities of sharing, comradeship, and personal satisfaction are stressed. However, the husband and wife in a colleague relationship recognize that there are role differences. Each assumes responsibility and authority for different areas of the marriage and fully recognizes the interests and abilities of the other. Deference is accorded when it is applicable.

Companionship and colleague-type marriages are frequently found among upper middle-class couples. Characteristically, these partners subscribe to the ideal of "togetherness" and share their interests and recreation, religious activities, sports, and sometimes their careers (Duberman, 1974).

FACTORS PROMOTING MARITAL HAPPINESS

In the minds of some people, two myths describe the popular image of marriage, one idealistic and the other quite cynical. The idealistic myth says, "and they lived happily ever after," implying that marriage is a continuous state of courtship and romantic love.

Figure 4–3.   (Copyright © 1959 by *The New Yorker Magazine.* Reprinted by permission.)

"We're not living happily ever after."

The second myth is that of the domestic "grind." It may portray the husband sitting behind the paper while the wife moves about in morning disarray. Or, it may portray the husband leaving for work while the wife spends the day tending to various household chores. As is the case with most myths, no one really believes either one of these, but they nevertheless leave an impression. Perhaps most newly married couples faintly hope to live happily ever after but actually fear that dreary domesticity will be their lot (Udry, 1966).

According to Sheehy (1976), the years of early adulthood are the "seesaw years" for the married couple. Although the ups are breathtaking and triumphant breakthroughs of "we can!", the "downs" are surprise "thuds". Most couples try to deny and dismiss the "downs"—the last thing they want at the peak of their illusions is to accept those things they can't handle or accomplish. Optimism during the early years of adulthood rides as high as expectations. Sheehy adds that the growth spurts experienced during these years will be, at best, uneven. When the husband is moving up, the wife is likely to feel herself slipping. And, when she feels "ready to soar," he may descend into the "sloughs of despondency." Trying to stabilize is what early married life is all about.

Numerous studies have been conducted to investigate the ingredients of successful marriages. One of the older, but more widely cited, studies was undertaken by Lewis Terman in 1938. In his field work, he attempted to discover what principal traits characterized the happy and unhappy husband and wife. Table 4–1 lists the characteristics Terman found most prominent in the couples he interviewed.

TABLE 4–1   CHARACTERISTICS OF HAPPY AND UNHAPPY MARITAL PARTNERS AS LISTED BY TERMAN*

Happy Wives	Unhappy Wives
Have kindly attitude toward others	Often have feelings of inferiority
Like to help underdogs	Tend to be defensive or aggressive
Tend to be conventional	Are easily annoyed, irritated
Are cooperative	Often join clubs only to get an office or
Have strong urge to save money	recognition in them
Are optimistic about life	Are extreme in their views
Do not take offense easily	Are more likely to be neurotic
Are less interested in social activities	Lose tempers easily
such as dances	Are impressed by thrilling situations
Like to teach children	Seek spectacular activities
Put less importance on clothes	Want to be on the move; are romance
Are systematic homemakers	seekers
Do less day-dreaming	Show little interest in others

Happy Husbands	Unhappy Husbands
Have greater stability	Often have feelings of inferiority
Are cooperative	Compensate by browbeating wife and
Get along well with business associates	subordinates
Are somewhat extroverted	Dislike details
Are conservative in attitudes	Are more radical about sex morality
Are willing to take initiative	Are inclined to be moody
Take responsibility easily	Are argumentative
Do not get rattled easily	Like recreations that take them away
	from home
	Are likely to be careless about money

*From Terman, 1938.

There have been other attempts to explore the predictors of marital happiness. Burgess and Locke (1953), for instance, uncovered certain criteria of marital satisfaction which include, among others, the couple's possession of positive personality traits (such as emotional stability), similarity of cultural backgrounds, a harmonious and stable family environment, a loving relationship developing out of companionship rather than infatuation, and wholesome attitudes toward sexual relations. In a review of the literature, Troll (1975) states that couples with traditional expectations for marriage report greater happiness than couples with more expressive expectations. Also, wives tend to report more marital stress than their husbands do; however, they also report more overall satisfaction. Kirkpatrick's (1955) analysis of factors related to marital happiness is presented in Table 4–2.

An excellent summary statement concerning the success of marriage has been provided by Bell (1975). Marital happiness and harmony, he believes, are determined by the amount of interaction between the two partners over the span of a given marriage. A marriage is not simply the sum of two individuals; rather, it is a *unity* of *two interacting personalities*. To state it another way, no single type of personality causes a failure in marriage; instead, two individual personalities, through interaction with one another, fail in

TABLE 4–2   FACTORS RELATED TO MARITAL HAPPINESS*

	Favorable	Unfavorable
Premarital factors		
1. Happiness of parents' marriage (high)	X	
a. Parents divorced		X
b. Parent or parents deceased		X
2. Personal happiness in childhood	X	
3. Ease of premarital contact with the opposite sex	X	
4. Mild, but firm discipline by parents	X	
5. Lack of conflict with parents	X	
6. Courtship		
a. Acquainted under one year		X
b. Acquainted over one year	X	
c. Approval of parents	X	
d. Similarity of age	X	
e. Satisfaction with affection of other	X	
7. Reason for marriage		
a. Love	X	
b. Loneliness		X
c. Escape from one's own family		X
d. Common interests	X	
Postmarital factors		
1. Attitudes		
a. Husband more dominant		X
b. Pair equalitarian	X	
c. Wife more dominant		X
d. Jealous of spouse		X
e. Feels superior to spouse		X
f. Feels more intelligent than spouse		X
2. Good relationships with in-laws	X	
3. Not living with in-laws	X	
4. Community of interest	X	
5. Desire for children	X	

From Clifford Kirkpatrick: *The Family—As Process and Institution,* 2nd ed. Copyright © 1963, The Ronald Press Company, New York.

marriage. Consequently, the successful marriage relies on the desire of the husband and wife to make their relationship work. How committed they are to meet one another's expectations will ultimately decide whether a marriage is successful.

EARLY MARRIAGES: TRENDS, CHARACTERISTICS, AND PROBLEMS

For a number of years, considerable concern has been generated over younger teenage marriage and the problems it presents to parents, educators, community welfare workers, and agencies that work with adolescents. Although the number of marriages in this age group has declined in recent years, as shown in Table 4–3, teenage marriage nevertheless represents a problem that needs continued attention and investigation (Dreyer, 1975; Landis, 1975).

HELPING TO CREATE A HAPPY MARRIAGE

Since every couple and every relationship is unique, Middlebrook (1974) states, there are no infallible rules for selecting a mate with whom a satisfying relationship can be maintained. Nevertheless, she offers the following general guidelines for building a happy marriage:

BEFORE MARRIAGE

1. Try to *distinguish sexual attraction from love.* Obviously, sexual attraction is an important component of love, but it is not enough to base an enduring relationship on.

2. *Examine your reasons for wanting to marry* this particular person. If you are marrying to escape from an unhappy homelife, to "reform" the other, to solve your own personal problems, or because all of your friends are marrying, don't. Analyze what you would gain and what you would lose should you marry.

3. *Keep the lines of communication open.* Discuss areas that will be important after marriage, such as the relationship between the two of you and your in-laws, money, religion, children, and the role of husband and wife. There should be no surprises in basic areas after the wedding ceremony. *Really get to know the other person.*

4. *Be analytical about the relationship you now have* with the other person. Patterns of interaction before marriage are your best clue as to what life with the other person will be like after marriage. Don't delude yourself that the other person will "change" after marriage. *What you see is what you're going to get.*

5. *Think about the characteristics of the other person.* Are you compatible in areas that are important to you? Complete similarity could lead to a boring relationship, but dissimilarity in important areas—such as attitudes about sex, religion, children, the husband and wife roles, and so forth—can be irritants after marriage.

AFTER MARRIAGE

1. *Be as concerned about the happiness, growth, and well-being of the other as you are about your own.*

2. *Keep the lines of communication open.* Don't store up grievances. Air important differences openly, but in a way that will not wound the self-esteem of your partner.

3. *Be tolerant.* Nobody is perfect. Accept the imperfections of the other that you can tolerate. Before criticizing the other, think about some of your own imperfections, and decide whether the issue is important enough to discuss.

4. *Don't try to make your partner into a carbon copy of yourself.* You married your partner because you liked and loved what was there; give the other person some breathing room. You'll both be more interesting to the other if you don't have total togetherness.

5. *Be aware of the other person's moods* and guide your reactions accordingly. Don't bring up an irritating subject when the other person is feeling tired or irritable.

6. *If you do get into an argument, keep the discussion limited to the issue at hand.* Hurtful remarks about areas irrelevant to the issue at hand will only interfere with the discussion. If you sense that the argument is escalating, break off the discussion. When tempers have cooled, resume the discussion.

7. *Be your partner's best friend.* Act in such a manner that the other person knows he or she is deeply loved. Be receptive to discussions of the other person's problems, but don't dwell exclusively on them. A marriage is not psychotherapy. Be sure you share pleasant events as well as problems.

8. *Be analytical about the meaning of your patterns of interaction.* Say what you mean and not what you think you should say. Be honest with one another.

9. *Make "marital rules" explicit.* Bargain openly and negotiate contracts about duties, obligations, and privileges. There are some unpleasant duties that must be performed, and how the chores are to be allocated should be made explicit.

(Middlebrook, 1974, p. 467)

Of the teenagers who marry, most are high-school juniors or seniors (Burchinal, 1965). The marriages are not usually characterized by elopement; on the contrary 92 per cent of the marriages studied were conventional and were performed by clergymen. Because the couples were not well educated and were of low socio-

**TABLE 4–3   PERCENTAGES OF MARRIED WHITE
MEN AND WOMEN AGED 15 to 20 YEARS IN U.S. POPULATION,
1910 to 1971***

Age	1910	1920	1930	1940	1950	1960	1971
			Women				
15	1.1	1.3	1.1	1.0	1.0	2.3	a
16	3.4	3.8	3.9	3.4	5.6	5.6	a
17	8.1	9.1	9.1	8.0	12.7	12.0	a
18	15.9	17.9	17.7	16.2	23.2	24.5	16.7
19	24.6	27.4	27.4	24.1	36.8	40.5	29.2
20	35.1	37.2	36.7	35.4	49.5	54.8	42.0
			Men				
15	0.1	0.2	0.1	0.1	0.6	0.6	a
16	0.1	0.3	0.2	0.3	0.6	0.9	a
17	0.3	0.8	0.6	0.6	1.2	1.9	a
18	1.2	2.4	1.9	1.9	3.4	5.4	4.4
19	3.4	5.9	5.2	4.9	8.8	12.9	11.5
20	7.9	11.5	10.5	9.9	17.5	24.4	19.2

*Adapted from Bureau of the Census, *Population Characteristics*
[a]Data not comparable

economic status, most early marriages Burchinal studied were financially unstable. The husband's occupational trade was frequently limited to unskilled or semiskilled work.

A number of factors, Burchinal (1965) states, contribute to early marriages. Among these are the glamorized and romantic image of marriage that is portrayed by the movies and television, the wish to accelerate achievement of adult status, dissatisfaction with home life, loneliness, and the tendency to become involved in early and serious dating. However, pregnancy is the most important factor in precipitating early marriages. In an investigation of high-school marriages, it was learned that 87 per cent of the girls who married did so because they were pregnant (Burchinal, 1960).

Although some early marriages are successful, most unfortunately are plagued with problems and maladjustment difficulties. Monahan (1963) estimates that the divorce rates for married adolescents will be between two and four times as great as those for couples who marry in their twenties. Glick (1957) discovered that those married before age 18 have divorce rates almost three times as high as those marrying between the ages of 22 and 24.

According to Cox (1974), four main problems are responsible for the failure of adolescent marriages. First, marriage always *reduces personal freedom.* For adolescents, this reduction of freedom often comes before the partners have had a chance to explore, adventure, and test themselves as individuals. Often, marriage comes before they really know who they are, since they are still in the midst of psychological and philosophical growth.

Another problem that arises is one of *finances.* Lack of money serves to further impede striving toward self-fulfillment. Moreover, financial strain greatly raises the level of conflict between marriage partners.

A third problem is that of *immaturity*. The earlier the marriage, the less chance the couple have of being mature enough to meet the challenges of decision-making, responsibility, and compromise that marriage offers.

Finally, the introduction of *children*, which is characteristic of most early marriages, exaggerates already existing problems. In general, the belief that children serve to bring together a marriage is faulty at best. Although children are wonderful additions to families and the major reason for the existence of the family as an institution, it should be recognized that they can create many additional problems for all parents, but especially for teenagers.

ALTERNATIVES TO TRADITIONAL MARRIAGE

Remaining single or pursuing a nontraditional form of marriage are alternatives available to all segments of the population. Among the nontraditional forms of marriage is contract marriage. Other alternatives include communal living, group marriage, and "swinging."

Single Adulthood

For various reasons, some people simply prefer not to get married (see Table 4–4). In 1960, for example, there were over 3 million men over 35 and 3 million women over 30 who had chosen to remain single (Duberman, 1974). In 1972, there were 1.4 million single men and 0.9 million single women between the ages of 25 and 29; there were 3.2 million single men and 2.8 million single women over the age of 30 (Kimmel, 1974).

Unfortunately, as Duberman (1974) points out, bachelorhood and spinsterhood are viewed with suspicion in the United States. Not only is social pressure to conform by marrying applied to single people, but the unmarried are treated differently and tend to think of themselves as different. "Ours is a two-by-two world," she states, "and there is little room in it for the unaccompanied individual. Furthermore, unattached people, especially women, are considered a threat to married people. To justify their own state, married people think of marriage as 'natural', and anyone who does not conform to this point of view is challenging the social values." (p. 115)

Yet, Kelley (1974) stresses that it is entirely possible to fill a satisfying and rewarding masculine or feminine role without entering into marriage. Although this has been traditionally easier for men, it is now becoming feasible for women as well, especially in light of the "women's liberation" movement. The single man or woman may occupy a prominent place in commercial, political, or professional worlds. Just as being single does not doom an individual to an unrewarding life, getting married is no guarantee of happiness. Single adults are capable of developing mature interests and constructing stable and satisfying interpersonal relationships.

TABLE 4–4 SINGLE PERSONS IN UNITED STATES ANALYZED BY AGE, SEX, AND STATUS (MARCH, 1972)*

Subject	Total 14 Years and Over	Age (Years)						
		14 to 24	25 to 34	35 to 44	45 to 54	55 to 64	65 to 74	75 and Over
Women								
In thousands	17,649	13,981	1321	522	514	550	470	292
Percentage	100.0	100.0	100.0	100.0	100.0	100.0	100.0	100.0
Head of household	14.4	4.9	42.5	47.5	52.7	57.6	60.0	63.8
Head of primary family	3.8	1.4	10.9	17.2	14.5	14.2	11.9	12.5
Primary individual	10.6	3.4	31.6	30.3	38.2	43.4	48.1	51.3
Living alone	8.7	2.2	24.4	26.6	35.3	41.4	45.3	49.8
With nonrelatives	1.8	1.2	7.1	3.7	2.9	2.0	2.8	1.6
Not head of household	85.6	95.1	57.5	52.5	47.3	42.4	40.0	36.2
In families	80.8	91.7	46.4	42.8	38.6	35.0	28.4	28.2
Secondary individual	4.7	3.4	11.2	9.7	8.7	7.3	11.5	8.0
Men								
In thousands	20,759	16,227	2108	903	613	452	314	141
Percentage	100.0	100.0	100.0	100.0	100.0	100.0	100.0	100.0
Head of household	12.6	4.3	32.3	32.6	51.0	66.1	73.1	79.5
Head of primary family	1.9	0.4	3.4	5.6	11.0	16.7	12.7	17.7
Primary individual	10.8	3.9	28.8	26.9	40.0	49.4	60.4	61.8
Living alone	8.3	2.2	22.1	24.0	34.8	46.5	57.6	58.7
With nonrelatives	2.5	1.8	6.8	3.0	5.2	2.9	2.8	3.1
Not head of household	87.4	95.7	67.7	67.4	49.0	33.9	26.9	20.5
In families	82.0	92.2	55.8	54.1	37.6	20.7	19.8	12.0
Secondary individual	5.3	3.5	11.9	13.3	11.4	13.2	7.0	8.5

*Source: U.S. Bureau of the Census (1972), Table 6.

Contract Marriage

Contract marriages are marriages in which the partners agree to remain together for a specified time. The contract is usually renewable, provided, of course, that both parties are agreeable. In most cases the contract is a private agreement rather than a legal document (Kelley, 1974).

Contract marriages seem to be attracting considerable public attention. In 1971, for example, a bill to permit three-year contract marriages with the option to renew was introduced in the Maryland House of Delegates by Hildegarde Boswell and Lena Lee. The proposal was aimed at helping the younger generation and averting the problems likely to develop in future marriages.

A contemporary marriage contract is usually one that is open and flexible and stresses the importance of continual self-growth for both marriage partners. Its underlying assumptions differ from the traditional marriage contract, which many couples still use to guide their individual marriages (see boxes).

UNDERLYING ASSUMPTIONS OF THE TRADITIONAL MARRIAGE CONTRACT

1. Marriage furnishes a means for the giving and taking of love, understanding, and for sexual fulfillment.
2. Sexual relations should take place only (or largely) between the two partners.
3. Marriage offers a measure of security, comfort, and stability, so that both partners soon learn to know what they can expect. Boundaries are set by husband and wife and it is their expectation that these will be respected.
4. Marriage involves a set of responsibilities and duties. It also involves certain roles—"what a husband is and should be" and "what a wife is and should be."
5. Marriage is for the raising and rearing of children and "having a family."
6. Marriage is a means of "weathering life's storms and ups-and-downs."
7. Marriage means companionship, someone to talk to.
8. Marriage is an insurance against a lonely old age.

(Otto, 1970, pp. 117–118)

In contrast to the traditional marriage contract, open contracts (among other features) do not place the partners in bondage to each other, diminish the individual identity of the partners, create a "couple-image", or enforce togetherness in the belief that only thus can the marriage be preserved. The open contract does not substitute new regulations for old ones; rather, it suggests ways in which couples can learn to communicate openly with one another in order to arrive at a fully understood and mutual consensus for living.

Communal Living

Recently, communal living has been in the news. According to Cox (1972), the concept of the family commune originated in antiquity. Utopians from Plato to Thoreau have suggested and often experimented with this type of family system. Today, there are approximately 3000 communes scattered throughout the United States.

THE CONTEMPORARY MARRIAGE CONTRACT IN OPERATION

The first years of married life are often sprinkled with squabbles as newlyweds work out the practical aspects of living together.

To avoid these irritations when they married, in June of 1972, Mary Lenth and Jere Gwin signed a two-year agreement spelling out who does what around the house.

The contract is three pages long and includes these specifications:

• Both of the couple's last names were combined to form a new family surname, Gwin-Lenth, because they agreed that Mary's name is a part of her identity that should not be lost.

• Husband and wife are to share equally in the weekly housework. The contract lists certain specific chores, including "a general picking up, mopping, vacuuming, dusting, and cleaning of toilets, sinks, tubs and mirrors."

This agreement is not legally binding but Mary and Jere say they will honor it as a symbol of their marriage. When it expires, they will decide whether to renew it or to seek a divorce.

Because of this expiration clause, the Gwin-Lenths are sometimes accused of using the agreement as a way of legitimizing a temporary affair. But the two say they want a lasting marriage. Mary says:

"We believe a permanent relationship is possible. But we don't think it is realistic, in a world where people grow and change rapidly, to assume it's going to happen."

The two say they place little value in the institution of marriage. They got married because they felt their friends and relatives expected it of them. Says Jere:

"What is important to us is our relationship itself."

(Reprinted from *U.S. News and World Report,* April 16, 1973. Copyright 1973, U.S. News & World Report, Inc.)

The basic underlying principle of the commune can be stated as follows. Single people or couples enter into this living arrangement with the expectation that a variety of sexual relationships will be available. The nature of the relationships formed depends on the type of commune entered and the amount of time spent there. Usually, five individuals or more gather in the commune in order to share certain features of common life, such as "a dwelling, economic maintenance, and social, cultural, educational, or spiritual life" (Kelley, 1974). Many people think of communal life as a means of becoming involved in the broader community and counteracting the belief that the outside world is hostile (Bell, 1975).

The success of communes in contemporary society is doubtful because of the intricacies of our economic system (Duberman, 1974). To be sure, Duberman writes, it takes a great deal of trust to surrender all one's economic resources to a group. Yet, it is unfair to write off this alternative to marriage as invalid, especially when there is considerable evidence that young people, as well as some older people, are experiencing a growing need for a sense of community. There are many who feel that our impersonal and bureaucratic society offers too little sharing. Others are actively seeking a sense of belonging. If the need for community becomes stronger than the need for economic success, this alternative life-style may well gain many followers.

Group Marriage

A group marriage is defined as a group of three or more persons in which the individuals consider themselves "pair bonded" or

EXPLORING THE COMMUNAL LIFE STYLE

At first glance, it looks like a movie set for *Walden Two*. There is a shop building called Harmony, a farm-house called Llano, and a dormitory called Oneida. Bulletin boards list upcoming cultural events, and young people lounge on hammocks, reading and engaging in serious discussions. The smell of farm-fresh cooking is everywhere. The resemblance to Walden Two is more than superficial. Twin Oaks, a 123-acre farm commune nestled in the foothills of Virginia's Piedmont, is a remarkable attempt to create a utopian community governed by Skinner's laws of social engineering.

Work is allocated by an intricate system of labor credits so that none of the 35 members have unequal burdens. Titles and honorifics have been done away with so that, in the words of the community's code, "all are entitled to the same privileges, advantages and respect." Private property is forbidden, except for such things as books and clothing, and even with that loophole, most members draw their clothing, right down to their underwear, from a massive community closet. No one is allowed to boast of individual accomplishments, to gossip ("negative speech") or to be intolerant of another's beliefs. . .

The use of tobacco and alcohol is . . . discouraged at Twin Oaks, and all drugs, including marijuana, are banned. So is television, which is considered a cultural poison. "We decided that we just weren't strong enough to stand up to television," says Kat Griebe, one of Twin Oaks' charter founders and, at 40, one of the oldest members. "Its powerful message is that of middle-class American values, which we reject—a high level of consumption, streamlined cosmetic standards of beauty, male dominance, the use of violence as a problem solver, and the underlying assumption that life should be a constant state of titillation and excitement. Life just isn't like that". . . .

All of the utopian ventures of the early and mid-19th century—from Indiana's New Harmony on the Wabash River to Massa-chusetts' famed Brook Farm—eventually foundered, and Twin Oaks, too, has its problems. The major one appears to be financial. "Skinner never wrote about a poor community," laments Gabe Sinclair. "He wrote about a rich one." After starting with only $35,000, Twin Oaks, four years later, still finds survival a struggle. The farm brings more emotional than monetary rewards: members would find it cheaper to work at other jobs and buy their food at the market. The community's chief source of income is the sale of hammocks stitched together in Harmony, but it is not enough to make ends meet; several members are forced to take outside jobs in Richmond and Charlottesville—a direct contradiction to Walden Two's basic premise that all time should be spent in a totally controlled environment.

Beyond economics, there are serious psychological problems at Twin Oaks, and few members have stayed very long. Turnover last year was close to 70 per cent. The ones who leave first, in fact, are often the most competent members, who still expect special recognition for their talents. "Competent people are hard to get along with," says Richard Stutsman, one of Twin Oaks' trained psychologists. "They tend to make demands, not requests. We cannot afford to reinforce ultimatum behavior, although we recognize our need for their competence. So often we have given in to them on little things, and then when a big demand arises we have to deny them." When they leave, the community not only loses their skills but also sacrifices a potential rise in its standard of living.

While it is still considerably poorer than Walden Two, Twin Oaks has gone farther toward the goal of behavioral control than might have seemed reasonably possible. It is too soon, however, to call the commune much more than a fascinating experiment.

(Reprinted by permission from TIME, The Weekly Newsmagazine, September 20, 1971. Copyright Time, Inc. 1971.)

"married" to at least two other members of the group. These marriages may be formed in various ways. A man and woman may ask a third person to join their existing relationship; two or three existing couples may join with each other or with a previously single man or woman, and so on (Burr, 1976). Thus, group marriage overlaps polygamy, polygyny (several wives) and polyandry (several husbands) (Kelley, 1974).

Ramey (1972), in a fairly extensive investigation of group marriages among middle-class and upper middle-class couples and individuals, reports:

> For some people the idea of being married to two or more individuals at once is overwhelming. But establishing a dyadic marriage involves a "growing together", not a spontaneous happening. The same is true for a group marriage which begins with a set of potentials that are developed fully only over time. To begin, all that is necessary is the assurance that everyone in the group can sustain multiple pair bonding. This is why the definition specifies that each individual in the group have at least two pair-bonds before the group can be called a group marriage.

(Ramey, 1972, p. 452)

According to Burr (1976), group marriages have several characteristics that distinguish them from other styles of marriage. First, intimate sexual activity (but not always) occurs in all of the cross-sex relationships. Occasionally, homosexual activities develop. Second, group marriage requires considerably more commitment, time, energy, and effort than do the simpler forms of marriage. Obviously, the larger the group, the more demanding the interpersonal relationships. "Given the tendency of humans to have such reactions as jealousy, feeling left out, resentments, and a need for esteem, group arrangements can be extremely complex." (p. 16) A final characteristic is that most of the individuals involved in group marriages are older adults. Very seldom are individuals under 30 involved in this type of living arrangement (Burr 1976).

"Swinging"

Swinging, also referred to as "wife swapping", is a relationship involving two or more married couples who decide to switch sexual partners or to engage in group sex. Research has indicated that swingers are usually upper middle class individuals who are employed in professional and white-collar ocupations. Ironically, most seem to be conservative in many ways, with the exception of their sexual behavior. The median age for men was 29 to 34 years and for women, 28 to 31 years (Bartell, 1970; Denfield and Gordon, 1971).

According to Denfield and Gordon, (1971) many swingers are attempting to find ways to strengthen an otherwise strained marital relationship. In support of this, the following four points are proposed:

1. Swingers have developed rules that serve to define the sexual relationship of marriage as one of love, of emotion.
2. Recreational swingers are occasionally known to drop out of swinging, at least temporarily, while the wife gets pregnant. By not swinging, the couple can be assured that the husband is the father of the child; unknown or other parentage is considered taboo. This reflects a traditional, middle-class view about the conception and rearing of children.

3. A common word in the swinger's vocabulary is discretion. Swingers desire to keep their sexual play a secret from their nonswinging or "square" friends. They want to protect their position in the community, and an effort is made to limit participation to couples of similar status or "respectability."

4. Some of the controls on jealousy are: (1) that the marriage commands paramount loyalty, (2) that there is physical but not emotional interest in other partners, (3) that single persons are avoided, and (4) that there be no concealment of sexual activities.

(pp. 9–11)

In general, swinging does not take place until several years after the wedding, although some couples have been known to adopt this style of sexual behavior prior to or from the beginning of their marriage. In contemporary society, most swingers adopt this type of relationship for only a short time. The actual form of sexual activity also differs from group to group. Whereas some participate only in "open sex" (in which everyone is always in the same room), others practice "closed sex" (in which couples are free to go into separate rooms). Swinging almost always begins with heterosexual activity, yet homosexual activity frequently occurs later. Homosexual participation in this type of arrangement is more common for women than for men (Burr, 1976).

Summary

It has been estimated that virtually 95 per cent of Americans will be married at least once. The motives for marriage are numerous and diverse, prompting one researcher to categorize them as "push" and "pull" factors. Push factors would include conformity, love, legitimization of sex, and legitimization of children, whereas pull factors include the need for companionship, sharing, and communication.

Several types of marriages can be identified, each stressing different statuses and roles for the husband and wife. These include the traditional marriage (the husband is recognized as the head of the household); the companionship marriage (no difference exists between female and male roles, and a great emphasis is placed on sharing); and the colleague marriage (similar to the companionship marriage as far as sharing is concerned, but role differences exist).

Numerous researchers have sought to identify the ingredients of successful marriage. In general, happy marriages are characterized by husband and wife cooperation, sharing of housework, empathy toward one another, similarity of backgrounds, and wholesome attitudes toward sexual relations. Most experts agree that marital happiness is determined by the amount of constructive *interaction* between the two partners. Teenage marriages have been characteristically plagued with maladjustment difficulties. Four main problems appear to account for the failure of these marriages: reduction in individual freedom, financial difficulties, immaturity, and the introduction of children.

Not all Americans choose the traditional form of marriage. On the contrary, some may decide to choose an alternative life-style: remaining single, contract marriage, communal living, group marriage, or "swinging." Of these alternatives, remaining single is the most popular.

Suggested Readings

1. Blood, R. O.: *Marriage.* New York, The Free Press, 1969.

   This well-known sociologist provides a balanced discussion of the key aspects of marriage in the United States. Especially well done are sections focusing on mixed and unmixed marriages, marital readiness, and occupational roles and marriages.

2. Burr, W. R.: *Successful Marriage.* Homewood, Illinois: The Dorsey Press, 1976.

   This "principles approach" text includes such topics as alternative marriage styles, communication and decision-making, and sexuality in marriage. Well supplemented by references and graphic material.

3. Cox, F. D., (Ed.): *American Marriage: A Changing Scene?* Dubuque, Iowa: Wm. C. Brown Company, Publishers, 1972.

   A collection of readings supplemented by the author's running commentary. Sections include "Tomorrow's Morality", "The Romantic Ideal", and "The Family of the Future".

4. Landis, P. H.: *Making the Most of Marriage.* (5th ed.). Englewood Cliffs, New Jersey: Prentice-Hall, Inc., 1975.

   This extremely successful text combines high readability with a wide range of current research findings. Of particular interest are chapters related to love, mate choice, and marriage adjustment.

5. Roleder, G. (Ed.): *Marriage Means Encounter.* Dubuque, Iowa: Wm. C. Brown Company, Publishers, 1973.

   This book exposes six areas of encounter which are relevant to all marriages: (1) premarital sex, (2) marital sex, (3) marital roles, (4) parenthood, (5) the new marriage, and (6) marital failure.

Jean Berlfein

UNIT 5

THE FAMILY: PARENTHOOD

Introduction

ADJUSTMENT TO PARENTHOOD

RESPONSIBILITIES OF PARENTHOOD

PARENTAL ROLES
    The Role of the Mother
    The Role of the Father

Summary

Introduction

One of the most important, most exciting developmental challenges young married couples encounter is parenthood. The arrival of a newborn infant in the household is characteristically a joyous occasion, the culmination of many long months of growing anticipation and preparation. For those who have experienced this event, words cannot capture the feelings of pride, love, and warmth that family members can share.

Quite likely, the transition from a dyad to a triad relationship is one of the most complex and dramatic changes most people will ever make in their lives (Burr, 1976). Some writers, such as Landis (1975), claim that no other experience can cause as much personality growth as being a parent. Furthermore, no single circumstance in the life of a child will be as influential as its relationships with its parents.

Williamson (1966) believes there are at least six motives for becoming a parent. The first is *ego expansion*—that is, the child

TRENDS IN FAMILY PLANNING

The current emphasis society has placed on ecology in addition to the problems of overpopulation appears to be reducing family size (Kelley, 1974). Although the two-child family seems to be the ideal of most Americans, there are indications that the number of childless marriages will increase in future years.

The accompanying chart shows that the birth rate in the United States for 1973 (1.9 children per family) was below the level of replacement (2.1 children per family). The level of replacement is the average number of lifetime births per woman necessary for the population to reach zero growth.

Why are birth rates declining? According to Duberman (1974), several noteworthy reasons can be cited. To begin with, more and more young adults are simply choosing to remain unmarried. Furthermore, some married couples are deciding to have children later. Other couples are limiting the size of their families. In addition, there are more women than ever before in the labor force, contraceptive techniques are more widely known and available, and abortion laws are being liberalized. Each of these factors contributes to the fact that Americans today are having fewer children.

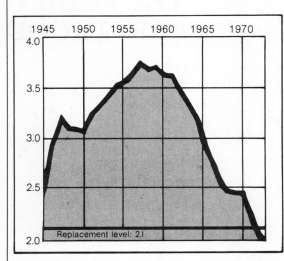

Figure 5–1. Declining birth rates in the United States. (U.S. National Center for Health Statistics; U. S. Census Bureau.)

gives the parents a greater sense of importance and a feeling of immortality. Second, parenthood offers the couple *the chance to be creative and attain a sense of achievement,* particularly through child-rearing practices. Third, parenthood fulfills *status and conformity* needs, particularly since the status of men and women in most societies is enhanced by proof of fertility. The desire for *control and authority* is a fourth motive, particularly when the couple desire dominance over others. Fifth, the need for *love or affection* appears to be one of the most important motives of young couples planning a family. Finally, parenthood fulfills the desire for *happiness,* since rarely does the new parent fail to experience a euphoric state.

ADJUSTMENT TO PARENTHOOD

Becoming a parent requires considerable adjustment and adaptation, to say the least. A number of researchers, including LeMasters (1957) and Dyer (1963), go so far as to label this time of life as a "crisis period". During the baby's first year—and frequently longer—the new mother may experience post partum depression and chronic fatigue because of loss of sleep, not to mention her concern over how well she is performing as a mother. The husband, on the other hand, may become concerned over his inactive sexual and social life as well as his new financial responsibilities and his new role as a father. Yet Hobbs' (1963) analysis of parenthood suggests that "crisis" may be too strong a term for this stage. Although it is indeed a period of demands and strain, most parents are able to weather its difficulties unless the child is born with unusual health problems.

Blood (1972) describes one of the many facets of adjustment required in becoming a parent:

> Prior to the first child's arrival, the family consists of two persons able to give their entire attention to each other. After he [the baby] arrives, the comfortable reciprocity of the dyad is destroyed. Henceforth, each adult must compete with the child for the attention of the spouse. The winner is likely to be the child. The younger he is, the greater his dependence on his parents. When he is an infant, his needs for food and clothing are at a maximum. Without attention, he would literally die. The spouse, however, can care for himself and therefore must be content with left-over time and energy after the baby's needs are met. Mature adults expect nothing else, but parents young enough or neurotic enough to have strong dependency needs may find the sense that 'three's a crowd' disconcerting.
>
> (Blood, 1972, pp. 377–378)

Rossi (1968) maintains that early parenthood looms as a crucial transitory stage today, perhaps more than marriage itself. For most couples, there are four principal reasons for difficulty in adjusting to parenthood. First, contemporary society appears to provide little preparation for parenthood. Although the values of American society suggest that every married couple should seek to have children, formal training in adjustment to this new lifestyle is lacking in the home and in the schools. Second, it appears that learning about

FOLKLORE ABOUT PARENTHOOD

LeMasters (1977) believes that many people living in modern civilizations are apt to think they do not believe in folklore—to have an unwarranted assumption that their behavior is based on sound, rational principles, when in fact they subscribe to a number of folk beliefs that romanticize parenthood. Some of these are:

1. *Child rearing is all fun and little work.* The truth of the matter is that raising children is probably the hardest and most thankless job in the world. Although few parents would deny that it is exciting, rewarding, and interesting, the tasks associated with child rearing are not always amusing.

2. *Children will turn out well if they have "good" parents.* Almost everyone knows of at least one nice family with a black sheep in the fold. Children and society are so complex that parents simply do not have the "quality control" one finds in industrial production. Skillful parents usually turn out a more reliable "product" than those with more modest talents—even for good parents there is no such thing as "zero defects".

3. *Today's parents are not as good as those of yesterday.* This belief is impossible to prove or disprove, of course, but it seems quite prevalent. It is true, however, that higher standards are applied to today's parents, and the modern world in which parents have to function is more complex than the world of yesterday. All of this tends to create the impression, LeMasters notes, that the abilities of parents as a group have deteriorated since the good old days. However, there is always a tendency to romanticize the past, and this appears to have done a real disservice to today's parents.

4. *Child rearing is easier today because of modern medicine, modern appliances, child psychology, and so forth.* Although some claim that modern parents have an easier time because they have access to such things as dishwashers and diaper services, the truth of the matter is that parents are in much more of a rat race today with their busy schedules than their grandparents ever imagined. And, in some cases, modern medicine and child psychology have made child rearing more difficult since parents are more aware of the terrible things that can happen to children

and are expected to recognize them early enough to take the proper preventive action. Although access to the services of the pediatrician or child psychologist may make parents glad they are living in the 20th century rather than the 18th, young adults frequently become saddled with anxieties and fears their predecessors never had.

5. *Children are appreciative of the advantages their parents are able to give them.* Oddly enough, the opposite seems to be the case: many children are today less appreciative than those of an earlier era, not more so. The same attitude seems to be characteristic of all who live in modern society; we take for granted such things as painless dentistry and religious freedom and complain when the system fails to deliver. In this sense, many parents derive little satisfaction from giving children all the modern advantages: they merely feel guilty when they *can't* deliver the goods.

6. *There are no bad children—only bad parents.* This may well be the most destructive bit of folklore related to parenthood. In *addition* to parents, numerous factors affect the destinies of children, including genetic heritage and the actions of siblings, members of the extended family, teachers, and peers. Unfortunately, parents are held unduly responsible for shaping the *total* destiny of their offspring.

7. *Love is enough to sustain good parental performance.* Unfortunately, love is not enough. It must be guided by knowledge and insight and tempered with self-control on the part of the parent. Yet, the reverse is also true: no amount of scientific or professional knowledge about child development will do parents (or their children) any good unless it is combined with love for the child and acceptance of the parental role.

8. *All married couples should have children.* This is a dubious proposition and one that few (if any) experts on childhood would support. Many married couples enjoy their own exclusive company and can sustain their marriage without the addition of children. Sometimes, marriages of this sort are strained or broken by the arrival of children.

(Adapted from LeMasters, 1977)

parenthood during pregnancy is limited. Most expectant couples, at best, participate in informal discussions with family members and make a few visits to the doctor. Third, an abrupt transition takes place as soon as the baby comes home from the hospital. Parents quickly realize that the newborn infant is completely dependent on them 24 hours of the day. Finally, formalized guidelines for successful parenthood are seldom available. Many young couples have to rely on the advice of parents and friends or "on-the-job" training.

While Rossi's (1968) emphasis on the need for parental role preparation appears to be well taken, Clayton (1975) believes Rossi's concern is too negative. He suggests that although most prospective parents are uneasy about the coming transition, they probably go through considerable anticipatory practice, at least at the talking level. To say the least, they have nine months to prepare for their new responsibilities. After initial anxieties about the demands placed upon them by the infant and about their caretaking responsibilities, most new parents begin to take pride in their accomplishments, such as changing diapers or feeding the baby. These represent joyful experiences and may quickly serve to neutralize those fears resulting from a lack of preparation. In this sense, the lack of explicit training and guidelines for parental behavior does not necessarily mean catastrophe for the new parent.

RESPONSIBILITIES OF PARENTHOOD

Parenthood calls for the execution of new tasks and the reorganization of daily routines. The responsibilities associated with early parenthood are numerous and diverse. The first and most obvious obligation is maintenance; that is, the parents are responsible for supplying their offspring with food, shelter, and clothing (Benson, 1971). Most American couples make changes in the family budget, putting aside extra money and setting up special funds for the baby's food and clothing, not to mention medical bills and other expenses. The purchase of certain household luxuries not essential to the life of a child, such as a color television set, a stereo system, or a new car, may be postponed. Living arrangements are changed, and a new house or larger apartment may be considered (Kelley, 1974).

Another responsibility is providing the baby with continual attention, since a newborn infant cannot be left alone and is seldom entrusted to someone else. As a result, Blood (1969) states, personal and social relationships become limited. The husband and wife are seldom able to enjoy each other's exclusive and unlimited companionship, and visiting with friends is likely to be restricted. The child's needs compete with those of the spouse, and as more children arrive, each family member's slice of attention becomes smaller. Yet, even though the couple's social life is curtailed, the change has its share of rewards and compensations:

The very fact of having a baby is a new activity—a kind of recreation as well as work. It is no accident that parents are often described as

Photo Trends

Figure 5–2. Parenthood requires a wide variety of responsibilities.

"proud". A baby represents not only a task but an achievement. He is "flesh of our flesh". Every development is an event for co-parent to hear about (and friends and relatives too). The first smile, first tooth, and first step highlight what is often a wearing but seldom a dull existence. If husband and wife go out less, they have more to stay in for. Instead of saying that social life is restricted, better say it is revised (except for those to whom bright lights are indispensable).

(Blood, 1969, pp. 440–441)

Associated with the need to provide close parental attention to the newborn child is the constant flow of infant-oriented tasks to be carried out. In most households, the majority of these chores are handled by the mother. Usually, if a woman shifts from full-time employment outside the home to full-time housekeeping, there are corresponding shifts in the allocation of domestic tasks (Blood, 1969). Immediately after the birth, the mother needs the help of the father as she is learning how to care for the baby. In traditional marriages, however, the division of labor has tended to become more pronounced once the wife recovers her strength and masters new skills. Because the wife is now a full-time domestic, the husband typically does less housework, the couple generally share fewer tasks, and role specialization increases.

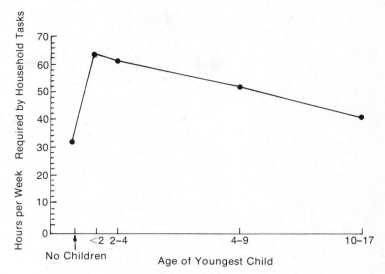

Figure 5–3. Amount of household tasks, by age of youngest child. (Adapted from Wiegand, 1954, p. 18.)

Many young mothers, according to Stroup (1966), report they are at first overwhelmed by all the tasks they are required to perform. Feeding and bathing of the baby and laundering diapers and clothing, added to the regular household routines of cleaning, cooking, and shopping, is a full day's work. Nevertheless countless other chores can be added to this list. Figure 5–3 indicates the extent to which housekeeping chores increase with the birth of a child. If the father shares in the household work, the mother's load is reduced considerably.

Because of the demands imposed on parents by the new child, it is sometimes necessary to reorganize daily routines to improve the efficiency of the household and of the marriage. Stroup (1966) points out that many couples, upon systematically examining their schedules, discover that certain changes can be made with resulting increases in efficiency and satisfaction. Tasks can be simplified if couples can plan in terms of their own needs, abilities, and desires in their own situation. Fitzsimmons (1950) suggests that couples should be concerned with the following areas:

1. Deciding on consuming and producing activities which must be fitted into each division of time so that they can be accomplished without undue effort or use of time, and the life family members lead will result in production which must be carried on; enjoyment of satisfactions desired; and the achievement of goals considered worthwhile.
2. Forming the habit of scrutinizing proposed activities or, from time to time, activities already undertaken to evaluate their worth for the individual or the family.
3. Discarding those which do not appear to offer sufficient returns in product or satisfaction to make them worth doing.
4. Improving the methods of doing the jobs which are retained.
   a. Setting reasonable standards for the product or outcome of all work processes whose attainment is possible in the time and with the amount of energy which can be devoted to that end.

b. Developing standardized procedures for all jobs which are repeated frequently and performing them each time according to
   this procedure.
c. Developing standardized procedures for all jobs which take a
   great deal of work, many operations, or a long time to perform.
d. Develop standardized procedures for consuming, as well as
   producing, activities where these are repetitive in nature.
   Examples are dressing, bathing, and preparing oneself for bed.

5. Watching for changes in goals which may make necessary some
   change in the choice of activities to be undertaken by family
   members.
6. Watching for changes in methods of performing tasks, new equip-
   ment or possible changes in working places which might enable
   family members to do their work with still greater reduction in expenditure of motions and time.
7. Making allowances for leisure and unassigned time, according to
   individual preferences, so that the process of planning, trying out,
   and continuing the best use of motions and time will not prove
   burdensome.
8. Relating activities consciously to goals desired so that feelings of
   fatigue may be reduced by awareness of progress toward goals.
9. Being aware that fatigue is a natural result of physical and mental
   effort and even of boredom.
10. Arranging a plan for time use which will provide work periods
    that are not so long as to cause excessive fatigue and free periods
    in which suitable rest or relaxation can be obtained.

(p. 423)

New responsibilities also arise as a result of changes in the power structure of the marriage (Blood, 1969). When the wife leaves the labor force, she becomes more dependent on the husband, who in turn is usually cast in the role of sole breadwinner. Although more and more mothers are returning to the labor force, a topic we will discuss shortly, the father usually must accept primary responsibility in providing financial support to his family. In general, the younger the mother is, and the more rapidly children are acquired, the more the husband is likely to dominate the family's power structure.

Finally, all young parents are responsible for developing proper parental emotional attitudes and adopting suitable child-rearing standards (Landis, 1975). The atmosphere surrounding the child—shortly after birth as well as in years to come—is of critical importance to the child's personality and social growth. "Impressions and attitudes resulting from these early experiences," Landis stresses, "carry over through the individual's lifetime, affecting many other relationships. The relationships between the parent and the child are important factors in the happiness of the child as he grows to adulthood and to his later success in marriage." (p. 430)

In summary: fulfilling the major responsibilities accompanying the stages of early parenthood—whether they be the provision of food or shelter or the reorganization of daily routines—requires the efforts of both the mother and the father. The successful execution of each of these responsibilities is essential to the overall welfare of the child and the marital harmony between husband and wife.

PARENTAL ROLES

Parenthood requires a major addition to a couple's set of roles, adding the parts of mother and father to those of wife and husband. Such a reallocation requires considerable resocialization. Let's turn our attention to the parental roles assimilated by the new mother and father.

The Role of the Mother

Cross-cultural studies reveal that the mother-child relationship considered normal in the American middle class is quite different from that found in most other cultures. In most traditional societies, maternal and paternal roles are sharply defined, primarily because the father is cast in an authoritarian and exalted position in relation to his family. In contemporary middle class American society, however, the distinction between maternal and paternal roles, at least in influencing and controlling the children, has for the most part disappeared (Bell, 1975).

This is not to imply that the wife does not have distinct status pertaining to her role as mother (Duberman, 1974). Among some social groups, nonmaternal responsibilities are considered secondary to maternal responsibilities and mothers are still expected to remain home and care for their children, especially in the early years of development. However, recent societal trends indicate that mothers are breaking with this tradition and seeking vocational involvement. Many women are capable of simultaneously performing the traditional role of mother and the less traditional role of wage-earner (Clayton, 1975).

MOTHERS AS BREADWINNERS: BREAKING THE TRADITIONAL ROLE BARRIER

In a suburb of Washington, D.C., a 6-year-old child was surprised to find that his playmate's mother was at home one noon, preparing lunch. The 6-year-old piped up: "What's the matter with your mother? Can't she work?"

Of all the social verities that have recently been called into question, none has crumbled quite so rapidly as the belief that a woman's place is in the home—full time. Today a record of 43 per cent of all U.S. women—32 million strong—are in the nation's labor force. . . . They now constitute 37.5 per cent of the work force and more are streaming into the job market every day. . . .

The most dramatic change has occurred among married women. Only 30 per cent of them were in the nation's work force a decade ago; today, more than 40 per cent of them are. The new trend is partly due to male willingness; one recent survey showed that half the men questioned would not object if their wives took a job. . . .

An increasing number of them have abandoned the notion that children need a full-time mother. Just under 50 per cent of all U.S. women who have school-age children also hold down jobs; so do 30 per cent of women who have children under 6 years of age.

. . . the rise of working women is caused at least as much by their desire for respect as for cold cash. If the trend to working mothers seems uncaring and unwise, defenders of it point out that a second paycheck often allows fathers to spend more time with their child. Not only is Dad freed of some pressure to work overtime and struggle for promotion, but he also feels an obligation to get home and help mother with the chores.

(Reprinted by permission from TIME, The Weekly Newsmagazine; copyright Time, Inc., 1971.)

One of the more difficult tasks of the female marriage partner is learning to balance her roles as wife and mother (Kelley, 1974). As Blood (1969) mentions, the adage "two's company and three's a crowd" epitomizes the difference between a couple capable of giving each other undivided attention and a trio whose attention must be divided. Because babies are dependent and mothers are directly responsible for them, the new triad may lack the symmetry that characterized earlier marriage.

Kelley (1974) believes it is quite natural to expect a shift in the relationship between husband and wife as a result of these role changes. However, it is important for the mother—as well as the father—to make the transition as smooth as possible. An evening's recreation without the baby and an emphasis on certain enjoyable experiences that husband and wife can share are important ways of making the resocialization process easier.

The Role of the Father

"Congratulations, Mr. Jones, it's a girl."

Fatherhood is going to have a different meaning and elicit a different response for every man who hears these words. Whereas some feel pride when they receive the news, others worry, wondering whether they will be good fathers. Although there are some men who like children and may have had considerable experience with them, others do not particularly care for children and intend to spend little time with them. Many fathers and mothers have been planning and looking forward to children for some time. For other couples, pregnancy was an accident that both husband and wife have reluctantly accepted (Dodson, 1974).

Whatever the reaction to the birth of a child, it is obvious that the shift from the role of husband to that of father is a formidable task. Yet, unfortunately, few attempts have been made to educate fathers in this resocialization process. Although numerous bestsellers have been written about American mothers, only recently has literature focused on the role of a father (LeMasters, 1977).

It is argued by some writers (Burr, 1975; Williamson, 1966) that the transition to the paternal role, although difficult, is not nearly as great as the transition the wife must make to the maternal role. Duberman (1974) concurs by stating that the maternal role requires a complete transformation in daily routine and highly innovative adaptation, whereas the father's role is less demanding and immediate.

Rogers (1969) believes that various influences are changing the concept of fatherhood. Shorter workdays and longer vacation periods are giving fathers more time to spend with their families. The ongoing depolarization of sex roles has also modified the husband's function in the family. Thus, many fathers have been able to acknowledge and develop their more familial traits, including a greater capacity for forming affectional relationships with their children, a factor that serves to narrow the psychological distance between

(Photo courtesy of Nancy Clark.)

Figure 5–4. The importance of the father's role in child rearing should not be overlooked.

parent and offspring. Of particular importance is the fact that the father may not feel compelled to remain aloof as the symbol of power and wisdom. Rather, as we learned earlier, it is becoming more common for mothers to pursue careers, requiring the father to help with domestic chores and child care (Rogers, 1969).

One young father attending graduate school vividly recalls how his role changed when his wife was required to work for economic reasons and he was called upon to look after his 9-month-old son while she was away. Of particular interest were his reactions to the household responsibilities that society labels as "feminine" and his reflections on being given full-time responsibility for care of his child.

> After the first month, I began to feel more comfortable in my role of caretaker for Jeremy, yet in some ways it was a paradoxical feeling. Although I became more confident, there existed an uneasiness in knowing that I spent each day with a person who was completely dependent upon me. While it represented a challenge, it also was a source of insecurity, an emotion I'm sure that many mothers feel.
>
> I found many interesting reactions concerning my continual contact with Jeremy from people in the neighborhood. For example, when going for walks, we often encountered other children walking and playing with their mothers. What did I have in common with these mothers? Many of them looked at me rather strangely wheeling a stroller. I had no recipes to swap and I was unaware of their interests, yet gradually we began to interact and found that we had other things in common. With time, conversation became easier. As a result, I found that their children became more accessible to Jeremy and me.

My experiences with Jeremy enabled me to fully appreciate the emotional reactions that accompany child-rearing. When I had work to do at home, I would become anxious in waiting for the proper time to undertake it. When my boy was asleep and my wife was working, I would sometimes become overwhelmed with feelings of loneliness. I sometimes became intolerant over Jeremy's untidiness. Yet, nothing surpassed the joys and happiness that I experienced in watching my son take one of his first steps or hearing my name spoken for the first time.

Those first few days of caring for Jeremy made me more aware of my child's needs and how I could deal with them as a person. Before the time that my wife went to work, she had performed most of the functions of childhood; she fed him, washed, and changed him. Being placed in this new capacity made me realize that there was more to parenthood than assisting my wife or merely babysitting.

Preparing meals for Jeremy, despite "practice sessions," and special instructions from my wife, proved to be an experience in itself. This was one task that I seldom envisioned myself doing. After carefully measuring and mixing, I was astounded when he would sometimes knock his bowl to the floor with reckless abandon. He would also become extremely intolerant over this interruption, screaming with an intensity that I had never before experienced. Changing diapers on a *continual* basis also became difficult for me to deal with, especially since I, probably like most fathers, had performed this task only occasionally. Many times, when I thought that I had perfected the procedure, things began to go wrong. During the second week it became apparent that when the pin was placed through the diaper it often did not connect both corners. To correct this, I changed the angle of the pin and successfully connected the corners, but in the process managed to prick my son's leg. In an effort to prevent this, I placed my index finger between the diaper and Jeremy's leg, the result being that the pin was now consistently being stuck in my own hand. During this trial and error process, I couldn't help but wonder if my wife had experienced such difficulties.

(Helms and Turner, 1976)

PARENTAL ROLES IN THE FUTURE

The last 25 years of this century will likely produce a more "unisexual" definition of the parental role. Fathers and mothers will be performing more and more of the same parental tasks either side by side or as a result of a negotiated division of labor that essentially ignores the traditional sex-role split of the past. If this does occur—and many social scientists think it will —the result will be a better quality of family life. Perhaps such a movement will also signal a convergence of the cultural definitions of manhood and womanhood.

To date the achievement of manhood and womanhood status has meant distinctly different achievements and characteristics. The traditional conception of a "man" has included sexual proclivity and success in the occupational sphere. The man in our society has been defined as someone who is rational and calculating, someone who is calm under stress and who does not openly express emotions and affection. The traditional evidence of achievement of womanhood has been marriage, and adequate performance of the wife role, and becoming a mother, once, twice, three or four times. The "woman" in our society is someone who is warm and affectionate, someone who openly expresses her emotions, sometimes in a direction opposite of rationality.

Perhaps a movement toward a greater mutual and shared involvement in a unitary parental role as opposed to the traditional and separate father/mother roles will produce a complementarity of behaviors and characteristics that are similar instead of opposite. Perhaps it will produce at least a partial reversal of the finding that marital adjustment and satisfaction suffer because of the onset of children.

(Reprinted by permission of the publisher, from Richard R. Clayton: *The Family, Marriage and Social Change.* Lexington, Mass.: D.C. Heath and Company, 1975, pp. 403–404.)

Kelley (1974) adds that in addition to sharing the responsibilities of parenthood, the new father must accept the change in his relationship with his wife. When the first child arrives, he must learn to share his wife's affection and must realize that love given to the child is not love taken away from him. Although it is quite common for both parents to go through a "honeymoon period" with the newborn baby and to develop strong emotional attachment to the new arrival, the feelings are usually more intense for the mother. As a result, the mother may make the child, rather than the father, the emotional center of her life. An insecure husband may feel neglected or rejected. It becomes the task of both husband and wife, therefore, to define the meaning of parental love and to strive for harmonious family relationships (Rossi, 1968).

Summary

People decide to have children for many reasons. Of all of the motives, six appear to be most prominent: ego expansion, creativity and achievement, status and conformity, control and authority, love or affection, and happiness. The transition to parenthood is difficult for most couples today largely because there is little preparation for parenthood in contemporary society, because couples apparently do not use the pregnancy period to learn about parenthood, because the change in lifestyle attendant upon the baby's arrival at home is very abrupt, and because there are no certain guidelines for successful child-rearing.

Parenthood makes it necessary to reorganize daily routines and carry out new responsibilities. Obvious among the responsibilities is the provision of food, shelter, and clothing for the new arrival. Other responsibilities include providing the newborn infant with continual attention, executing infant-oriented tasks, allocating other domestic chores, reorganizing and adapting to changes in the power structure of the marriage, and developing proper parental emotional attitudes and suitable standards of child rearing. The major addition of the roles of mother and father to those of wife and husband also requires considerable adaptation, not to mention the resocialization involved.

Suggested Readings

1. Brazelton, T. B.: *Toddlers and Parents*. New York: Dell Publishing Company, Inc., 1974.

   Written by a distinguished pediatrician, this softcover book is a most practical reference guide for new parents. Particularly interesting topics explored include sibling rivalry, the withdrawn child, the hyperactive child, and the toddler's growing awareness of the self.

2. Dodson, F.: *How to Parent*. New York: Signet Books, 1970.

   Dr. Dodson's book addresses itself to new parents and the problems they might encounter. His experiences as a parent and as a psychologist are interspersed throughout.

3. Gordon, S., and Wollin, M.: *Parenting, A Guide for Young People.* New York, Oxford Book Company, 1975.

This book of fifteen compact chapters introduces young adults to the facts, problems, and ideas most relevant to parenthood in the United States today.

4. LeMasters, E. E.: *Parents in Modern America,* 3rd. ed. Homewood, Illinois: The Dorsey Press, 1977.

A well-referenced and topical text that should be on the bookshelf of any serious-minded student of psychology or sociology. Particularly well done are chapters on folklore about parenthood, parents and the behavioral sciences, parents without partners, and counseling with parents.

5. Pickarts, E., and Fargo, J.: *Parent Education.* New York: Appleton Century Crofts, 1971.

The authors propose a method for meeting the need for parent education programs. The book is designed for people in the educational and mental health fields who deal in some way with the confusion parents experience about child rearing.

Jean Berlfein

UNIT 6

VOCATIONAL DEVELOPMENT

Introduction

All young adults, in some way, must establish themselves as worthwhile and significant individuals. Historically, this has usually been accomplished within the world of work. Status and recognition have typically been achieved by becoming a wage-earner and serving some useful purpose in the labor force. Although this traditional emphasis is being challenged today, employment remains an important function of the individual for the present and the near future (Kowitz and Kowitz, 1971).

Davis and Hackman (1973) point out that because we are living in a work-oriented society, it is expected that individuals, at a reasonably early age, will arrive at a vocational choice. When making vocational commitments, people are, in most instances, predicting their future vocational adjustment. If the choice is made in a reasonably rational manner, a person typically assumes that the occupation selected will satisfy whatever criteria were used in making the choice.

THE COMPLEXITY OF TODAY'S WORK WORLD

The complexity of today's vocational world and the pressures imposed by society make the career selection process a most difficult one. Many younger adults remain confused and bewildered over the mere thought of choosing and then entering a profession. The pressure is especially unreasonable for those of college age, who have not yet learned enough about themselves or about possible occupations to be able to make a satisfying choice the first time (Breger, 1968). A surprisingly large number of older adults are not at all satisfied with the career choices they have made and must therefore find a different vocation or live with their discontent (Wollman et al., 1975). In relation to this, Bernard and Fullmer (1977) suggest that typical workers will make six or seven major changes during their total work lives, usually before age 35 or even age 30.

Hackman and Davis (1973) suggest that today's young adult must grapple with at least five questions related to career planning: Can I succeed at the job or learn it? (a question of aptitude); Will I like it and be satisfied? (a question of satisfying one's interests); How can I decide between this and some other job? (a question involving decision-making); Will I amount to something? (a question implying status); and, Will the job enable me to be of worth to myself and others? (a question entailing an examination of one's self-concept). Obviously, each of these areas requires considerable contemplation.

Shertzer and Stone (1976) bring into focus several factors that underscore the need for careful career planning and decision making. Each of these adds further support to the belief that young adults are confronted with a most difficult task in deciding what they want to do with the rest of their working lives.

The first is an *accelerated increase in human knowledge*. Although a strictly quantitative analysis is not possible, Shertzer and

EVALUATING YOUR CAREER CHOICE: A SELF QUIZ

By the time a person reaches the young adult years, it is expected that some type of career commitment will have been made. Yet, Sachs (1975) states that the vocational selections made in early adulthood are often discarded later in life because the young adult's level of aspiration is found to be inconsistent with his or her abilities and opportunities. Many young adults fail to examine essential qualities about *themselves* critically in relation to the careers they have chosen, not to mention examining the various facets of the job itself. One researcher (Steckle, 1957) has suggested that career-minded individuals should ask themselves the following questions before committing themselves to a particular occupation:

About You

1. What are the educational needs of individuals who are engaged in this occupation? Is my present educational status sufficient, or will I need more? If so, can I obtain it?

2. Is my intellectual ability sufficient to meet the educational and occupational demands this vocation makes of its participants? Will I be able to cope with such specialized training as may be expected of me?

3. What, if any, special abilities, talents, or aptitudes are requisite for success? If such exist, do I possess them? If not, is there any way by which I may?

4. Will my present array of interests, likes, dislikes, aims, and ideals be compatible with those needed for happiness in this work?

5. Is my general personality structure such that the work will be congenial? Will I fit in with those who are already so engaged? Does this work make any special personal or character demands? If so, what are they and how will I fit in?

6. Have I any annoying traits that might argue against success? Any deficiencies or disabilities that would limit me? If so, can I do anything to overcome them?

About Your Job

1. What are the opportunities in this field? Where, in the range of income, must I start? What may I expect as my skill increases? If special rewards exist, what must I do to obtain them?

2. What about constancy of employment? Is it hazardous, seasonal, intermittent, or variable? What degree of personal security does it offer?

3. Is it a blind alley job? Is advancement possible and regular if one does well? Is the job itself a kind of training program for better ones?

4. What is the relationship between supply and demand in this work? Are more people being trained than the work can accommodate? Will I be faced with competition too strong for me to meet? Am I a good competitive worker, or do I become too discouraged with "second place?"

5. In what kind of community will I probably be living if I enter this field? Will it be one well adapted to domestic living, the rearing of children, and the happiness of my spouse?

6. What is the social prestige of the job? Does success in it bring approval by others? Are the skills demanded by the work those which "not just anyone" may develop?

(Steckle, 1957, pp. 272–273)

Stone (1976) believe that humanity's knowledge has accelerated at an ever-increasing rate. Historically, they postulate that human knowledge doubled from A.D. 1 to 175; doubled again by 1900, again by 1950, and still again by 1960. As far as careers are concerned, this means that newer fields of specialization are continually emerging, many of which require elaborate training programs or some type of college education.

A second aspect of the contemporary vocational world that deserves attention is the *changing role of women*. New career opportunities are awaiting women, as the once traditional sex-role barrier is rapidly disappearing. As we discovered in the foregoing unit, more and more women, unmarried as well as married, are active members of the nation's labor force. Currently, every third worker is a woman. Shertzer and Stone (1976) estimate that eight out of every ten American women will be working for pay outside the home at some point in their lives. Yet while some barriers to women's working have been removed, it is only fair to say that there are still large discrepancies of income and occupational level between men and women.

Kimmel (1974) provides an interesting comparison of the female worker in the 1970s with her earlier counterpart. In 1890, 13 per cent of female workers were married; in 1970 this figure rose to 58 per cent. In 1940, only 1 out of every 10 female workers had children under 18; in 1970, the figure was 1 out of 3. Furthermore, the

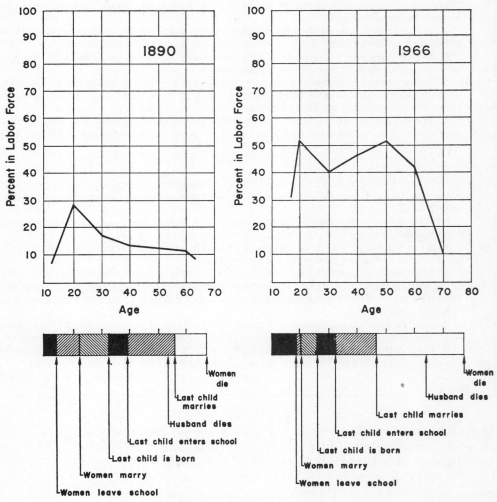

Figure 6–1. Work as it relates to the significant stages of a woman's life. (Adapted from Neugarten, B. L. [ed.]: *Middle Age and Aging.* © 1968, The University of Chicago Press.)

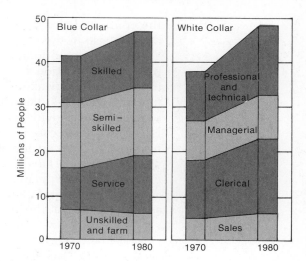

Figure 6–2. Projected employment by occupation between 1970 and 1980. The need for unskilled and farm laborers will decrease, while skilled workers will be in demand.

The chart reflects the Bureau of Labor Statistics' projection of changes in occupational structure from 1970 to 1980, assuming G.N.P. growth of about 4.3 per cent a year. Should full-employment growth be substantially less, demand for skilled white-collar and service workers is likely to increase less than projected; much higher growth than 4.3 per cent, conversely, may create more high-skill jobs than projected. (*From* Mayer, L. A.: "New questions about the U.S. population." *Fortune,* February, 1971. Source: U.S. Census, 1970. Reprinted by permission; © 1971 Time Inc.)

contemporary woman is likely to enter the labor force earlier and to work considerably longer than the woman employed in 1900. Figure 6–1 illustrates the manner in which work relates to significant stages in the lives of women.

Career-minded young adults should carefully consider a third factor mentioned by Shertzer and Stone (1976): *labor power changes.* Population changes between 1970 and 1980 will be reflected in the demands made upon the labor force, causing major shifts in the occupational structure that bear important implications for the vocational planning of young adults. Among the changes cited by Shertzer and Stone (1976) are (1) a diminishing need for unskilled laborers; (2) geographical shifts of industries; (3) job insecurities due to accelerated technological development; (4) a decline in goods-producing industries; (5) a decline in agricultural occupations (see Figure 6–2); (6) an increase in service occupations; (7) an increase in the number of jobs that demand more education or training; (8)

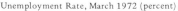

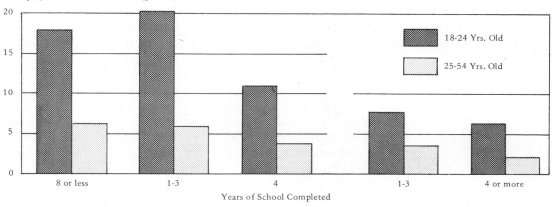

Figure 6–3. Unemployment rates are highest for members of the younger adult population. (*From:* Bureau of Labor Statistics, *Occupational Outlook Handbook,* 1974–1975 ed., United States Department of Labor, Washington, D. C., 1974, p. 22.)

the continued rise of youth unemployment (see Fig. 6–3); and (9) the increase in the number of youths entering the labor force.

A final factor demanding attention is the role that *automation* plays in the vocational structure. Shertzer and Stone (1976) maintain that, generally speaking, automation will reduce human effort for monotonous work, require fewer unskilled and semiskilled factory workers, and provide shorter work weeks with longer periods of leisure. In some cases, many workers have been displaced or have had to be retrained for other jobs as a result of automation; conversely, new jobs have been created because of this industrial trend. For young adults, planning in an age of automation must take into account an interpretation of today's industrial developments as well as a prediction of future changes.

WORK AND THE FULFILLMENT OF HUMAN NEEDS

In the contemporary world, at all levels of rank and wealth, and in virtually every walk of life, millions of men and women share a common fate. Whether they are members of the young adult generation or the middle-aged population, factory workers or accountants, teachers or laborers, they have all committed their lives and part of their identity to one of the vast organizations that produce and distribute goods, that explore the frontiers of science, or inform, educate, and govern mankind (Steinberg, 1975).

Involvement in the world of work—in whatever facet—will produce diverse individual reactions. Men, in particular, concern themselves with "making it" in a particular profession (Sheehy, 1976). Women, conversely, seem to exhibit mixed concerns toward their careers and have more difficulty maintaining them. Many young women, Horner (1972) asserts, fear to succeed in a profession because they are taught that being competitive and successful is unfeminine. Both men and women may reap a sense of pleasure or fulfillment from work or may feel blocked, frustrated, or dehumanized by it (Keniston, 1963).

What motivates individuals to work? According to Neff (1968), this is a most difficult question to answer, one that still plagues the most ardent researchers. However, he believes the answer lies in part in the needs that work itself fulfills, including *material needs, self-esteem, activity, respect by others,* and the *need for creativity.* Let's examine each of these needs a bit more closely.

Work fulfills a *material need* since people obviously work for money. Work is, by its nature, an instrumental activity, carried out in order to procure the necessities of existence, no matter how broadly the term "necessities" is interpreted. "In the modern industrialized society," Neff states, "whether capitalist or communist, money is the essential medium of exchange and the prerequisite for material existence. While the love of money may be the root of all evil, money is also the chief means by which people estimate the quality and quantity of their work. (p. 142) Without doubt, the time

and money invested in education and specialized training can increase one's future earning power and value as an employee (Riker
and Brisbane, 1970).

Yet, it must be stressed that all people do not work for monetary
motives alone. Some workers may function ineffectively even when
monetary rewards are readily available. Others may de-emphasize a
meager salary if the rewards inherent in the job are truly fulfilling
and satisfying. As Neff (1968) notes, the sphere of human work is an
arena for various types of human interactions and involves many
different kinds of motives.

Work also fulfills the need for some degree of *self-esteem*. Being
unemployed is seldom a happy condition and receives support from
family and society only to the degree that it is regarded as temporary.
Being employed as a worker is a condition for full membership in
most societies and provides a guarantee of some degree of autonomy
and self-respect. Sometimes being a nonworker is a sign of "second
class citizenship" and is associated with reduced feelings of personal worth.

Self-esteem has a tendency to vary according to the amounts of
prestige associated with various careers and with levels within each
occupation. Senior executives, for example, enjoy more prestige
than junior executives, journeyman carpenters more than their ap-
prentices. However, as in the case of material needs, self-esteem is a
complex and elusive variable, somewhat difficult to measure and
quite interrelated with other factors; it is not uncommon for individuals at the same occupational level to differ greatly in the degree
to which their self-esteem is fulfilled or frustrated by their work.
Furthermore, it would be inaccurate to assume that members of a
low-status occupation have, as a consequence, low feelings of personal worth.

Work enables us to fulfill the need for *activity*, to avoid boredom, to fill up the day with things to do. One of the more serious
consequences of forced unemployment or retirement, at least for
those who are accustomed to working, is the inability to find enough
to do. In the same vein, wealthy individuals who have no compelling
need to work may seek employment just to alleviate an intolerable
restlessness. Individuals whose need to work is strong tend to find
vacations boring or guilt-producing and to rush back to work with a
feeling of relief. Some people also find that working dispels their
anxieties, draining off anger or hostility, and taking their minds off
their troubles.

Neff (1968) objects to phrases such as the "need for activity" or
"freedom from boredom." To be sure, *what* is being done is at least
as important as the mere *doing*. Certain types of work are intrinsic-
ally monotonous, so that no mere expenditure of energy can prevent
feelings of the most intense boredom. But let us not forget that what
is intensely boring for one person may be relatively stimulating for
another. For mental and physical health each must find work that is
absorbing and satisfying (Allport, 1955).

A fourth need apparently fulfilled by work is *being respected by others*, which must be distinguished from the need for self-esteem. These needs, Neff insists, are interrelated but separate:

> The two needs reflect quite different questions, *viz.*, "What do I think of myself" versus "What do others think of me"! It is certainly possible to encounter persons in whom these two views are quite dissonant. They may have a very low opinion of their worth as persons but believe that others think well of them. Perhaps more frequent are the cases of individuals who place a quite high evaluation on themselves but perceive others as giving them insufficient respect. In its extreme form the latter kind of case presents the thought process of the paranoid psychotic, in whom delusions of grandeur and persecution are simultaneously present. For the majority of people, however, the opinions of others are a factor in their self-esteem, so that the latter fluctuates within rather wide limits according to whether they receive criticism or praise. Nevertheless, these two sets of opinions are not perfectly correlated across individuals and cannot be treated as identities. (pp. 146–147)

Whether the need for respect of others is gratified by work depends on what values are prevalent in a society and the extent to which the individual accepts them. In the United States, the amount of respect an occupation is accorded is generally related to such factors as the duration and kind of formal preparation the job re-

Figure 6–4. Work fulfills the need for some degree of self-esteem as well as the need for activity.

quires; the level of payment; the degree to which a worker is "his own"; the economic, social, and political power the position commands; and the value the society places on the work itself. In general, people in occupations of higher status expect to receive respect for the work they do and the position they occupy, whereas people employed in jobs of lower status are reduced to wanting to be respected for their personal qualities, and not for their work.

Finally, work can fulfill a *need to be creative,* or what Fromm (1941, 1955) would call man's need for *transcendence.* The four other needs described by Neff (1968) can be met by virtually any type of work, but the need to create is satisfied by some occupations and frustrated in others.

Usually, we think of an act of creation as being quite idiosyncratic, expressive of the unique characteristics of an individual. According to this concept, creativity would be possible only in vocations such as art, scholarship, or science.

Yet creativity is also involved in more mundane work. Such work may consist of rearranging traditional components in a new pattern. Or it can consist of producing more of a familiar object. Thus an industrial worker may feel that he is creating something, even though the machine he operates has been developed by someone else. The object being produced is evidence enough that the worker's labor has not been fruitless. When automation proceeds so far that the worker's connection with the product becomes weakened, however, he or she feels alienated or useless.

Individuals with a strong desire to be creative may become quite frustrated in work environments that are countercreative. Unfortunately, only a handful of workers in contemporary society are lucky enough to find an opportunity to create something genuinely expressive of their unique talents (Neff, 1968).

THE VOCATIONAL COMMITMENT: WHY WE CHOOSE THE WORK WE DO

Needs may motivate an individual to work, but what driving forces account for the *kind* of work he or she enters? What compels a person to undertake a career in business administration or medical technology? What prompts a college graduate to pursue a postgraduate degree in marine biology, or a 25-year-old high school drop-out to return to a trade school to undertake a career in automotive mechanics? Numerous theories have been proposed to explain the mechanisms behind the career selection process. In order to understand why young adults choose the type of work they do, it is important to recognize what may have *predisposed* them to certain fields. Brammer and Shostrum (1977) have summarized the more widely recognized theories of vocational choice.

Ginzberg (1951) maintains that career choice is a process that encompasses three fairly distinct phases: *fanciful* (6 to 11 years), *tentative* (12 to 17 years), and *realistic* (18 years onward). The *realistic* phase, of particular relevance to this text, can be divided into three substages. In the "exploration" phase, a person attempts to acquire the experience needed to resolve his or her occupational selection. The "crystallization" phase enables individuals to evaluate critically all the factors involved in the selection process and eventually to commit themselves to the selected field. Finally, the "specification" phase allows the individual to review the alternative positions within a given field carefully and to arrive at some type of specialization.

Roe (1956) believes that basic human needs and early family experiences affect subsequent career choices. She has proposed a theory that emphasizes the importance of the child's early experiences with parents, the relationship between parental attitudes and beliefs and need satisfaction, and the manner in which the child is reared. Each of these factors nurtures within the individual a general, broad vocational orientation. For example, a warm, loving household with close interpersonal relations may foster an individual's interest in socially oriented occupations. The cold, rejecting household may motivate an individual to reject close interpersonal relationships and pursue careers that are not related to people. As Roe phrases it:

> Depending upon which of the home situations is experienced, there will be developed basic attitudes, interests and capacities which will be given expression in the general pattern of the adult's life, in his personal relations, in his emotional reactions, in his activities, and in his vocational choice.

(p. 217)

Carter (1944) claims that vocational interests develop from the efforts of individuals to adapt to direct family and social pressures and to their own perceptions of their needs and capacities. Interests are nurtured from identification with a particular occupation and are confirmed by experimenting with it. In time, individuals incorporate occupational demands into their self-concepts, and career interests become relatively stabilized.

That occupational choices are implementations of one's self-concept is the focal point in Super's (1951) theory. When individuals express a vocational preference, Super believes, they put into occupational terminology the kind of person that they perceive themselves to be. A selected job allows for the implementation of the self-concept (the occupation makes possible the play of a role appropriate to the self-concept) and enables one to achieve self-actualization.

Holland's (1966) theory of vocational development operates on the assumption that the occupational structure can be categorized into specific personal types or themes, namely realistic, intellectual, social, conventional, enterprising, and artistic. Holland has devised empirical goals, role preferences, activities, and self-concepts for each of these types for both men and women. For example, realistic individuals prefer physical and technical activities, hold conventional economic values, and accord social and esthetic values little importance. Most perceive themselves to be practical, conventional, submissive, and uncreative. Such a classification theory, he

YOUNG ADULTHOOD AND THE FIRST-JOB DILEMMA

As we have suggested since the outset of this discussion, a young adult is quite likely to experience frustration and disillusionment when embarking on his or her first job. This dilemma of successfully meeting all educational requirements in college and yet being unable to find a position that promotes personal satisfaction and personal creativity plagues numerous college graduates, reports Schein (1970).

Schein's study indicates that within five years almost every large company loses more than half the college graduates hired. In an investigation of graduates holding master's degrees from the Massachusetts Institute of Technology management program, he found that half the members of the 1964 graduating class had already left their first jobs, two thirds of the 1963 graduates had changed jobs, and a remarkable 73 per cent (nearly three quarters) of the 1962 class had left their initial position, with some working on their third or fourth jobs.

What factors can be cited to explain the young adult's "first-job dilemma"? Contrary to popular belief, it is not always caused by the graduate's desire for a higher salary. The roots of the dissatisfaction that leads to resignation appear to be far deeper.

To gather as much evidence as possible concerning job dissatisfaction among new graduates, Schein analyzed both employee and employer complaints. Among the graduates, a universal complaint was that their "good ideas" were frequently rejected, undermined, sidetracked, or even sabotaged. Other complaints included difficulty in learning to accept emotionally the reality of the organization's human side, the lack of adequate manager feedback on job performance, learning to determine to whom in the company loyalty was owed, and coping with the frustrations associated with the new work itself. After the first year, many graduates also complained that they had little opportunity to test themselves and that the work, for the most part, was unchallenging.

Managers, on the other hand, too often had a "stereotyped image" of college graduates: overambitious, unrealistic in their expectations, wanting too much money and responsibility too soon, and immature. The psychology of the manager also tended to be seen as a problem. Many managers were less educated than the new subordinates, resentful that the graduates commanded a far higher starting salary than the manager once did, and threatened by all the new management theory the graduates brought with them (much of which the boss found difficult to understand).

Schein offers several recommendations for change that may prove helpful in the future. It must be realized that the new graduate's first supervisor exerts the strongest influence in shaping the attitude of the young adult toward the organization. Supervisors of graduates should be mature and secure in their knowledge, understanding fully the characteristics of young adults and the expectations they hold. Also, young adults who aspire to executive positions must come to terms with their own immaturity. They must learn to cope with the organization emotionally and intellectually. In some cases, emotional "unlearning" might be in order. Relearning must also take place in order that the graduate can learn to manage people.

Schein suggests, too, that we need to prepare the graduate better for the realities of the occupational world. An apprenticeship program as part of the student's curriculum might be a solution to this problem. Also, job recruitment procedures can stand reform. Schein stresses that "a better dialogue is necessary between the university, the student and the hiring organization. Many of the unrealistic expectations that new graduates bring with them to their first job are built up by the recruiter's sales pitch" (p. 55). The eager and ambitious worker does not need glowing pictures of challenging work that too frequently have a remote connection with reality. An honest, realistic portrayal of the company may help to prevent future job dissatisfaction and promote more harmonious working conditions within an organization.

believes, will assist the individual to consider the complex personality dimensions of occupations in a systematic and realistic fashion.

Summary

By the young adult years, it is expected that most individuals will arrive at a vocational choice. However, it is fairly well accepted that the pressures imposed by society and the complexity of today's vocational world make the career selection process a most difficult one.

There are several attributes of the vocational world that underscore the need for careful career planning. These include an accelerating increase in man's knowledge, the changing role of women in the labor force, significant labor power changes, and the role that automation plays in the overall vocational structure.

We are motivated to seek employment, according to one researcher, because of the needs that work fulfills. The more important include material needs in addition to the need for activity, respect by others, and creativity. To explain why we choose the *specific* work we do, several key theories have been proposed. These are Ginzberg's developmental approach, Roe's theory of early experience, Carter's theory of family and social pressures as well as individual needs, Super's self-concept theory, and Holland's vocational and personal "type" (or theme) approach.

Suggested Readings

1. Marland, S. P., *Career Education*. New York: McGraw-Hill Book Company, 1974.

   Marland offers a comprehensive examination of past, present, and future trends of career education in the United States.

2. Neff, W. S.: *Work and Human Behavior*. New York: Atherton Press, 1968.

   An insightful analysis of the nature of work and its implications for mankind. Neff pays particularly close attention to the psychological aspects of work as well as its practical issues, two areas that represent the strength of his presentation.

3. Osipow, S. H., *Theories of Career Development* (2nd ed.). New York: Appleton-Century-Crofts, Inc., 1973.

   A most thorough and detailed examination of the key theories of vocational choice. An excellent resource text.

4. Shertzer, B., and Stone, S. C.: *Fundamentals of Guidance* (3rd ed.). Boston: Houghton Mifflin Company, 1976.

   Chapters 12 and 13 of this textbook offer an excellent presentation of the work world, including vocational choice theories, dynamic factors influencing career development, and career planning and placement.

Section B The Middle Years of Adulthood

Fred Weiss

UNIT 7

PHYSICAL AND INTELLECTUAL DEVELOPMENT

Introduction

Middle age seems to be a paradox. It is a time of turbulence, a time of quiescence; a time of success, a time of failure; a time of joy, and a time of sadness. Yet youngsters, oldsters, and those in between seem to agree that the middle years represent the prime of life (Taylor, 1976).

There are two almost diametrically opposed interpretations of the nature of middle age. To some it is a crisis, a period of self-evaluation (frequently with negative conclusions), unhappiness, and even depression. Evidently, to many, reaching age 40 (or thereabouts) means "over the hill". Consequently, jokes about the "middle-aged" individual proliferate, for example, the running gag by the great comedian Jack Benny, who spent nearly half his life stating his age as "39".

The brighter side of middle age has been touted in such books as *Life Begins at 40*, writings that stress the "now you are free" and "do your own thing" themes. This viewpoint also emphasizes that middle age is a developmental period when individuals come into their own, people are more accepting of themselves, and most people mature into more nearly perfect harmony with the universe as they develop a broader perspective. Thus, in many respects, middle age is what each person makes of it.

Following the years of early adulthood, middle age has a tendency to "creep up" on many people, seemingly without warning. No longer can one stay up all night, engaged in uproarious activity, for now the body demands its rest. The middle-aged person finds that the more hectic pace of youth and early adulthood must be replaced by a more regulated life-style, including routine sleeping hours, although this does not necessarily mean more hours of sleep. Indeed, there is evidence that the older one gets, the less sleep one needs.

Within our culture, middle age is generally associated with higher income, a factor that affects one's physical life-style. Many can now afford more beer, wine, and snacks, and more elaborate meals; accompanying this richer diet there is often a reduction of physical activity. Many, unfortunately, eat too much and exercise too little. A "middle-age paunch" may make its appearance as muscle tone slowly deteriorates in people who do not exercise (Birren,

Figure 7–1.   © King Features Syndicate, Inc., 1976.

1964). As Taylor (1976) states, many of the middle-aged select foods of borderline nutritional value, consumed in unbalanced quantities and eaten at the wrong time of day. Triglycerides (fat molecules) and cholesterol build up as a result of excessive intake of fatty foods, and the heart, lungs, and other organs must work harder. Consequently, the middle-aged adult must begin to slow down and work for shorter periods when engaged in strenuous activities. However, having to moderate work activities may not be particularly upsetting, since this is a very gradual process. Moreover, most people readily compensate by working at their own pace and being sensible about the activities they undertake (Belbin, 1967).

AGING DURING THE MIDDLE YEARS

Aging is a process that is little understood. We do know, however, that part of the aging process is influenced by heredity, whereas some of it is influenced by environment. Because each of us is genetically different, we age at different rates. For some, the

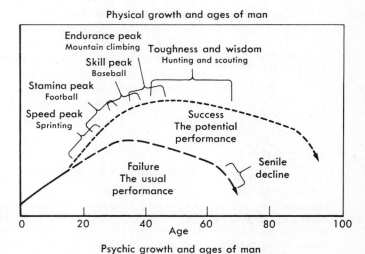

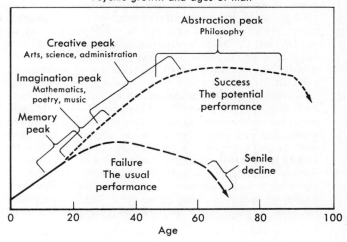

Figure 7–2. The upper lines indicate the physical and psychological potentials of normal people; the lower lines indicate how most people fail to measure up. (Modified from Still, J. W.: "Man's potential and his performance." Copyright 1975 by The New York Times Co. Printed by permission.)

process is very gradual and barely noticeable on a year-to-year basis, whereas others appear to age rapidly before our very eyes.

Most of these signs of aging are manifested in the exterior of the body, primarily the hair and skin. Hair does not grow as rapidly and may become thin. During the forties, the hairline recedes, particularly in men (Troll, 1975). As less pigment is produced, hair also turns gray and loses its luster. The skin is no longer able to stretch quite so tightly over the muscles, which, as we have previously noted, may become flabby. Wrinkles make their appearance at the corners of the eyes (laugh lines or crow's-feet), or around the mouth, and on the forehead.

What can be done to help the body best adjust to the aging process? Basic guidelines include a balanced diet and appropriate exercise to help attain an overall streamlined and healthy appearance. Avoiding excess sun will also keep the skin from drying out too quickly. In addition, there are ointments, creams, special vitamin diets, hair transplants, health spas, gymnasiums, and weight-loss groups. There is also "plastic" or cosmetic surgery, which can range from rhinoplasty (simple "nose job") to blepharoplasty (the tightening of drooping eyelids) to full face-lifts. Some undergo surgical removal of large fat deposits from the "bay window" and even removal of sections of the intestinal tract in intestinal by-pass operations that reduce absorption of digested products into the bloodstream, causing weight loss. In the United States, many middle-aged and older citizens are sufficiently concerned about their outward physical appearance to spend considerable time, energy, and money trying either to maintain the status quo or to reverse the natural aging process, and all this means big business.

MIDDLE AGE AND SENSORY CAPACITY

Vision, the sense we most depend upon, changes noticeably during the middle years, especially after age 40. This is the age when many people begin holding newspapers and books farther in front of them, and bifocals make their appearance to compensate for *presbyopia,* a condition of farsightedness (Burg, 1967; Farnsworth et al., 1965). According to Troll (1975), recovery from glare and adaptation to darkness also take longer in middle age, making night driving more difficult.

Hearing is another sense that may start declining by age 40, and while Americans do not seem embarrassed to wear eyeglasses as vision declines, we are apt to remain "tuned out" rather than wear a hearing aid. The ability to hear low-pitched sounds seems to remain constant in adulthood, but men, especially, lose auditory acuity for the higher pitches. This loss, as we mentioned in Unit 2, may begin as early as young adulthood. Farnsworth and associates (1965) suggest that the auditory difference between the sexes may be caused, at least in part, by men's greater exposure to noise in association with certain traditionally male occupations such as truck driving, mining, auto assembly line work, and the like.

The senses of *taste, touch,* and *smell* in adulthood have not been extensively investigated—in fact, relatively little empirical evidence seems to be available. These senses seemingly decline at least somewhat over the years, but because we rely on taste and smell so little, and because they are difficult to study in the first place, the evidence is at best general. Farnsworth and associates (1965) found that the ability to distinguish tastes (sweet—sour—salt—bitter) remains reasonably constant; nevertheless, the taste threshold rises or taste sensitivity declines, resulting in a slight difficulty in distinguishing among these four basic tastes.

**TABLE 7–1   FUNCTIONAL CAPACITY OF MEN AGED
30 TO 80 (Based on 100 Per Cent at Age 30)**

Physiological Characterisitc	Age					
	30	40	50	60	70	80
Nerve impulse speed	100	100	96	93	91	87
Basic metabolic rate	100	98	95	92	86	83
Body water content	100	98	94	90	87	81
Work rate	100	94	87	80	74	—
Heart output (at rest)	100	93	83	70	58	--
Renal efficiency	100	98	90	82	77	59
Lung capacity	100	92	78	61	50	41

Based on data from Shock, 1962.

MENSTRUATION AND BEHAVIOR

It is fairly well recognized that throughout adulthood, women experience mood swings during their menstrual cycles (Paige, 1973). Some investigators believe that women feel especially competent and optimistic at midcycle, a time when the estrogen level is at its peak, but when the level of estrogen is lowest (just before and during menstruation), women tend to be depressed, anxious, or even hostile. Paige states that there is little argument over these symptoms, except that there is some question concerning what proportion of the female population actually experiences them. She notes that some studies indicate that an enormous 95 per cent of all women report having such symptoms, whereas others suggest that a mere 15 to 20 per cent do so. The recording of such vast differences suggests that while there obviously is a hormonal base for behavioral changes, some may be caused by social or cultural influence. Paige's studies seem to support this hypothesis.

Paige's first group of respondents consisted of 56 Protestants, 18 Catholics, and 13 Jews. Almost all the Catholics and Jews reported that they would never engage in sexual intercourse during menstruation, whereas less than half the Protestants made this statement. Furthermore, Prostestants exhibited little change in anxiety levels between midcycle and premenstruation, but Catholics showed extreme increases in anxiety just prior to the menstrual flow. Jewish women appeared to be more anxious than the other two groups during the whole month. Paige concluded that the differences in the intensity of anxiety could not be attributed strictly to estrogen levels, since all normal women secrete approximately the same hormones. Differences in anxiety levels, she felt, must instead be related to religious beliefs. Among the Orthodox Jews, women are not allowed to have intercourse for the seven days succeeding the onset of menstruation. They are considered "unclean", and they must take a ritual bath in the *mikvah* after their periods to establish their return to cleanliness. The fact that Catholicism also encourages abstinence during the menstrual period might account for the common occurrence of "menstrual blues" in Catholic and Jewish women.

TABLE 7–2 SYMPTOMS ASSOCIATED WITH MENSTRUATION AS REPORTED ON THE MENSTRUAL DISTRESS QUESTIONNAIRE (Paige, 1973)

Physical Changes	Per Cent
Cramps	57
Backaches	33
Skin problems	26
Weight gain	25
Headaches	22
Breast tenderness	20
Emotional Changes	**Per Cent**
Mood swings	27
Irritability	27
Tension	24
Depression	22
Restlessness	17
Crying	16

Further replication investigations including 181 Protestants (a diverse grouping), 54 Jews (mostly Orthodox or Conservative), and 63 Catholics (who attended Mass on a regular basis) supported Paige's earlier findings. A Menstrual Distress Questionnaire (MDQ) designed in 1968 by Rudolf Moos was administered to this group of women, producing the results found in Table 7–2. The findings indicate that social, cultural, and religious views may indeed influence emotions, especially anxiety, during the menstrual period.

BELIEFS ABOUT MENSTRUATION

Most societies have considered menstrual blood to be dangerous, sometimes to women, but especially to men. Therefore, some societies like the Arapesh of New Guinea isolate their women in small "menstrual huts". The menstruating woman must remain in a crouched position and is not allowed to eat, to sleep, or even to touch her own body. Men keep their distance from these huts for fear of dying.

Other cultures prohibit women from participating in everyday functions such as preparing meals, attending religious ceremonies, or engaging in sexual intercourse. Even the Bible states:

And if a woman have an issue, and her issue in her flesh be blood, she shall be put apart seven days: and whosoever toucheth her shall be unclean until the even.

Leviticus 15:19

And from the Code of Manu (Hindu Law):

A woman during her menstrual period, shall retire for three days to a place apart.

During this time, she shall not look at anybody, not even her own children, or at the sight of the sun. On the fourth day, she shall bathe.

The Koran tells us:

They will ask Thee also concerning the courses of women; answer, They are pollution; therefore separate yourselves from women in their courses, and go not near them until they be cleansed.

In modern America "the curse" is still viewed as something mysterious and unclean. Products such as Kotex, Moddess, and Tampax are advertised in such a way as to suggest that they will bring "peace of mind" to the user. The very term "sanitary napkin" connotes the idea of uncleanliness. Other products are advertised as remedies for the undesirable side effects of menstruation, such as "period puffiness", cramps, headaches, and iron deficiencies.

(Adapted from Paige, K: "Women Learn to Sing the Menstrual Blues." *Psychology Today*, September 1973.)

MENOPAUSE AND CLIMACTERIC (CHANGE OF LIFE)

Menopause can be simply defined as the cessation of menstruation. This is a straightforward medical definition, making absolutely no reference to the *physiological* changes that occur in *all* women, or to the many *psychological* changes that occur in *some* women.

Menopause generally occurs during the late forties or early fifties, though some women have been known to experience it as early as the midthirties. The period from the onset of irregularity of the menses to total cessation (menopause) is called the *climacteric*. The female climacteric may last only a few months or may be extended over several years. During the climacteric, ovulation, menstruation, and reproductive capacity gradually cease (Kinsey et al., 1953).

Menopause is caused by the "burning out" of the ovaries; that is, after 30 to 40 years of menstrual cycles a woman has released almost all her ova (eggs). Although the male continues to produce new sperm throughout adulthood, the human female is born with a fixed number of ovarian follicles (immature ova and their cases). The number of follicles present at birth is estimated to be 750,000. By puberty this figure has been reduced to about 400,000, of which only about 450 will mature to expel ova. The rest will deteriorate. By approximately age 45, a woman's supply of follicles is nearly depleted, and only a few remain.

As the number of follicles decreases, there is an accompanying decline in production of the female sex hormone estrogen. When estrogen production nears the zero level, the climacteric culminates in the complete cessation of cyclic ovarian activity—the menopause (Ruch and Fulton, 1960). Because of the rapid decrease in secretion of the hormones estrogen and progesterone, mammary glands atrophy, as do the uterus and vagina in varying degrees (Fig. 7–3).

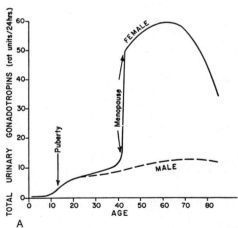

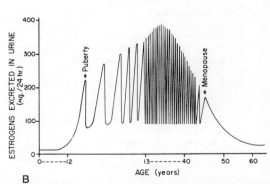

Figure 7–3. *A,* Total rates of secretion of gonadotropic hormones throughout the sexual lives of females and males, showing an especially abrupt increase in gonadotropic hormones at the menopause in the female. *B,* Estrogen secretion throughout sexual life. (*From:* Guyton, A. C.: *Textbook of Medical Physiology,* 5th ed. Philadelphia, W. B. Saunders Co., 1976.)

There are two distinct periods when women experience the psychological effects of long-term hormonal changes. One occurs *during the climacteric,* the other occurs *upon reaching menopause.*

During the climacteric, a woman "must readjust her life from one that has been physiologically stimulated by the production of estrogen and progesterone to one that is devoid of these feminizing hormones" (Guyton, 1976). Loss of these hormones may cause such symptoms as hot flashes (moments of feeling warm and uncomfortable, often accompanied by perspiration); irritability, including frequent mood changes and even depression; fatigue and anxiety; and often sensations of dyspnea (labored or difficult breathing). It has been estimated that between 50 and 85 per cent of all women experience some of these symptoms (Bardwick, 1971). It is not known, however, whether these conditions result solely from hormonal changes or are in part a reflection of societal beliefs such as those that affect menstrual mood swings (Paige, 1973).

The concept of hormones as part of a cause-effect relationship is supported by Masters and Johnson (1970), who state that menopausal symptoms can be reduced by taking estrogen. Hormone

TABLE 7–3   ATTITUDES TOWARD MENOPAUSE: BY AGE

Illustrative Items	Percentage Who Agree,[a] in Age Groups			
	A 21–30 (N = 50)	B 31–44 (N = 52)	C 45–55 (N = 100)	D 56–65 (N = 65)
I. **"Negative Affect":**				
28. Menopause is an unpleasant experience for a woman	56	44	58	55
34. Women should expect some trouble during the menopause	60	46	59	58
33. In truth, just about every woman is depressed about the change of life	48	29	40	28
II. **"Post-Menopausal Recovery"**				
24. Women generally feel better after the menopause than they have for years	32[b]	20[b]	68	67
27. A woman gets more confidence in herself after the change of life	12[b]	21[b]	52	42
17. After the change of life, a woman feels freer to do things for herself	16[b]	24[b]	74	65
35. Many women think menopause is the best thing that ever happened to them	14[b]	31	46	40
III. **"Extent of Continuity":**				
12. Going through the menopause really does not change a woman in any important way	58[b]	55[b]	74	83

replacement is used by some women to eliminate such physiological symptoms as hot flashes, hair loss, atrophy of the breasts and vagina, and loss of skin elasticity (Kirby, 1973). However, Guyton (1976) states that while alleviating the symptoms, such treatment will also prolong their duration. It also may increase the risk of cancer.

In addition to physiological and psychological symptoms occurring during the climacteric, the individual woman's overall attitude regarding what the climacteric and menopause actually *mean* to her must be considered. About half of all American women (pre-

TABLE 7–3   ATTITUDES TOWARD MENOPAUSE: BY AGE *(Continued)*

Illustrative Items	Percentage Who Agree,[a] in Age Groups			
	A 21–30 (N = 50)	B 31–44 (N = 52)	C 45–55 (N = 100)	D 56–65 (N = 65)
IV. **"Control of Symptoms":**				
4. Women who have trouble with the menopause are usually those who have nothing to do with their time	58	50[b]	71	70
7. Women who have trouble in the menopause are those who are expecting it	48[b]	56[b]	76	63
V. **"Psychological Losses":**				
18. Women worry about losing their minds during the menopause	28[b]	35	51	24[b]
11. A woman is concerned about how her husband will feel toward her after the menopause	58[b]	44	41	21[b]
VI. **"Unpredictability":**				
6. A woman in menopause is apt to do crazy things she herself does not understand	40	56	53	40
10. Menopause is a mysterious thing which most women don't understand	46	46	59	46
VII. **"Sexuality":**				
3. If the truth were really known, most women like to have themselves a fling at this time in their lives	8[b]	33	32	24
19. After the menopause, a woman is more interested in sex than she was before	14[b]	27	35	21

[a]Subjects who checked "agree strongly" or "agree to some extent" are grouped together.

[b]The difference between this percentage and the percentage of Group C is significant at the 05 level or above.

From Neugarten, B. L., Wood, V., Kraines, R. J., and Loomis, B.: "Women's attitudes toward the menopause." *Vita Humana.* 6:140–151, 1963. Reprinted by permission of S. Karger AG, Basel.

menopausal, climacteric, and post-climacteric) consider menopause to be a depressing and unpleasant experience, whereas the other half actually feel relief when menstruation is over (Neugarten et al., 1963).

SEXUALITY

Decreases in sexual responsiveness wtih age are probably due to psychological causes rather than physiological ones. Although there is no menopause in men comparable to that which women experience, the possibility of a unique male menopausal stage has recently received attention (Lear, 1973). While there is a very gradual decrease in the secretion of the male hormone testosterone, extremely low levels are not reached until old age, and even then, men produce fertile sperm and thus are capable of fathering children. Men do, however, decline in their ability to have repeated orgasms, and, according to Masters and Johnson (1970), the incidence of sexual inadequacy in males rises sharply after age 50. The male's inability to engage in intercourse, or even to produce an erection, can be attributed to a number of causes, including job-related anxiety or worries about sexual adequacy or imagined loss of sexual powers; boredom; or overindulgence in food or drink. In the absence of these inhibiting factors, a man should be capable of enjoying sex until he is in his seventies or even his eighties (Masters and Johnson, 1970).

A woman remains capable of sexual activity throughout her life, and women become more responsive to sexual stimuli during their middle years. Some authorities believe that this is because an increase in blood circulation resulting from earlier pregnancies enhances the possibility of orgasm (Sherfey, 1972).

HEALTH PROBLEMS OF MIDDLE AGE

Of all the preventable disorders of middle age, obesity looms as the most threatening. For anyone who is 30 per cent or more overweight, the probability of dying in middle age is increased by more than 40 per cent. Disorders attributed wholly or partially to excess weight include hypertension and complications due to diabetes, as well as digestive disorders (gallstones and liver dysfunction). In one screening study of supposedly healthy middle-aged Americans undergoing routine checkups at a major health care center, 16.3 per cent were overweight by 30 per cent or more; 7.8 per cent suffered from hypertension, and 2.8 per cent from diabetes (Smith and Bierman, 1973).

Health problems associated with chronic smoking also appear in the middle years of adulthood. Cancer of the mouth, throat, and lungs, pulmonary emphysema, and cardiovascular diseases all begin making their appearance, especially between the ages of 45 and 55. Statistics indicate that nonsmokers have only half the health prob-

Figure 7–4 *A,* **Disorders of middle age.** *(From:* Collen, M.F.: "Automated multiphasic screening." *In* Sharp, C., and Keen, H.: *Presymptomatic Detection and Early Diagnosis.* London: Pitman Medical Publication Company, Ltd., 1968.) *B,* **Leading causes of death in middle age, as percentage of total deaths between ages 45 and 64.** *(From: Vital Statistics of the United States, 1968.* Vol. 2, Part B: Mortality. Rockville, Maryland: U. S. Department of Health, Education, and Welfare, 1971.) *C,* **Percentages of deaths caused by cancer of various types in younger and older middle-aged men and women.** *(From: Mortality from Malignant Neoplasms, 1955–1965.* Part I. Geneva, Switzerland: World Health Organization, 1970.)

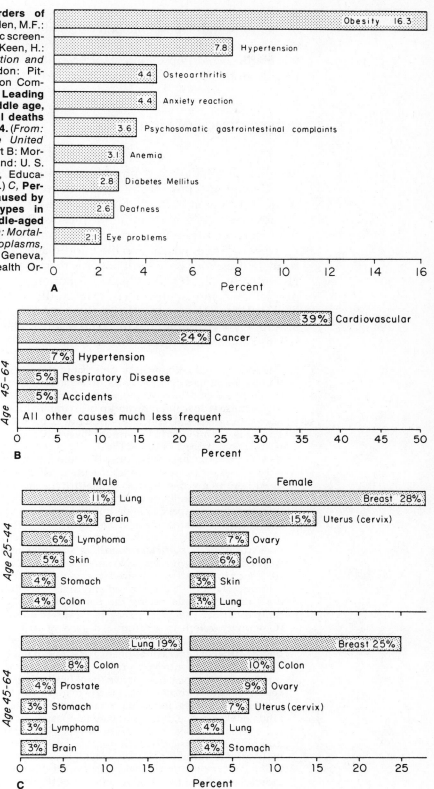

lems that the heavier smokers have. Whatever the reasons (smoking or otherwise), the most common cause of death in the late fifties is cardiovascular disease, which strikes down a total of 38 per cent of the middle-aged population. Moreover, the death rate accelerates rapidly in the late middle years (Fig. 7–4).

INTELLIGENCE IN MIDDLE AGE

Earlier, it was suggested that psychologists disagree about whether intelligence remains constant, increases, or declines with age. Seemingly, few young adults concern themselves with this issue, but to many older adults either approaching middle age or already there, it is a meaningful question. To some, the idea that there is a decline in memory arouses considerable anxiety.

Intelligence (whether in the middle-aged individual, the young adult, or the child) is difficult not only to measure but even to define. Historically, the IQ (intelligence quotient) test was designed to predict academic achievement (McCandless et al., 1972), which it does rather well—especially for those who are very like the white, middle-class children on whom the test was standardized. Ausubel (1968) makes some interesting remarks regarding intelligence:

> The concept of intelligence, by definition, clearly excludes level of functioning in all *noncognitive* areas of behavior. This definition renders largely irrelevant the commonly voiced criticism that the IQ is misleading because it does not indicate an individual's capacity for coping with nonrepresentational, concrete, mechanical, or interpersonal problems. The IQ is not intended to represent these latter capacities, and no claim is made that it does. In fact, if the intelligence test were modified so that it *could* perform these functions, it would automatically lose whatever effectiveness it possesses as a measure of cognitive ability. The argument here is not that indices of maturity level in other noncognitive areas are theoretically or practically unimportant, but rather that it is utterly naive to expect a single instrument adequately to measure several largely unrelated kinds of abilities.
>
> Also irrelevant in much the same sense is the criticism that the IQ does not indicate *particular* cognitive strengths and failings or *typical* ways of attacking problems. No single *summary* score could possibly do so. If such information is desired it is available in the detailed test protocol from which the IQ is derived and in the qualitative observations of the examiner. Quite beside the point, also, is the frequently-voiced complaint that the intelligence test fails to identify *creativity*. . . . [C]reativity refers to a unique degree of originality in some *substantive* area of human endeavor, and not to the possession of a high degree either of general intelligence or of one of its component abilities.
>
> Much futile controversy rages over the issue of whether or not the intelligence test measures *native* (genetically determined) *cognitive endowment*. Although an effort is made to maximize the influence of *genic* factors by using test items that presuppose only very *generally available* kinds of experience, it is obviously impossible to rule out the differential effects of exposure to different types of cognitive experience, to different levels of cognitive stimulation, and to different personality and motivational variables. Hence, intelligence can be regarded only as a *multiple-determined functional capacity*, the level of which in a given individual reflects the relative potency of these various factors as they

exist and interact in his particular case. Most general intelligence tests, for instance the Binet type, explicitly attempt to avoid the impact of *particular* kinds of past experience by presenting the subject with relatively *novel* tasks. Even so, however, many of the component sub-tests, such as vocabulary, obviously reflect the influence of environmental factors, for example, of social-class membership and cultural deprivation. Special aptitude tests, such as language usage, are even more dependent on the nature of prior experience and social-class background.

(pp. 226–227)

Thus, we begin to see some of the problems encountered in assessing adult intelligence. Since the principal purpose of IQ tests is to predict academic achievement, the test loses value when applied to adults, since it may not be a true indicator of adult intelligence.

Some investigators have inferred that significant changes in the brain occur during the aging process. However, there is virtually no evidence that any physiological changes occur in the brain during the middle years of adulthood (Welford, 1965). As already explained, however, reaction times slow down and senses become less acute as an individual ages. This, of course, will affect test scores if speed is a factor in the assessment. In fact, Kimmel (1974), in evaluating intellectual functions, notes that there are several areas in which performance is judged to be poorer simply because it is slower. Thus, many older studies report that intelligence as measured on IQ tests declines with age. However, more recent work questions these conclusions. The middle-aged person, while slower than the young adult in grasping and solving a problem, can call more practical experience to his or her assistance (Welford, 1951). Having had a wider range of life experiences, the intelligent middle-aged adult, in particular, will recognize more variables in a given situation, thus taking more time. Young adults confine themselves solely to the problem, whereas middle-aged adults utilize a broader perspective—a perspective that in some cultures might be called wisdom.

The middle years may in fact represent the peak years for many types of intellectual functions. Zubek and Solberg (1954) analyzed electroencephalograms and reported that some people may not even reach full brain development until the age of 30.

Lehman (1953) reported that the peak of intellectual productivity was reached at ages 30 to 40. The job performance of many people in their thirties was rated as being of "very high quality", whereas the work of those in their forties was more often given a rank of "worthy". Another researcher, however, analyzed total work productivity and concluded that the most productive and creative period of life is between ages 40 and 50, although there were differences according to vocation (Dennis, 1968). For instance, productivity declined more rapidly after age 40 in creative artists than in scholars in the humanities, whose intellectual abilities appeared to remain consistently high even into their seventies.

Although debate on the subject continues, most researchers presently believe that the majority of people reach the height of their

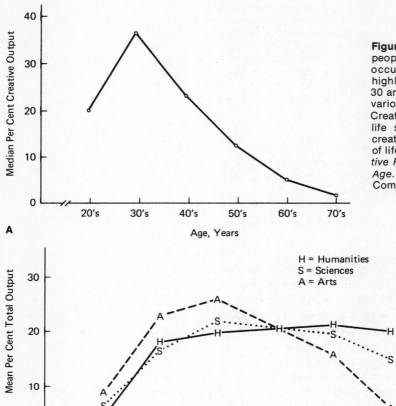

Figure 7–5. *A,* Creative output of people in scientific and academic occupations. Such people are highly creative between the ages of 30 and 40. *B,* Peaks of creativity in various intellectual occupations. Creativity occurs throughout the life span, but different kinds of creativity occur at different stages of life. (*From:* Botwinick, J.: *Cognitive Processes in Maturity and Old Age.* © 1967 by Springer Publishing Company, Inc., New York.)

productive and creative capacities between the ages of 30 and 45 or perhaps 30 and 50.

Other factors besides speed influence results of intellectual tests. For instance, on the average, higher IQ scores are achieved by those adults who are in the higher social classes, by those who have more education, by those who are healthy, and, of course, by those who had higher IQ scores as children (Botwinick, 1967).

According to Botwinick (1967), memory, the area of concern for so many middle-aged people, does indeed appear to decline over the life span. Why this is so is not clear, but other studies (e.g., Canestrari, 1963) have indicated that if middle-aged adults are allowed more time to learn tasks requiring memorization, they can do as well as younger adults (note, again, the importance of the time factor). This idea is supported by test results suggesting that short-term memory is more adversely affected by aging than long-term memory (Botwinick, 1970).

While short-term memory and reaction time are declining during the middle years, other intellectual functions are reaching their peak. The creative process is approaching new heights for some, but, it must be added, not for others. There is abundant evidence that certain gifted individuals, especially those working in disciplines such as advanced mathematics, reach their creative zenith in their early or mid twenties and then spend the rest of their lives sorting, explaining, and elaborating upon their earlier ideas. For others, vocabulary continues to increase, and verbal reasoning skills continue improving well into the middle years and possibly even into late adulthood (Birren, 1964).

In conclusion, it appears that the ability to be flexible in thinking, to comprehend, and to create actually improves during middle age, but short-term memory and certain motor skills and eye and hand coordination wane during this developmental stage (Baltes and Schaie, 1974).

Summary

The middle years of adulthood are a stage of life that generally begins with a modest decline in physical abilities and a number of bodily changes such as graying or loss of the hair, development of a paunch, loss of skin elasticity, and development of facial wrinkles. For those who keep themselves physically fit, there is little decline in athletic ability. However, great sums of time and money are spent annually on attempts to "look young".

The little-understood processes of aging also affect the sensory capacities of the middle-aged. The eyes lose some of their ability to accommodate near objects, hearing acuity may decline, and although the senses of taste, touch, and smell are difficult to investigate, currently available evidence indicates a decline in these senses as well.

The behavior of women is affected by the level of estrogen in the body, which is related to the female sexual cycle. However, some research indicates that emotional states may be affected by religious and cultural beliefs about the nature of menstruation.

Another factor that may affect the behavior of the middle-aged woman is the climacteric, or change of life—hormonal changes that lead to irregular menses and finally cessation of menstruation (menopause). During these months or even years, the rapid decline in estrogen and progesterone levels may be accompanied by "hot flashes", irritability, anxiety, and other symptoms. These changes do not preclude sexual activity, however, for a woman may remain sexually active all her life. Among males and females, decreases in sexual responsiveness as aging takes place are most likely due to psychological rather than physiological factors.

Intelligence is difficult to measure, but it does appear that those who utilize their intellectual functions (e.g., professors, scientists) have little if any loss of intelligence, whereas those who do not engage in such mental activities may decline in intelligence. The older one gets, the better one can draw upon previous experience—a perspective that can be termed *wisdom*.

Suggested Readings

1. Dennis, W.: "Creative productivity between the ages of 20 and 80 years" in *Journal of Gerontology*. 21(*1*), 1966.

   An investigative account focusing on the manner in which creativity unfolds throughout adult life.

2. Masters, W. H., and Johnson, V. E.: *Human Sexual Response*. Boston: Little, Brown and Co., 1966.

   Chapters 15 and 16 of this highly acclaimed book focus on the sexual responses of the aging man and woman.

3. Paige, K. E.: "Women learn to sing the menstrual blues" in *Psychology Today*. 7 (*4*), 1973.

   This article explores how cultural attitudes, rather than hormone secretion, may account for a woman's depression, hostility, and anxiety during menstruation.

4. Sears, R. R., and Feldman, S. S. (Eds.): *The Seven Ages of Man*. Los Altos, California: William Kaufmann, Inc., 1973.

   Chapter 16 of this text deals with the physical growth changes that transpire in the body during the middle years of life.

5. Smith, D. W., and Bierman, E. L., *The Biologic Ages of Man*. Philadelphia: W. B. Saunders Co., 1973.

   Of special interest in Chapter 9 of this book are the common physical problems of the middle-aged individual.

Section B   The Middle Years of Adulthood

Lance Canon

UNIT 8

PERSONALITY AND SOCIAL LEARNING

Introduction

The psychology of middle adulthood is a relatively new area of investigation, and developmental psychologists have really just begun to formulate theories concerning the midlife period. Unfortunately, much of the early literature describing middle age was based on casual observation and clinical evidence, which tended to distort the realities of this critical time of life (Nye and Berardo, 1973; Rappaport, 1976). In addition, past theories of adult personality have usually been derived from the young and arbitrarily applied to older subjects (Botwinick, 1973). Few of the theories developed so far fully account for the interrelationship of physical aging and changes of personality. As Gould (1975) has pointed out, we are many years away from acquiring the store of information needed to give us an understanding of the adult personality comparable to our present understanding of childhood and adolescence.

Analyses of adult personality development may be based on any of three alternative theories of personality formation (Troll, 1975). One theory contends that the self is *stabilized early in life*. From this perspective personality development is seen as a striving for a consistent identity that can minimize the disturbing effects of environmental events. A second theory interprets personality as a *response to situations*. As life situations fluctuate, so too does the personality. A third theory maintains that the self-system does not seek to minimize changes; it incorporates them and thus is transformed into a *new and different whole* (Troll, 1975).

With these three perspectives in mind, how do we best explain personality changes during adulthood? Is the adult personality characterized by continuity or change? Unfortunately, the answer to these questions is somewhat elusive. As Troll (1975) indicates, some personality characteristics remain unaltered throughout adult life, but others change idiosyncratically or as a consequence of environmental experiences. Bischof (1976) suggests whether the adult personality is viewed as remaining stable or changing depends on a number of factors, including who defines the concept and how this problem is studied. While each of these theories of adult personality development can be substantiated to some degree, which theory best explains the adult personality has yet to be determined.

IS THERE A MIDLIFE CRISIS?

Some writers prefer to view the middle years as a chaotic period filled with numerous conflicts. They emphasize the many changes that take place at this time, such as the permanent departure of children from the home, vocational adjustments, and necessity of coping with the physiological and psychological consequences of aging. As in previous stages of life, certain developmental tasks must be met (see box). Under certain conditions, conflict may arise over the individual's inability to exhibit successful accommodation. However, other researchers deny the existence of such conflicts, claiming that middle adulthood is something of a euphoric stage. It is a time when individuals have been for the most part relieved of major social and economic burdens, not to mention the responsibilities of parenthood. Consequently, middle age seems to promise a period of new-found freedom (Nye and Berardo, 1973). Nevertheless, most researchers agree that middle age is marked by reflective introspection (Rappaport, 1976).

DEVELOPMENTAL TASKS OF MIDDLE AGE

1. Helping teen-aged children to become responsible and happy adults.
2. Achieving adult social and civic responsibility.
3. Reaching and maintaining satisfactory performance in one's occupation.
4. Developing adult leisure-time activities.
5. Relating oneself to one's spouse as a person.
6. Accepting and adjusting to the physiological changes of middle age.
7. Adjusting to aging parents.

Adapted from Havighurst (1972).

Those who face conflicts should be reassured that this midlife phenomenon, like adolescence, is a normal crisis.

It may be acute, with depression and anxiety, but it is more likely to be quiet. It may even be enjoyable, for change means variety and the opportunity for exploration. An individual is not likely to pinpoint the crisis, for it probably occurs in stages over a period of years. It may be linked with external circumstances like change in work, but it is more likely to be private and internal.

(Rayner, 1971, p. 232)

A growing number of researchers are seeking to explain the midlife crisis (Brim, 1976). Many suggest that such a crisis begins with an awareness of physical and psychological cues, signals that symbolize approaching middle age. As we learned earlier, the aging process and one's awareness of it may very well be affected by a "social age clock", a built-in psychological mechanism that may retard or accelerate later stages of adulthood (Neugarten, 1968). One writer, attempting to describe the timing of the middle-age crisis humorously believes that it occurs when people aren't sure whether to blame their midlife troubles on their parents or their children.

Sheehy (1976) believes the midlife crisis can be charted sometime between the ages of 35 and 45, a period she calls the "deadline decade." The continuity of the life cycle is interrupted, Sheehy proposes, and energies, instead of being focused on external goals or ideas, turn inward toward the self. People become acutely aware of their physical being and of new aches and pains (some may even develop a minor case of hypochondria). Whereas in the twenties death seemed fairly distant, something that only happened to others, by age 40 it seems very close and personal. Consequently, the middle-aged adult becomes intensely preoccupied with signs of aging and premature doom. (Many at this age begin to read the obituary columns with regularity.) This kind of self-awareness prompts many to question their youthful dreams and aspirations and their actual accomplishments and fulfillments.

The midlife crisis may well be characterized by evaluation and concern about the future. In the early thirties, most people are goal-oriented and are working hard to achieve their aspirations (Levinson et al., 1974). By the time the thirties and forties are reached, life may look more complex and difficult than it did earlier, largely because of increased responsibilities, role strain, and goal confusion (Gould, 1975).

How does one resolve the midlife crisis? Most experts agree that successful resolution depends on an ability to reassess and readjust. This may be a painful procedure for many, but it is important to renounce some dreams while critically evaluating modes of life that are possible and available (Rayner, 1971). This type of reassessment, according to Levinson and associates (1974), may well lead to greater self-fulfillment in later adult life.

THE FEMALE MIDLIFE TRANSITION

Sheehy (1976) believes that women enter midlife earlier than men do (approximately by age 35), setting off a "my last chance" sense of urgency. What a woman feels it is her "last chance" to do, however, is affected considerably by the life pattern she has followed so far.

It is suggested that at least six facts related to female life combine to bring a "sense of deadline" to the surface at this particular age.

1. Thirty-five is when the average mother sends her last child off to school.
2. Thirty-five begins the dangerous age of infidelity.
3. Thirty-five is when the average married American woman reenters the working world.
4. Thirty-four is the average age at which the divorced woman remarries.
5. Thirty-five is the most common age for runaway wives.
6. Thirty-five brings the biological end to childbearing closer.

When these factors converge, many women begin to feel the need to change to a midlife perspective. However, whether the woman *acts* on her life assessment at this age and what part her husband may play in this psychological process are separate issues.

THEORIES OF MIDLIFE PERSONALITY DEVELOPMENT

The middle years of life appear to represent a turning point for most people. The concept of time is restructured, and new perceptions of the self and the environment are formed. Introspection and self-evaluation are characteristic of this period. The reflection that transpires during middle age is not the same as the reminiscence that characterizes old age, but perhaps it is its forerunner (Neugarten, 1968; Rappaport, 1976).

According to Kimmel (1974), personality becomes more balanced in middle age. On the one hand, the individual's social world is no longer expanding rapidly, and ways of dealing effectively with it have been devised. On the other hand, greater knowledge of the self has been acquired, along with relatively comfortable ways of integrating the internal and external aspects of the personality. "In the ideal case," Kimmel writes, "this leads to a smoothly functioning, competent fit between the individual and the environment that allows some striving for the goal of self-actualization" (p. 305). However, the tendency toward rigidity and resistance to change may also appear at this time.

Several noteworthy theories of midlife personality development have been proposed. Of particular interest are those developed by Erik Erikson, Robert Butler, Else Frenkel-Brunswik, and Charlotte Buhler.

Erik Erikson's Theory

Erikson (1963) considers the essence of personality development during the middle years to be the conflict of *generativity versus stagnation*. Erikson posits that not only do young children need and depend upon their parents, but the older generation is also dependent upon the younger. "Mature man needs to be needed, and maturity needs guidance as well as encouragement from what has been produced and must be taken care of" (pp. 266–267).

The key element in Erikson's theory is *generativity*, one's concern with guiding the next generation. Although not all adults are personally motivated to rear a new generation, Erikson points out that this drive does not necessarily apply to one's own offspring. The concept of generativity may seem synonymous with *productivity* and *creativity*, yet neither can replace generativity in the Eriksonian sense. The force countering generativity is stagnation, which may take the form of self-absorption, egocentrism, or self-indulgence.

Robert Peck's Theory

Peck (1968) has added an interesting dimension to Erikson's work. Believing that Erikson placed too much emphasis on the psychosocial crises of childhood and adolescence and not enough on the last 40 or 50 years of life, Peck suggests that it might be useful to divide middle age into several phases of psychological adjustment. Four such adjustments include *valuing wisdom versus valuing physical powers, socializing versus sexualizing in human relationships, cathectic flexibility versus cathectic impoverishment,* and *mental flexibility versus mental rigidity.*

Valuing Wisdom versus Valuing Physical Powers.   After the late twenties, one of the inescapable consequences of aging is a decrease in physical strength, stamina, and attractiveness (if "attractive" is defined as "young looking"). Yet, the sheer experience acquired through living longer may enable the middle-aged adult to accomplish considerably more than a younger counterpart. The term wisdom sums up this increment in judgmental powers that living longer brings. Wisdom is not the same as intellectual capacity. It is perhaps best defined as the ability "to make the most effective choices among the alternatives which intellectual perception and imagination present for one's decision" (pp. 88–89). Such choice-making is affected by several factors, including emotional stability, unconflicted or conflicted motivation set, and mental ability. Individuals who age most succesfully are those who "invert" their previous hierarchy of values, giving mental ability a higher position than physical prowess, both as their standard for self-evaluation and as their primary means of problem solving.

Socializing versus Sexualizing in Human Relationships. This adjustment focuses on the sexual climacteric, which coincides with general physical decline but is partially separate from it. The climacteric may motivate men and women to value one another as individual personalities rather than primarily as sex objects. As Peck states:

> If a person takes positive action at this point, redefining men and women as individuals and as companions, with the sexual element decreasingly significant, it would at least be understandable that inter-personal living *could* take on a depth of understanding which the earlier, perhaps inevitably more egocentric, sex-drive would have tended to prevent to some degree.
>
> (p. 89)

Cathectic Flexibility versus Cathectic Impoverishment. Psychological development in this sense means the ability to be emotionally flexible—to be able to shift emotional investments from one person or activity to another. Emotional flexibility is crucial in middle age because of psychologically critical developments such as the loss of parents, the departure of children from the home, and the death of friends and relatives of similar age. Unfortunately, some people experience an increasingly impoverished emotional life because, as their cathexis objects disappear, they are unable to reinvest their emotions in other people or pursuits. Adapting positively by finding new objects of emotional focus is required to overcome this crisis.

Mental Flexibility versus Mental Rigidity. It is important for middle-aged people to remain flexible in their opinions and actions and to be receptive to new ideas. The elderly are often said to be "set in their ways", but "hardening of the mental arteries" is likely to appear at midlife—a point when people may have achieved peak status and have devised a set of "answers" to life, tempting them to forgo the mental effort of envisioning novel solutions to problems. Some people become dominated by their experiences and use them as the basis for fixed rules that almost automatically govern their subsequent behavior. The flexible individual will strive to master life's experiences, to achieve some degree of detached perspective on them, and to use them as provisional guides to the solution of new problems.

Else Frenkel-Brunswik's Theory

Another theory of personality development has been proposed by Frenkel-Brunswik (1968). She divides life into five stages: childhood, adolescence, young adulthood, middle age, and old age. Her observations of middle-age personality dynamics are especially relevant to our present discussion.

In many respects, middle age is a time when activity diminishes and "negative dimensions" (such as sickness and loss of associates) appear. The death of a friend or relative, which might have been less emotionally disruptive earlier in life, when new attachments were constantly being formed, now has considerable psychological impact. The middle-aged adult may also be affected by other losses, personal or economic. Physical deterioration is another cause for concern. Furthermore, vocational dissatisfaction may prompt a career switch at this time.

Consequently, according to Frenkel-Brunswik, the transition to middle age is a period frequently characterized by a psychological crisis. There is a tendency to change and to exhibit discontent or even complete negation. Certain observations seem to bear this out:

> We find, for instance, the most frequent occurrence of trips taken for rest or recuperation between the ages of 45 and 48, with a decrease lacking until the age of 60. This can be looked upon as renewal of unrest, showing itself in an intensified wanderlust, and a frequent change of residence. In the short time between the 45th and 48th years there is further a transitory inclination toward daydreaming and loneliness to be found. Unspecific activities, such as literary interests, a tendency toward retrospection, which otherwise first appear at 60 years, are also to be noticed here as a transitory condition.
>
> (Frenkel-Brunswik, 1968, p. 81)

Frenkel-Brunswik also notes that creativity frequently reaches its culmination at this time. Social activities shift into new areas, with a new emphasis on philanthropic activity. In the area of physical activity, athletic participation appears to decline and interest in nature increases.

Other Theories of Midlife Personality Development

Buhler (1972) places considerable emphasis on goal formulation. The years preceding adulthood are primarily devoted to the establishment of goals, whereas the remaining years of the life cycle are devoted to fulfilling these ambitions or reassessing them. Acknowledgment of success or failure is especially acute during the middle years. Buhler believes that fulfillment of goals may depend on four factors: satisfaction of needs, ability to expand creatively, adjustment to limitations, and consistency of the inner self.

Kuhlen (1964) has proposed a personality model similar to Buhler's. He postulates that growth expansion motives or goals (such as achievement, power, and self-actualization) play an instrumental role in the first half of life, but these motives may very well change by the middle years because they have been satisfied or have "contracted". In this repect, Kuhlen views the life cycle as a curve of expansion and contraction.

Kuhlen and Johnson (1952) illustrated the shift of goals that may take place during adulthood (Fig. 8–1). Studying a group of public-school teachers, these researchers asked the question "What would you most like to be doing ten years from now?" Marriage was an expansion goal among young single women, whereas young married

Figure 8–1.   Middle age is frequently characterized by reflective   Ted Dobson
introspection.   Camera Press, London

women wanted to acquire a house and become housewives. After age 30, career advancement was an expansion goal. By the middle years (approximately age 45), most of the single women were concerned about retiring, an example of a contraction goal. Married women seemed to formulate contraction goals earlier: at 40, many spoke of retiring. Among men, retirement was often not mentioned until age 50, leading the researchers to believe that married men maintain expansion goals longer than the other groups queried.

Each of the theories we have considered has provided us with a better understanding of the personality of the middle-aged person. We know from the writings of these authorities and others that middle age is a time of questioning, evaluation, and intro-spection. For some, a mid-life crisis may occur.

Despite the psychological crises and developmental tasks to be met during middle age, there is a positive side to this stage of life. Many middle-aged adults succeed in "discovering" themselves in a healthy manner. They are in a position to evaluate their strengths and weaknesses, interests and talents. Middle-aged people may have self-doubts, but they have acquired a fund of life experiences on which they can draw to answer their questions. Most have de-veloped mature cognitive and social skills that enable them to make sound decisions regarding vocational, family, and community is-

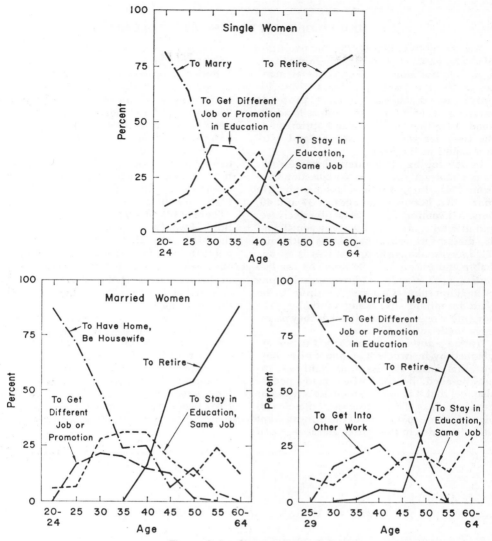

Figure 8–2. Changes in goals with age among public school teachers. (*From:* Kuhlen, R. G., and Johnson, G. H.: "Changes in Goals with Adult Increasing Age." *Journal of Consulting and Clinical Psychology, 16*:1–4, 1952. Copyright 1952 by the American Psychological Association.)

sues. Being less socially oriented (and more selective in joining groups or organizations), they don't feel the pressures of conformity as much as they once did. The end result of the self-evaluation that takes place in middle age is frequently a gratifying sense of personal growth and maturity (Neugarten, 1968).

THE SELF-ACTUALIZING PERSONALITY

Throughout the course of adulthood, many people strive to reach a psychological ideal, a harmonious integration of their per-

THE ADULT'S GROWTH TOWARD SELF-TOLERANCE

According to Gould (1975), the evolution of a personality continues through the fifties and does not stop at adolescence as many psychologists believe. In a thought-provoking discussion, Gould proposes seven stages of personality unique to adulthood, from the confidence and optimism of the twenties to the mellowing and self-acceptance of the fifties.

In developing his theoretical framework, Gould analyzed responses to a questionnaire from 524 white, middle-class people. He found that between the ages of 37 and 40, personal comfort and satisfaction decrease, and marital comfort is low. Between 40 and 43, discomfort and unhappiness with oneself increase, suggesting that this is an unstable and uncomfortable time. By the late forties, both friends and loved ones become quite important. Children continue to be quite important, and many adults begin to have more regrets about mistakes they might have made in child-rearing.

Young adults in their early thirties are plagued by insufficient amounts of money, but this issue is less important for the middle-aged. By the forties, many people also feel that it is too late to make any major career changes. The feeling that "there's still plenty of time to do most of the things I want to do" recedes in the forties and is replaced by a sense "of reconciliation of what is with what might be."

Between the ages of 41 and 43, many of the respondents felt that their personality was fairly well set. From 44 to 50, life seems to "settle down" for most people. There appears to be a tolerant acceptance of the new ordering of things.

The fifties are characterized by stability tempered by concern about the passage of time. Aware that half their adult lives had been used up, the respondents were increasingly pessimistic about the statement, "There's still plenty of time to do most of the things I want to do" and increasingly agreed that "I try to be satisfied with what I have and not to think so much about the things I probably won't be able to get." Concern about health also rises at this stage, and many agreed that they couldn't do things as well as they once had.

Gould stresses that these descriptions are generalizations that reflect the average of considerable personal variation. Although he believes that such a sequence applies to the majority of people, precise ages for the developments proposed are a reflection of total personality, life-style, and subculture. How these changes are expressed and dealt with will depend on the individual.

sonality. Attaining self-actualization requires considerable ego strength and the ability to make use of all potentialities and capabilities. In those who reach self-actualization, we can expect to find a highly refined dimension of growth that is characterized by autonomy, individuation, and authenticity. Of course, not everyone reaches self-actualization, and the criteria for self-actualization may vary (see box).

An extensive description of self-actualization has been provided by Maslow (1954; 1968; 1970), who defines the need for self-actualization as "the desire to become more and more what one is, to become everything that one is capable of becoming." He argues that human behavior is motivated by far more than hedonistic pleasure-seeking and pain-avoidance or mere striving to reduce internal tension. Maslow does acknowledge that many motives are generated by the tension in the organism and that higher forms of behavior are possible only after the tension level has been reduced.

Maslow suggests that several preconditions must be satisfied before self-actualization can be attained. Individuals must be relatively free of mundane worries, especially those related to survival.

MASLOW'S HIERARCHY OF NEEDS

At the heart of Maslow's theory is the assumption that human needs (and consequently motivations) exist in a hierarchy, from the most basic to the most advanced. The further one progresses up this motivational pyramid, the more distinctly "human" one becomes. Higher motives will develop only when the more basic ones have been satisfied.

The most basic needs are for *physiological well-being* and *safety*. To fulfill these two needs, adequate rest, nourishment, and shelter must be found, and individuals must strive to achieve a sense of security. When these two needs have been satisfied, psychic energy can be directed to the need for *be-longingness and love.* Belongingness may be defined as the need to be part of a group and to experience sharing. *Esteem* is the fourth level of the hierarchic pyramid. By this, Maslow means that individuals must receive feedback from others (in the form of respect and assurance) in order to realize that they are worthwhile and competent. The fifth need, *self-actualization,* means fulfilling one's individual nature in all its aspects. To reach the fulfillment of one's potential, all previous needs have to be met adequately. An essential component of self-actualization is freedom from cultural and self-imposed restraints.

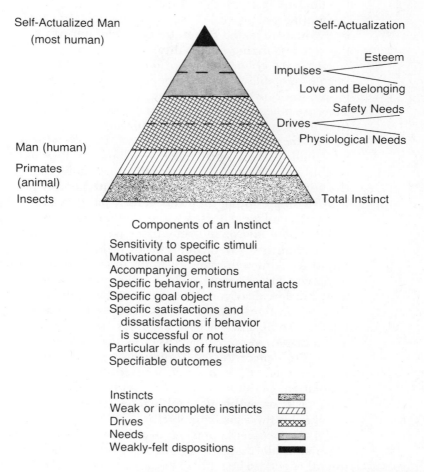

Figure 8–3. (*From:* Di Caprio, N.: Personality Theories: Guides to Living. Philadelphia: W. B. Saunders Co., Inc., 1974.)

They should be comfortable in their vocation and should feel accepted in their social contacts, whether these be with family members or associates at work. Furthermore, individuals should genuinely respect themselves.

It may very well be that self-actualization is not attained until the middle years of adulthood. In the years prior to middle age, energy is frequently dissipated in diverse directions, including sexual relationships, educational advancement, career alignment, marriage, and parenthood. The need to achieve financial stability during these young adult years consumes considerable psychic energy. By middle age, though, many people have managed to fulfill most of these needs and can spare the energy to strive toward ego maturity.

In order to study the self-actualizing personality, Maslow selected 48 individuals who appeared to be making full use of their talents and were at the height of humanness. His subjects were students and personal acquaintances, as well as historical figures. In the final analysis, he described 12 "probable", 10 "partial", and 26 "potential or possible" self-actualizers. His analysis of these individuals revealed fifteen traits that he felt were characteristic of the self-actualizing personality.

1. *More efficient perception of reality.* Many self-actualizing persons are able to perceive people and events realistically. That is to say, their own wishes, feelings, or desires do not distort reality. They are objective in their analysis of the environment, and are able to detect that which is dishonest or false.

2. *Acceptance of self and others.* People with self-actualizing personalities lack such negative characteristics as guilt, shame, doubt, and anxiety—characteristics that sometimes interfere with the perception of reality. Individuals with healthy personalities are capable of accepting themselves for what they are and know their strengths and weaknesses without being guilty or defensive.

3. *Spontaneity.* Self-actualizing people are relatively spontaneous in their overt behavior as well as in their inner thoughts and impulses. Although many conform to societal standards, there are those who are unconcerned about the roles society expects them to play. Maslow discovered that some self-actualizing people develop their own values and do not accept everything just because others do. While others may accept the status quo, self-actualizers perceive each person, event, or object as it really is and weigh it accordingly.

4. *Problem centering.* Unlike the ego-centered personality, who spends much time in such activities as introspection or self-evaluation, problem-centered individuals direct their energies toward tasks or problems. Problem-centered persons are also likely to consider their goals important.

5. *Detachment.* Maslow discovered that his subjects needed more solitude than the average person. The average person frequently needs to be with others and soon seeks the presence of other people when left alone (this reflects the need for belongingness and esteem derived from others). Self-actualizers, on the other hand, enjoy privacy and do not mind being alone.

6. *Autonomy.* As can be inferred from nearly all the other characteristics of the self-actualized personality, such people have a certain independence of spirit. Individuals are propelled by growth motivation more than by deficiency motivation and are self-contained personalities:

> They [self-actualizers] are dependent for their own development and continued growth on their own potentialities and latent resources. Just as the tree needs sunshine and water and food, so do most people need love, safety, and other basic need gratifications that can come only from without. But once these external satisfiers are obtained, once these inner deficiencies are satiated by outside satisfiers, the true problem of individual human development begins, e.g., self actualization.
>
> (Maslow, 1970, p. 162)

7. *Continued freshness of appreciation.* Self-actualizing people have the capacity to continually appreciate all of nature and life. There is a naivete, a pleasure, even an ecstasy about experiences that have become stale to others. For some of the subjects studied, these feelings are inspired by nature; for others the stimulus may be music; for still others, it may be children. But, regardless of the source, these occasional ecstatic feelings are very much a part of the self-actualizing personality.

8. *The mystic experience.* Self-actualizers are not religious in the sense of attendance at formal worship, but they do have periodic peaks of experience that Maslow describes as "limitless horizons opening up to the vision, the feeling of being simultaneously more powerful and also more helpless than one ever was before, the feeling of great ecstasy and wonder and awe, the loss of placing in time and space with, finally, the conviction that something extremely important and valuable had happened, so that the subject is to some extent transformed and strengthened even in his daily life by such exeriences" (Maslow, 1970, p. 164).

THE QUEST FOR SELF-ACTUALIZATION

The examples used to illustrate self-actualization are often lofty and very specialized talents. Assuredly, it must be intensely gratifying to have and use such abilities, but how many people are even potentially great artists or scientists?

It is not necessary to possess some dramatically creative talent or devote oneself to a scientific pursuit to be a self-actualizing person.

Furthermore, everyone has a variety of capabilities and probably no one can utilize all of them to their maximum. It is necessary to choose some and exclude others. There just is not enough time in life to be or do everything imaginable. People who experience real fulfillment in their occupations or sidelines *or* recreations *or* families may well be self-actualized. Using mechanical skills to tinker with the car or repair appliances, building furniture for the home, engaging in athletic events, or simply helping other people are all examples of self-actualization for those who derive personal satisfaction from doing them.

The point of all this is that one doesn't have to be Pablo Picasso, or Jonas Salk, or Golda Meir to be self-actualized. Ordinary people who enjoy their lives and achieve fulfillment in what they do are equally likely candidates.

(McMahon, 1977, p. 195)

9. *Gemeinschaftsgefühl.* This German word, first coined by Alfred Adler, is used by Maslow to describe the feelings toward mankind that self-actualizing persons experience. This emotion, which might be loosely described as "the love of an older brother", is an expression of affection, sympathy, and identification.

10. *Unique interpersonal relations.* Self-actualizers have fewer "friends" than others, but they have profound relationships with those friends they do have. Outside of these friendships, they tend to be kind to and patient with all whom they meet. An exception is the harsh way they sometimes speak to hypocritical, pretentious, or pompous people. However, for the most part, what little hostility they exhibit is based not on character but on situation.

11. *Democratic character structure.* Maslow found that without exception, the self-actualizing people he studied were democratic, being tolerant of others with suitable character regardless of their social class, race, education, religion, or political belief.

12. *Discrimination between means and ends.* Unlike the average person, who may make decisions on expedient grounds, self-actualizing people have a highly developed ethical sense. Even though they can not always verbalize their moral positions, their actions frequently take the "higher road". Self-actualizers distinguish means from ends and will not pursue even a highly desirable end by means that are not morally correct.

13. *Philosophical, unhostile sense of humor.* The humor of self-actualizers is not of the ordinary type. As Maslow (1970) describes it:

> They do not consider funny what the average man considers to be funny. Thus they do not laugh at hostile humor (making people laugh by hurting someone) or superiority humor (laughing at someone's else's inferiority) or authority-rebellion humor (the unfunny, Oedipal, or smutty joke). Characteristically what they consider humor is more closely allied to philosophy than to anything else. It may also be called the humor of the real because it consists in large part in poking fun at human beings in general when they are foolish, or forget their place in the universe, or try to be big when they are actually small. This can take the form of poking fun at themselves, but this is not done in any masochistic or clownlike way. Lincoln's humor can serve as a suitable example. Probably Lincoln never make a joke that hurt anybody else; it is also likely that many or even most of his jokes has something to say, had a function beyond just producing a laugh. They often seemed to be education in a more palatable form, akin to parables or fables.
>
> (pp. 169–170)

14. *Creativeness.* Without exception, every self-actualizing person that Maslow studied was creative in some way. This creativity is not to be equated with the genius of a Mozart or an Einstein, since the dynamics of that type of creativity are still not understood. Rather it is what Maslow calls "the naive and universal creativeness of unspoiled children." He believes that creativity in this sense is possibly a fundamental characteristic that we all are born with but lose as we become enculturated. It is linked to being spontaneous and less inhibited than others, and it expresses itself in everyday activities. Described quite simply, it is a freshness of thought, ideas, and actions.

Figure 8–4. According to Maslow, self-actualizing people are usually middle-aged or older.
(Courtesy of Nancy G. Turner.)

15. *Resistance to enculturation.* Self-actualizers accept their
culture in most ways, but they still, in a profound sense, resist
becoming enculturated. Many desire social change but are not rebel-
lious in the adolescent sense. Rather, they are generally independent of their culture and manage to exhibit tolerant acceptance of
the behavior expected of their society. This, however, must not
be construed as a lack of interest in making changes they believe
in. If they feel an important change is possible, their resolution and
courage put them at the forefront of the battle. Maslow believes that
the self-actualizers he describes are not revolutionaries, but they
very easily could be. He further states that they are not against
fighting for social change; rather, they are against ineffective
fighting.

The subjects studied by Maslow were for the most part highly
intelligent and possessed several or even many of the characteristics
so far presented. However, this does not mean they were perfect. In
fact, Maslow (1970) noted a number of human failings associated
with self-actualized people. Some can be boring, stubborn, or vain,
have thoughtless habits, be wasteful or falsely proud. They may have
emotions of guilt, anxiety, or strife, may experience inner conflicts.
They are also "occasionally capable of an extraordinary and unexpected ruthlessness." This ruthlessness may be seen when they feel
they have been deceived by a friend or if someone has been dishonest with them. They might, with a surgical coldness, cut the person
verbally or abruptly sever the relationship.

Summary

Research focusing on the nature of personality development during the middle years has been limited. Early efforts were either clinically based or loosely developed via casual observation, approaches that tended to distort the realities of this stage. Most experts agree that an effective theory must take into account the mechanisms of aging and the personality changes that correspond with them.

Three alternative perspectives can be adopted in studying the course of adult personality development. One approach emphasizes the *stability* of adult characteristics. A second perspective interprets personality as a *product* of the situation, and a third emphasizes the incorporation of personality *changes* so that the self-system becomes a new and different whole. Although each of these viewpoints can be substantiated to some degree, conclusive findings concerning which theory best explains the adult personality have yet to be reached.

The midlife crisis may be caused by a number of factors, including the realization of one's aging process, the growth of younger generations, career dissatisfaction, and an awareness of the imminence of death. Such a self-awareness may prompt middle-agers to question their youthful dreams and compare them with their actual accomplishments. Successful resolution of the midlife crisis usually relies on an ability to reassess and readjust goals and aspirations.

Several noteworthy theories concerning adult personality development have been proposed. Erikson places considerable emphasis on the psychosocial stage known as *generativity versus stagnation,* a period when harmonious living is characterized by a concern for future generations. Peck has added a further dimension to Erikson's work by suggesting that four kinds of psychological adjustments have to be made by the middle-ager. These adjustments are called *valuing wisdom versus valuing physical powers, socializing versus sexualizing in human relationships, cathectic flexibility versus mental rigidity.* Frenkel-Brunswik stresses the concept of a middle-age psychological crisis, a period when the adult may exhibit discontent, negation, sorrow, and dissatisfaction toward certain environmental events. Buhler and Kuhlen both place considerable emphasis on goal formulation and the manner in which these goals are assessed by the adult.

Adulthood represents a time when many individuals strive for self-actualization, a highly refined dimension of growth that is characterized by autonomy, individuation, and authenticity. According to Maslow, self-actualization is at the pinnacle of a "hierarchy" of basic needs. In ascending order, the others are physiological, safety, belongingness, and esteem needs. Characteristics of self-actualizing individuals appear to be (1) more efficient perception of reality, (2) acceptance of self and others, (3) spontaneity, (4) problem-centering, (5) detachment, (6) autonomy, (7) continued freshness of appreciation, (8) mystic experiences, or the oceanic feeling, (9) *Gemeinschaftsgefühl,* or social interest, (10) unique interpersonal relations, (11) democratic character structure, (12) discrimination between means and ends, (13) philosophical sense of humor, (14) creativeness, and (15) resistance to enculturation.

Suggested Readings

1. Brim, O. G.: "Theories of the male mid-life crisis." *The Counseling Psychologist,* 6:1, 1976, pp. 2–9.

   An informative and well-researched account of the middle-aged psychological phenomenon.

2. Gould, R.: "Adult life stages: Growth toward self-tolerance." *Psychology Today,* 8:9, 1975, pp. 74–78.

   On the basis of study of 524 men and women, Gould suggests that personality development continues through early and middle adulthood in a series of unique stages. His ideas are most thought-provoking.

3. Kimmel, D. C.: *Adulthood and Aging.* New York: John Wiley and Sons, 1974.

   Kimmel presents the reader with a thorough investigation of adult personality processes. Topics include continuity and change in personality, conceptualization of the adult personality, and psychopathology.

4. Neugarten, B. L. (Ed.): *Middle Age and Aging: A Reader in Social Psychology.* Chicago: The University of Chicago Press, 1968.

   Part 2 of this reader emphasizes the psychology of the life cycle and the personality dynamics of the middle-aged adult.

Nancy Turner

UNIT 9

THE FAMILY

Introduction

Most marriages begin in early adulthood, and children are added to the primary family unit shortly thereafter. By the time most parents reach middle age, their children are teenagers or young adults, and their families are probably stable with respect to number of children.

During this time, parents and teenagers face a number of important developmental tasks (Havighurst, 1972). First, parent and child must communicate effectively. Lack of communication is considered to be the cause of the "generation gap", a popular metaphor for the alienation that occurs when two generations are unable rationally to reach any mutual understanding of their differing viewpoints.

Psychologists disagree about the nature of the generation gap and about whether it is characteristic of the family with adolescents. For example, Feuer (1969) and Reich (1970), although proceeding from entirely different premises, both believe that a generation gap indeed exists. Others, such as Adelson (1970), point out that advocates of the "great gap" position largely overlook differences *among youths*—differences that are every bit as great as the alleged differences *between adolescents and adults*. Adelson professes that the generation gap is a myth. Although there is conflict and strife within our society, he says, the gap is ideological, not generational.

Parent-adolescent communication must, of course, work two ways. Teenagers as well as parents are responsible for developing meaningful interaction skills, and this can be the most difficult of all the developmental challenges that face both parties. Success in parent-child communication may well depend on the degree of successful parenting exhibited when the children were younger. (Indeed, experience seems to support the conjecture that success at parenting depends on how successful one's own parents were.)

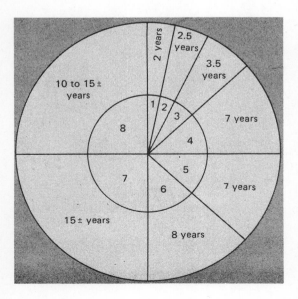

Figure 9-1. The family life cycle. (*From:* Duvall, E. G.: *Family Development.* 4th ed. Philadelphia: J. B. Lippincott, 1971.)
1. Married Couples (without children).
2. Childbearing Families (Oldest child, birth—30 months).
3. Families with Preschool Children (Oldest child 30 months—6 years).
4. Families with Schoolchildren (Oldest child 6–13 years).
5. Families with Teenagers (Oldest child 13–20 years).
6. Families as Launching Centers (First child gone to last child leaving home).
7. Middle-aged Parents (Empty nest to retirement).
8. Aging Family Members (Retirement to death of both spouses).

Another task of middle-aged parents is supporting adolescents in their search for identity (Erikson, 1963). At this point in their lives, teenagers are struggling to find their places within their own generation, and this may push them away from the family. Thus, "parents are faced with the responsibility of giving their teenagers guidance and support, and often develop the feeling common to many parents that their sons and daughters resent their help" (Perry and Perry, 1977). Some parents, especially those in the middle class, continue trying to mold their offspring to standards of behavior that facilitate functioning smoothly in society. Many parents stress morality and sexual restraint (Landis, 1975).

Handing down suitable values is a difficult task. In the past, children adopted many of their parents' values, but now teenagers are quick to conclude that times have changed since their parents were young. Indeed, the younger generation today encounters problems that the older generation may not have faced. Liberal sexual attitudes and the widespread use of alcohol and drugs are but two examples. Margaret Mead (1970) goes so far as to claim that today's youth are a "new breed," totally unlike any previous younger generation. In many respects they have created a "prefigurative culture" wherein youths are the "natives" and adults are "foreigners". Furthermore, it is the role of the "foreigners" to learn from the young rather than to teach them.

Parents also try to nurture independence, autonomy, and responsibility on the part of their children (Havighurst, 1972). Some parents, employing pressure to attain these desired attributes, may turn this into a most stressful period. They may prod the adolescent excessively to make a vocational commitment or to select a college or training school. The result may be friction, resentment, and in some cases, hostility.

Thus, in the middle years of adulthood, as children become teenagers, the family structure changes. While adolescents seek to develop their own individuality, parents in turn strive to reassert their position of control and authority. Wise and understanding parents recognize that the successful outcome of this period depends on their ability to anticipate and share their children's progress from early dependence into later independence and maturity (Kelley, 1974).

POST-PARENTAL LIFE—THE EMPTY-NEST STAGE

When all the children in a family have grown and departed, the middle-aged couple are suddenly left alone, sometimes living in a house that is now too big for two (and one that is filled with memories of their departed children). Middle-aged parents frequently experience feelings of restlessness, disillusionment, or dissatisfaction. Time once devoted to parenting must be reallocated to other meaningful activities.

This phase of family life, which is called the "empty-nest" stage, may loom as a major crisis for some middle-aged couples. This is

THE MIDDLE YEARS AND FAMILY HARMONY

The conditions that foster a favorable home environment during the middle years of the family cycle are, in most respects, the same conditions that were favorable for the family during earlier stages. Such conditions include the following:

1. *Democracy*. In democratic homes, adolescents learn self-respect primarily because they themselves are respected. Furthermore, there is seldom a condition of subservience to the will of someone else and there are no feelings that any individual counts for little in the home. It is through this kind of home atmosphere that parents are able to make adolescents develop self-confidence and social responsibility.

2. *Lack of serious emotional conflicts*. While differences of opinion between parents and adolescents are frequent in virtually any household, few lasting unpleasant emotions arising over conflicting viewpoints develop in favorable home environments. A continual atmosphere of quarreling, bitterness, and vindictiveness not only breeds unpleasant emotional states but also teaches the adolescent unfavorable ways of interacting with others.

3. *Consistent, fair, and objective discipline*. The reaction to error or mistakes should not be, "You have disgraced the family", "I don't like you", or "I am disgusted with your behavior". Rather, the parents might say, "You've made a mistake. We don't believe in what you've done. What should we do about it?" In this way, the adolescent will learn that there are standards of right and wrong behavior and will realize that discipline is not a matter of the whim of the parents, but instead is a means of teaching these standards.

4. *Affection and comradeship*. Adolescents who feel that they are loved and respected as individuals will feel free to become themselves. In some homes, affection ebbs and flows (it may flourish only when the one who is loved is particularly pleasing, or it may be given or withdrawn as a method of reward and punishment). In good homes affection is consistent. By providing comradeship, parents come to know their growing sons or daughters better, and the whole family can take joy in doing things together.

5. *Effective personal adjustment on the part of the parents*. When parents are maladjusted, their negative influence will be felt by adolescents as well as younger children. Many times such grown-ups will be gloomy and depressed, quick to take offense, jealous of others, overdependent, or disagreeable or unreasonable in any number of other ways.

6. *Development of the parents*. Effective and understanding parents develop *with* their children. This being the case, the parent's concept of what is best and proper for the adolescent will reflect objective standards instead of arbitrary custom. This will prevent unnecessary and surreptitious teenage behavior that may lead to guilt feelings. Certainly one cannot expect comradeship, understanding, and confidence to develop between teenagers and parents if the parents are living according to ideas that cannot be understood and accepted by teenagers.

7. *Gradual release of responsibilities*. As adolescents become able to assume responsibilities, they are gradually released by the parents. For example, they are given home duties that they are capable of performing, and they are allowed to be on their own whenever it is possible. In effective home environments, adolescents are also allowed to make more and more decisions for themselves and are consulted regularly on family matters.

(Adapted from Malm and Jamison, 1952)

more often true of the mother, who has focused all or too much of her time and attention on the children. Those mothers who totally wrap themselves up in their children discover that when their families reach the empty-nest stage, they have little left to live for (Bart, 1970). Fathers may be better able to cope with the departure of their children because they have spent much time away from the home (and their children) while working. However, many fathers report stress during the empty-nest stage (Perry and Perry, 1977).

If parents cannot accept the fact that their children are now

Figure 9–2. The empty-nest stage is an important developmental period for the middle-aged couple. (Courtesy of Nancy G. Turner.)

THE MOTHER'S ADJUSTMENT TO THE EMPTY-NEST STAGE

Some women may experience considerable adjustment difficulties during the empty-nest stage of the family cycle. This generally occurs in the late thirties or early forties, when a mother has acquired considerable free time. After what seems like a lifetime of caring for others, she may long to feel that she is still needed and serves some practical function. Her identity crisis becomes a time of self-evaluation and assessment ("Who am I?," "What is the meaning of my life?"). Unfortunately:

Too many married women arrive at middle age without having looked and planned far enough ahead, and experience difficulties in making the transition from motherhood to other socially useful occupations. Ministers, doctors, lawyers—those whose professions give them insights into personal lives—know that there are an appalling number of unhappy over-forty women. They also know that many of these could be helped if they could find a sufficient purpose for their lives. These women are simply at a loss to know what to do with themselves when they reach the point where their children are no longer dependent on them. Usually, these are the ones who have been the most devoted mothers. Not a few of them feel a quiet desperation in their desire to be of greater usefulness, but they are at a loss to know why. They have not foreseen what their later years would be like and have not planned for them. Too often their only relief is in some form of occasional social diversion which provides them an escape. Integration of the several parts of their lives has not been achieved.

(Harbeson, 1971, p. 139)

According to Sheehy (1976), it is not through more caretaking that the married woman with grown children expects to replenish the second half of her life. Rather, it is by cultivating talents left half-developed or following through on ambitions once curtailed because of family responsibilities. (This does not imply that the woman will stop caring about others; on the contrary the empty nest frees her so that she can extend her concern for future generations in a variety of civic and social forms.) Many will enter or reenter the work force to help satisfy their need to be useful and productive. In support of this, the 1970 population census reveals that 51 per cent of all women aged 30 to 54 were employed.

grown and ready to lead independent lives, they may try to keep them tucked under their wings. Jersild (1963) provides an excellent account of parents who find it difficult to "let go" of a child:

> Ever since the youngster was an infant they have had him in their care. The habit of watching over him is strong and the desire to continue so is also likely to be strong. It is especially hard for parents to let go an offspring in adolescence if they have not gotten into the habit of gradually allowing the youngster to have more and more freedom and self determination. . . . A mother who has given her all for her children may become anxious at the prospect of being without a mission in life. A parent who has lived his life through his children, so to speak, seeking through them to achieve, by proxy, pleasures he has never enjoyed or ambitions he never realized, may be very troubled when his offspring want to go their own way. A parent who has leaned on his children for emotional support, using them as though they were as much *his* parents as he theirs, may feel insecure and abandoned at the thought that his offspring are now moving on into other relationships. Again, a parent who has not been realistic in facing the fact that he is getting older may feel threatened by the reminders of age that come when his own children are becoming adults and want to enjoy the privileges of adults. (pp. 236–237)

It appears that those parents who best weather the empty-nest stage are those who do not try to foster dependency on the part of their children but rather encourage autonomy and independence. Parents who believe that their children are mature enough for the work world, college, or marriage are more apt to let go than parents who still perceive their young adults as immature. Ideally, parents recognize their children as separate individuals in their own right and strive to show genuine care and concern, but not to the extent of overinvolvement (Goethals and Klos, 1970). In some cases, the fewer long-range goals parents (especially the mother) have developed for their children, the sooner the parental phase of life will be successfully completed (Spence and Lonner, 1971).

Some parents may be fortunate in being able to adjust to the empty-nest stage on a gradual basis. For instance, college, military service, or extended trips away from home may separate young adults from their parents for relatively short periods of time. This allows the parents to experience a household with one less child—or no children—without the anguish of believing they will never see the child again. Thus, even though the "nest" is "semi-empty", the experience is at least softened by the expectation that the child will return. Gradual adjustment to the empty-nest stage also gives parents time to evaluate themselves and their goals.

CHANGES IN MARRIAGE DURING THE MIDDLE YEARS

The departure of the children may bring the realization that the husband and wife have drifted apart over the years. Now that they are left alone, they may be surprised at the changes that they see in one another—changes that might have gone undetected for some time. Thus, for some couples, the problems of the post-parental years and the empty-nest stage are intensified by growing reservations about the marriage itself. In many cases, this happens to those couples who stayed together "for the sake of the children" and masked growing differences with a veneer of cordiality (Perry and Perry, 1977).

In a study done by Blood and Wolfe (1960), over 900 couples were questioned regarding their marital status. The families studied represented virtually the full range of socioeconomic and occupational statuses. It was discovered that while many middle-aged husbands and wives found pride and satisfaction in their children, their jobs, and various other facets of life, few found satisfaction in their spouses. More specifically, young wives displayed a high rate of spouse satisfaction; 52 per cent were satisfied, whereas none were extremely dissatisfied. Among wives who had been married for more than 20 years, however, satisfaction declined substantially; only 6 per cent were fully satisfied with their marriages and 21 per cent were conspicuously dissatisfied. Much of this dissatisfaction was attributed to a decrease in the time spent doing things for one another. In a similar study, marital problems reported by middle-aged couples who sought counseling were compared with those described by newly married couples (Brayshaw, 1962). Sexual difficulties (reported by 40 per cent) were the chief cause of disturbance for the newly married, followed by living conditions (24 per cent) and parental influence (22 per cent). Ill health ranked fourth (14 per cent). On the other hand, ill health ranked first (29 per cent) for those married 18 years or more, followed by infidelity (26 per cent), incompatibility (23 per cent), and sex (15 per cent). Financial difficulties ranked last in both groups.

If couples find themselves dissatisfied with their marriage and discover they no longer really "know" each other, it is difficult for them to offer mutual support and understanding during the critical middle years. Some couples, assuming a pessimistic attitude, believe their functions and responsibilities as parents are finished and thus view their lives as practically over. Some feel there is little left to do with a life that has become devoid of meaning.

For other couples, however, the post-parental stage is the happiest and most rewarding period of their life (Deutscher, 1964). One husband reports:

> We get along better—we always got along very well, but we get along so much better since we're by ourselves. I know I appreciated and enjoyed her company more in the last year or two than I did before. The main change is like with myself; she's not as nervous since the children left home.
>
> (Deutscher, 1964, p. 56)

Those couples who manage the middle years of adulthood gracefully are usually those who have communicated with each other over the years and whose relationship is characterized by mutual love, understanding, and support. For these couples the post-parental stage will bring more companionship in daily routines and a closer affectional relationship (Kelley, 1974). Moreover, the relief from the economic burden of supporting children enables middle-aged parents to indulge in more luxuries, such as travel, recreational activities, or hobbies. Because of life-style changes such as these, there are some who refer to the post-parenthood years as a second honeymoon.

DIVORCE AND SEPARATION

The dissolution of a family by separation or divorce can be a major crisis for all its members. Although death is the leading cause of marriage dissolution in the United States (Davis, 1973), divorce rates are rising with alarming frequency. In 1975, the divorce rate was higher than at any period in our history except during WW II.

Perhaps a few statistics will indicate the severity of the problem. In 1960, there were 2.2 divorces per 1000 population in the United States. By 1975, the rate had risen to nearly 5 per 1000. Over a million divorces were recorded in that year, compared to 393,000 in 1960. Moreover, in 1960, 4.4 marriages were performed for every divorce recorded, whereas in 1975, the ratio of marriages performed to divorces granted dropped to less than 2 to 1.

It is estimated that if divorce rates continue to rise at the current rate, 1 of every 3 marriages will end in divorce. The rate of divorce is not, however, the same for all segments of the population. The poor and the poorly educated, members of the working class, and those who marry young have higher divorce rates than better-educated middle-class professionals (Glick, 1975).

Causes of Divorce

The causes of divorce are as many and varied as there are divorces. Unfortunately, we cannot learn the causes directly from court records, since persons in pursuit of divorce are more

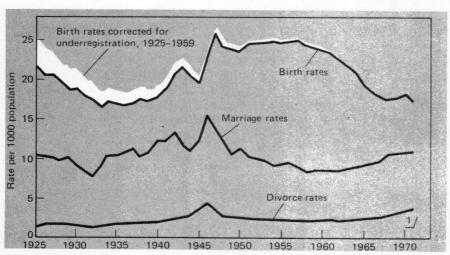

Figure 9–3. Vital statistics rates, 1925 to 1971. (*From:* U.S. Bureau of the Census: *Statistical Abstract of the United States,* 1972. 93rd ed. Washington, D.C., U.S. Government Printing Office, 1972.)

often than not forced into stating reasons that fit the laws of a particular state rather than the facts. However, despite the nearly fifty available legal grounds for divorce, the majority of American divorce suits are based on cruelty, which can be phrased in a number of ways, including "intolerable cruelty", "cruel and barbarous treatment", or "mental cruelty". In actual practice, the term includes bickering, quarreling, or even name-calling. Some statutes even define "incompatibility" as an aspect of cruelty (Kephart, 1977).

One of the more extensive investigations of the complaints leading to divorce was undertaken by Levinger (1966). In his study, Levinger used a sample of 600 couples applying for divorce in Cleveland, Ohio. The reasons for divorce cited appear in Figure 9–4.

As we might expect, the most common complaint for both husband and wife was mental cruelty, followed closely by neglect of the home and children. Other noteworthy complaints of the wives were financial problems and physical abuse, while the husbands cited infidelity and sexual incompatibility.

GROUNDS FOR DIVORCE IN THE UNITED STATES

Each of the United States has its own divorce code. The following is a list of existing grounds for divorce in our states and territories. Many of them are never used.

Abandonment
Adjudication of mental incompetence
Adultery
Any cause rendering the marriage void
Application following decree of divorce from bed and board
Attempt to corrupt son or prostitute daughter
Attempt to murder spouse
Bigamy
Consanguinity
Conviction of a felony
Crime against nature
Cruel and inhuman treatment
Desertion
Deviant sexual conduct
Drug addiction
Force, menace, or duress in obtaining the marriage
Fraud
Gross misbehavior and wickedness
Habitual drunkenness
Idiocy
Impotence
Imprisonment
Incapability of procreation at time of marriage
Incest
Incompatibility
Incurable physical incapacity
Indignities
Infection of spouse with communicable venereal disease
Insanity
Intolerable severity
Irremediable breakdown of marriage
Membership in sect believing cohabitation is unlawful
Mental cruelty
Mental incapacity at time of marriage
No reasonable likelihood of marriage being preserved
Nonsupport
Physical incompetence at time of marriage
Proposal to prostitute wife
Refusal by wife to move with husband to this state
Seven years' absence, absent party not being heard from
Sodomy or buggery
Treatment seriously injuring health or endangering reason
Unnatural sexual intercourse with person of the same sex or of a different sex or a beast
Vagrancy by husband
Voluntary separation
Wife being pregnant by another man at time of marriage without knowledge of husband
Wife being prostitute prior to marriage without knowledge of husband
Willful neglect

Kephart, 1977, pp. 449–450

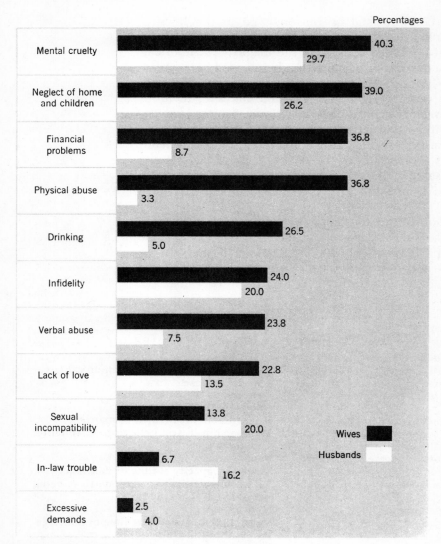

Figure 9–4. Complaints of 600 divorcing couples about their marriages. (*Adapted from:* Levinger, G.: "Sources of marital dissatisfaction among applicants for divorce." *Am. J. Orthopsychiatry, 36*:803–807, 1966.)

Which party fares better during divorce proceedings is a difficult question to answer, since so many variables come into play. Traditionally, the law pits the couple against one another in a contest to determine which party shall be judged guilty and which shall be held blameless (even though it is widely known that the majority of embattled husbands and wives have *both* committed acts that are grounds for divorce). Fairly typically, couples arrive at some kind of tentative agreement regarding the terms of the divorce before the suit reaches the court. For example, one will stay in the house or the apartment, and the other will move. Furniture and automobiles will be distributed in a certain way (Leslie and Leslie, 1977). Some courts are abandoning the "adversary concept" of divorce proceedings (in

THOUSANDS FINDING MARITAL RELIEF IN "NO FAULT" DIVORCE

Los Angeles (UPI)——Mr. Leon, a gray haired man in his forties who works for an electronics firm, was on the witness stand for less than 20 seconds.

"Have irreconcilable differences developed in your marriage?" his lawyer asked.

"Yes."

"Have those differences brought a breakdown of your marriage?"

"Yes."

"Is there any chance of a reconciliation?"

"No."

"Do you wish to avail yourself of marriage counseling services?"

"No."

That was it. The judge ruled that the marriage was dissolved and a union that had lasted 19 years was broken. Mrs. Leon didn't say a word. The couple had stipulated the division of their property and the husband agreed to pay $30 a month alimony plus support of the two children whose custody was awarded to Mrs. Leon.

It sounds cold and callous but the chief judge of the domestic relations courts in Los Angeles hails California's "no fault" dissolution of marriage system as one of the most sensible approaches to the ceaseless battle between the sexes that could have been legislated.

Superior Court Justice William Hogoboom said that fears that such a relatively easy means of dissolving marriages, with no reason except incompatibility, might lead to an avalanche of broken homes have proved unfounded.

Applications for dissolution of marriage went up 8.8 per cent in Los Angeles County in the year of 1970 when the new law went into effect, compared with suits for divorce in 1969, he said. But this year the rate has dropped to only 4–5 per cent above 1969.

Hogoboom said he feels the most important thing is that husbands and wives who have lived together in bitterness and even hatred rather than go through the trauma of public accusations can start new lives.

"They don't have to prove that the other has done something terrible," he said.

"And they can go their ways before rigid divorce laws force the man to start sleeping with another woman or his wife to hit him on the head with a frying pan."

California was the first state to put such "no fault" divorce into effect. Iowa followed suit with a similar law and Texas has such legislation approved. New York, which until only a few years ago had adultery as the only grounds for divorce, is studying the same approach.

Hogoboom said, in fact, that the California experiment is unique in the whole Western world culture.

The question of fault in a broken marriage enters into the California system only in the case where there is a dispute over custody of the children. Usually the mother is granted custody but there are exceptions when testimony is produced that she is unfit.

Community property is split right down the middle regardless of why the marriage broke up. Alimony and support are based on the two criteria of need and ability to pay. Battles between wealthy couples still lead to long, drawn out court fights.

It is now so simple to get a dissolution of marriage in California that one mate can go to the county clerk's office and get three forms, fill them out and institute suit without ever consulting a lawyer.

There is a standard questionnaire which asks for vital statistics and then leaves four lines open to answer the question: "What do you feel is wrong with this marriage?"

Hogoboom said one of the more encouraging trends under the new law is that the number of couples seeking reconciliation rose by 12.5 per cent during 1970. He said 33 per cent did reconcile and followups showed that a year later 75 per cent were still maintaining a home.

Hogoboom also said the new law has enabled the domestic courts to cut down on the backlog of cases since dissolutions now are being handled twice as fast as previously.

The judge acknowledges that the relatively more easy endings to marriage may lead some young couples to break up before really putting themselves to the test of adjusting to the marital status, but he does not believe that is often the case and that, at any rate, it is far overbalanced by the cases of couples who should have ended unhappy liaisons years ago.

It still takes six months for the dissolution to become final. Under the previous divorce law, that term was one year.

Jack V. Fox, Ontario-Upland *Daily Report*. Reprinted by permission of United Press International.

1969 the concept of "no fault" divorce was implemented in some states—see box), but the woman generally receives custody of the children. Consequently, many men suffer at least a partial loss of their children's company in addition to having to meet alimony or child support payments.

Sequel to Divorce

Like any crisis, divorce forces individuals to reevaluate their identities, plans, and future goals. Because of the intense emotions often involved in divorce, however, it is a time when level-headed thinking may be difficult to achieve. For many, divorce has numerous side effects: it may bring a sense of failure, pain, loneliness, and some degree of social awkwardness (Leslie and Leslie, 1977).

The divorced man and woman must adopt new life-styles. Just as one learns to be married, one must learn to be unmarried (Kimmel, 1974). The man is usually faced with the necessity of paying rent on an additional house or apartment, and he must undertake household chores such as laundering and cooking. He may attempt to perform these housekeeping chores himself, but, as Nye and Berardo (1973) state, men are usually not socialized to household tasks, and most lack both the skills and the attitudes necessary to perform these duties adequately. Frequently, a divorced man will hire someone to do the cleaning and laundering and will solve the problem of cooking by eating in restaurants—luxuries that may bring additional financial pressures.

Women, especially those who are housewives as opposed to working women, experience more of an adjustment problem than their ex-husbands. If a woman has children to care for, she may encounter difficulties in dating and trying to remarry. Some other adjustment problems are described by Perry and Perry (1977):

> Often the divorced woman must get a job, find housing, and rebuild her social life. The married friends with whom she and her husband had associated visually fade out of her life because she has become a "fifth wheel." Then, too, her legal problems do not end with the divorce decree. She frequently finds it difficult to establish credit. Banks, stores, and others treat her income differently from that of a man who is in similar economic straits.
>
> (p. 181)

Divorce usually causes adjustment problems for the children. In some cases, if the home was an openly unhappy one, no one has to tell the children that something is wrong with their parents' relationship; they may know it all too well and yearn for the relief that a divorce can bring. In other instances, children will be vaguely uneasy about their parents without really knowing why. The news that their parents are separating may precipitate an emotional crisis for them. In still other situations, children know virtually nothing about their parents' relationships until the fateful day comes when one parent, or perhaps both, sits them down to describe the marital situation (Leslie and Leslie, 1969). A substantial number of divorces involve children; the number of children affected by divorce each year has been rising.

There are some who believe that a divorce should never occur while dependent children are still at home. Advocates of this position must realize that the stresses of marital discord may force children into roles that can exact a tremendous emotional toll. Others feel that children are better off if unhappy parents do get a divorce, thus terminating the marital war and removing the children from the crossfire (Clayton, 1975). Either course, according to Epstein (1974), poses problems to the children. They are subjected to continual quarreling and tension if the parents stay together, or they are brought up by a single parent (usually a mother), who is often in an emotionally shaky state and plagued by financial worries, not to mention the fact that she may be holding down a job that takes her away from the home for the better part of the day.

According to Clayton (1975) children in a home where a divorce occurs are faced with at least four serious problems. First, children have a difficult time in understanding why two people they love do not love each other any more. Most youngsters, including adolescents, cannot fully understand the complexities of the strains that lead to a breakdown in the marital bond. More specifically, they usually cannot comprehend the physical-sexual aspects of the tie that no longer binds their parents together.

Second, children usually cannot understand why one parent has to leave the home, since home to them is "where we all live". Divorce requires that children formulate a new—and sometimes alien—definition of home and family.

A third problem for children is that they frequently have to bear the brunt of displaced aggression from their parents in terms of sarcastic remarks and unreasonable demands. Children may also be persuaded to "take sides" when quarreling begins, something that may cause them to feel guilty, alone, or frustrated. (This problem may also occur if parents stay together.)

Fourth, many youngsters feel that they are somehow stigmatized. They must explain to their friends why their parents are

PARENTS WITHOUT PARTNERS

An organization called Parents Without Partners has assisted divorced and widowed parents to develop wider social contacts and to receive support from others in similar situations. Although the motivation to join undoubtedly stems from the opportunity to meet prospective marriage partners and enjoy adult social relationships, overtly the organization strives to provide substitute relationships for the children in broken homes. For instance, a divorced male member may serve as a "foster father" to the children of a divorcée, spending considerable time with them and assuming some of the social roles of the natural father.

Divorce undoubtedly places a greater strain on the woman, especially in regard to seeking a new mate. The man can date either younger or older women without incurring social disapproval, and the population from which he can draw acceptable partners is larger than the population available to the woman, who characteristically looks for someone roughly her age or older. Also, since women are more frequently given custody of young children, their parental responsibilities can interfere with meeting prospective husbands. Thus, programs such as Parents Without Partners have greater appeal for women (Freeman and Jones, 1970).

separating when they themselves do not fully understand the meaning of divorce or its future consequences.

All in all, Clayton (1975) states, divorce is not a healthy experience for children, emotionally or physically. In some cases, children whose parents are divorced develop signs of physical and emotional disorders. Many are more aggressive than children from stable home environments (Loeb and Price, 1966). In many respects, divorce may create a state of disorientation for children that may leave many unpleasant memories.

Remarriage

The stereotype of divorced individuals living in a prolonged state of unhappiness and loneliness is generally false. While it is true that there are some divorced people who are maladjusted and unhappy, so are some never-married and married people. Moreover, most divorced people remarry, and for the most part, this is done rather quickly (Leslie and Leslie, 1977). Unlike marriages for previously unwed people, remarriages include interesting combinations, such as:

Divorced man/single woman
Divorced man/divorced woman
Divorced man/widowed woman
Single man/divorced woman
Single man/widowed woman
Widowed man/single woman
Widowed man/divorced woman
Widowed man/widowed woman

Approximately four out of five divorced people eventually remarry (Glick, 1975). It is estimated that about 25 per cent of all current marriages are remarriages, and it is likely that this figure will

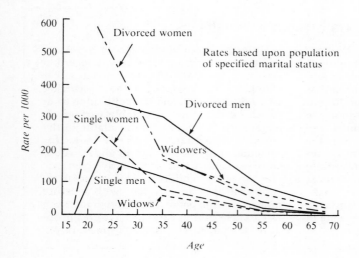

Figure 9–5. Remarriage rates. (*From:* Carter, H., and Glick, P. C.: *Marriage and Divorce: A Social and Economic Study.* Copyright © 1970 by the President and Fellows of Harvard College. Reprinted by permission of the publisher, Harvard University Press.

increase (Kephart, 1977). Of the total number of divorced people who remarry, a quarter do so within one year of their divorce, half within three years, and three quarters within nine years (Glick and Norton, 1971). Three quarters of divorced men will eventually remarry, while two thirds of the women will do the same. It should be noted that some people divorce and remarry several times. This distorts the statistics, making it appear that more people are getting divorced and remarried than is actually the case. (For instance, if 25 out of 100 marriages end in divorce, and 15 of the couples then divorce after remarrying, statistics might show 40 divorces for the 115 marriages—certainly a misleading figure.)

A divorced person encounters some difficulties in attempting to marry for a second time. Women have a particularly difficult time in meeting eligible men, since much of their time is devoted to the upbringing of their children and possibly holding down a job. Many men tend to marry a woman who is not in the process of raising children. A divorced woman without children or one whose children are already grown has a better chance of remarriage than one who has dependent children still at home.

Statistically, divorced persons seem to be greater marital risks than single persons entering their first marriage. Statistics also indicate that the remarriages of divorced women are more apt to end in divorce than the remarriages of divorced men (Landis, 1975). (This trend does not hold true for widows who remarry.) Remarriage may also create problems in regard to the stepchildren involved, although some children adjust quite well (Duberman, 1973). Nevertheless, many divorced persons are successful in their second marriages, and some report high levels of happiness (Schlesinger, 1970). Some studies indicate that 60 per cent of second marriages last until death, and some recent data derived from more sophisticated evaluations of remarriage suggest that when "repeaters" are eliminated from consideration, the prognosis for second marriages is much better than previously thought. Moreover, the marriages of divorced people who are middle-aged (35 or older) when they remarry actually have a somewhat better chance of success than first marriages do (Hunt and Hunt, 1977). Evidently, divorce for these people had a maturing effect, and they were better able to make marriage work the second time around.

It is obviously unfair to suggest that remarriage is necessarily characterized by disharmony or failure. As Kelley (1974) suggests, more data are needed in order to evaluate remarriage fairly.

Summary

The middle-aged couple is faced with several noteworthy family tasks. During these years, it is important to be able to communicate effectively with adolescent sons and daughters, to support them in their search for identity, and to assist them in becoming responsible, independent, and well-adjusted adults. Characteristics of favorable home environments for adolescents are democratic policies, lack of serious emotional conflicts, consistent and objective discipline, affection and comradeship, effective personal adjustment on the parents' part, parental development, and the gradual release of responsibilities.

Frequently, as children grow older and leave the home, parents, and especially the mother, experience the "empty-nest" stage. This difficult time is marked by restlessness, dissatisfaction, and disillusionment, especially if the mother has had little else to do with her life besides being a parent. After the children leave the home, both parents are in a position to "rediscover" one another and may become aware of changes that had gone unnoticed for some time. Some may come to the realization that they really haven't been communicating effectively over the years that their children were at home and must consequently make adjustments. If they have drifted too far apart, there may be marriage difficulties.

Those who gracefully weather the empty-nest period are usually the parents who have encouraged their children to be independent. Furthermore, these parents are more apt to recognize their children as separate individuals in their own right. If a parent believes the teenager or young adult is mature enough to meet the tasks of work, college, or marriage, the crisis is reduced considerably.

For middle-aged parents who don't experience this crisis and have a solid marriage, the later middle years may become one of the happiest periods in their life. The financial burden of raising children is over, and now that they have more free time available, they are able to pursue travel, hobbies, recreational and leisure-time activities, and other luxuries.

Divorce is a crisis that affects the whole family. Of all the grounds cited for divorce, cruelty is the most prevalent. As with any crisis, adjustments have to be made. The woman is frequently faced with having to get a job and parenting at the same time, since she typically receives custody of the children. The man, among other adjustments, encounters financial difficulties and must undertake a variety of domestic chores. Children, in particular, face numerous problems when divorce occurs, especially confusion over why their parents have separated. Divorce may create a state of disorientation for children that may leave many unpleasant memories.

Most divorced people will remarry, although the figure is higher for men than for women. Statistically speaking, divorced persons seem to be a greater marital risk than singles entering their first marriage. However, there are many who report high levels of satisfaction during their second marriages, and remarriages in middle age are likely to be successful. Most experts agree that more data are needed to evaluate remarriages objectively.

Suggested Readings

1. Fullerton, G. P.: *Survival in Marriage.* New York: Holt, Rinehart, and Winston, 1972.

   A well-written account of various aspects of marriage and the family. The topics of divorce and remarriage are especially well handled.

2. Otto, H. A., (Ed.): *The Family in Search of a Future*. New York: Appleton-Century-Crofts, 1970.

   This book contains an excellent collection of readings designed to focus on alternatives to monogamy and the prevailing family structure. Contributors, among others, are Sidney Jourard, Albert Ellis, and Margaret Mead.

3. Rheinstein, M.: *Marriage Stability, Divorce and the Law*. Chicago: University of Chicago Press, 1972.

   An excellent account of contemporary trends in marriage and a thorough description of divorce are the strengths of this book.

4. Roleder, G., (Ed.): *Marriage Means Encounter*. Dubuque, Iowa: Wm. C. Brown Company, 1973.

   Section 3 of this reader focuses on marital roles while Section 6 deals with marital failure.

Section B   The Middle Years of Adulthood

Raimondo Borea

Horst Schäfer
Photo Trends

UNIT 10

VOCATIONAL DEVELOPMENT

Introduction

Historically, Western society has expected individuals to adhere to the "work ethic", a value system and pattern of behavior that stresses hard work and long-range planning (Albee, 1977). As a society we have expected the harder-working members to advance up the socioeconomic work ladder and have believed that hard work is its own reward, its own fulfillment. The work ethic was probably crucial to the emergence of an industrial society.

The occupational commitments of many middle-agers are characterized by stability and maintenance, but contemporary thought, buttressed by research indicates that growing numbers of middle-aged workers are realigning their careers. Those workers with relatively stable career interests perceive the middle years of adulthood as a plateau, largely because of the prevailing belief that by this time most people have attained their career ambitions or have settled for less success than was originally anticipated. Yet, this assumption about career stability is most applicable to those at the top of the social, educational, and occupational scales, particularly those who have attended institutions of higher education or who are employed in professional or managerial positions. The assumption of midlife career stability also does not take fully into account the dynamics of rapid change in the values and economic structure of our society (Hiestand, 1971).

More recent studies focusing on midlife career development indicate that many middle-aged workers are disenchanted and disillusioned with their jobs. Some are switching careers in an effort to find happiness and satisfaction. Thus, the middle years portend a period of career renegotiation, a time for reasserting control over the direction of one's life and consciously realigning one's future (Mills, 1970). Proponents of this view regard the belief that one's career course is fixed after an initial job has been taken as a myth (Ginzberg, 1972; Heddescheimer, 1976). Some prefer to consider the middle years a critical period in career development (Bender, 1971; Brown, 1972; Tiedeman, 1976). In addition to feeling frustrated, disappointed, and confused by failure to attain earlier career goals, the worker with a monotonous, unfulfilling job may become quite depressed (Brim, 1976). This "boxed-in" feeling appears to be just as common—and as devastating—for women as for men (Schlossberg, 1977).

MIDLIFE CAREER DEVELOPMENT: A TIME OF TRUTH?

Kimmel (1974) relates this critical midlife phase of the occupational cycle to the adjustments young adults have to make when they first enter a vocation. In particular, it involves adjusting one's idealistic hopes to realistic possibilities in light of how much time is left for pursuing an occupation. (For example, the university professor who hopes to be famous in his field and to contribute many scholarly writings decides at age 50 that he had better begin if he is to attain this goal.)

THE SEARCH FOR CAREER RELEVANCE IN MIDLIFE: CASE STUDIES

Some time ago a minister in his midforties blurted out:

> For twenty years I have been thinking about quitting. I mean really thinking about it, day in and day out. You are the first person I have even told about it. I am guilty of being unfaithful to my call, dishonest with my parishioners and my colleagues and myself. I don't believe in most of what I preach anymore and I don't believe in *me* anymore.

Pressed about his feelings, this man revealed that while he yet held a belief in Christ and felt a commitment to the church, he had moved away from his earlier conservative theological precepts. Nevertheless he continued to preach them because the congregation "thought I was conservative when they called me. They could not deal with some of my new thoughts if I shared them."

This man was depressed, cynical, filled with anger, and showed signs of decreasing effectiveness in his work. He received very little in the way of satisfaction or a sense of fulfillment from his endeavors, although he was a hard worker and outwardly "successful."

A combination of psychotherapy, theological study and counseling has enabled him to remain in the ministry, in fact, in the same parish, but he is today preaching more of what he really believes and he reports that he feels "like a free man in Christ for the first time in my life!" . . .

Another person in his late thirties is today a leading creative producer in children's television. Three years ago he was an effective but increasingly frustrated pastor searching for meaning in doing what he felt he "ought" to do rather than what would give greatest vent to his creative urges. An evaluation of his abilities, a review of alternative ways to fulfill his value commitments and an investigation of real possibilities led to his decision to enter his present field.

A woman, 54, concerned about retirement and searching for a way to live meaningfully until and after retirement, worked out plans for retirement preparation which would also give enhancement to her professional work until then. She began training for a post-retirement career and shifted from fearing her later life to looking forward to it. This was done, not at the expense of her present life and responsibilities—they were instead enhanced, and life took on new meaning.

In the first case marital difficulties added to the problems this man faced. . . . The [second man] had anxieties related to life other than in the professional arena that called for therapeutic intervention. And the woman was beginning to experience some of the early symptoms of arteriosclerotic involvement.

None knew how to incorporate into his life planning all of the factors which had to be considered and how to arrive at a suitable decision. [Some] needed assistance in implementing the decisions once they were made. Yet all were very intelligent, well-educated, responsible persons.

They were all searching for a new sense of purpose in life and for a way to deal effectively with the *process of* life. None were overly concerned about maintenance of their present life position. They were in a search for *meaning,* for a new sense of vocation.

(Brown, 1972, pp. 1–2)

However, Kimmel (1974) believes that this midlife career reassessment differs from the adjustments of young adulthood in its emphasis on what might be called a *career clock.* (The career clock is similar to the "social clock"; it represents the person's subjective sense of being "on time" or "behind time" in career development.) Middle-aged individuals are often acutely aware of the number of years left before retirement and of the speed with which they are reaching their goals. If individuals are "behind time" or if their goals are unrealistic, reassessment and readjustment are necessary. Before it is too late, the individual may very well decide to change jobs. It should be noted, however, middle-agers who decide to make career changes vary considerably in their attitudes, underlying motives, and value orientations (Thomas et al., 1976).

A number of studies support the idea that middle-age career reevaluation is a "time of truth". A four-year study of 40 men between the ages of 35 and 45 revealed that most subjects gave considerable thought to the amount of career success they had had. Many expressed concern over the disparity between their earlier career aspirations and their actual attainments (Levinson et al., 1974). According to another study, middle-agers experiencing career dissatisfaction frequently ask themselves if they have done the right thing with their lives and whether there is still time to make a career change (Gould, 1972). In one investigation, responses to questionnaires distributed to over 1000 teachers and school-staff members showed that many of the middle-aged respondents not only were generally dissatisfied with life but also had diminished self-concepts (Horrocks and Mussman, 1971).

Does any particular sequence of events lead to a midlife career change? Robbins and Harvey's (1977) study of 91 middle-aged adults indicates that the process of deciding to change careers has four stages: (1) struggling with the problem, "What do I want to do with my life?"; (2) taking stock of oneself; (3) talking about the change with friends, associates, and family; and (4) scouting the career possibilities available. In making the change, most of the people in this study tended to build upon skills, education, or hobbies already acquired. Some, however, actively pursued additional formal education to acquire the skills necessary to change vocation. The longer one spent in planning for or contemplating the career change, the more successful the change appeared to be.

Factors Promoting Midcareer Changes

According to Heddescheimer (1976), mid-career changes may be the result of pressures from the *environment*, particularly familial, vocational, and societal changes, as well as pressures from the *self*.

Environmental Pressures. A number of *family* events may precipitate change in the work situation of the middle-aged husband

Figure 10–1. © Copyright 1976 by Chicago Tribune New York News Syndicate, Inc. All rights reserved.

or wife, although in most cases these changes affect the woman more. Divorce or the husband's death may force the woman to leave the home and return to work, or to switch from a part-time to a full-time job to make ends meet. The departure of the last child from the home may prompt the former full-time housewife to search for a meaning-ful career that can reaffirm her sense of usefulness and self-worth.

Changes in *job situations* may motivate individuals to consider different kinds of employment. According to Heddescheimer (1976), these changes include mandatory retirement from the military, loss of a job due to dismissal or technological obsolescence, or a demand from an employer to upgrade one's skills so that a job can be retained.

To improve their vocational skills, many middle-agers are enroll-ing in institutions of higher education. In 1972, approximately 780,000 persons over 35 years of age were attending colleges or universities, while an estimated 570,000 were enrolled in trade or vocational schools (Young, 1973). Hiestand (1971) suggests that further education leads to the acquisition of major work-related skills and permits at least four significant changes in the nature of one's career to take place. Further education may enable the individual (1) to enter a different occupation for the first time; (2) to make a sig-nificant upward movement within a particular profession; (3) to enter a different, perhaps newly emerging, field in which he or she was previously engaged; and (4) to enter a different profession.

Societal trends may also prompt career changes. An emphasis on job satisfaction appears to make middle-agers more aware of the discrepancy between their own less than ideal work and possibly

Figure 10–2. Many middle-aged adults seek to upgrade their vocational skills by enrolling in institutions of higher education.

more satisfying work situations. In speaking of the nature of our rapidly changing society, Hiestand (1971) writes:

> Within a period as short as a decade, substantial changes occur in the attractiveness of particular fields of work, both to those already in them and to those who might enter them. Particular companies and public organizations wax and wane, and with them the attractiveness of particular jobs. Moreover, rapid changes take place in the content and working methods in the professions and management. This raises the specter of technological obsolescence, heretofore primarily a matter of concern to blue-collar workers. If we look more carefully, we see that many at the professional level are subject to more change than is commonly assumed. We soon see that significant numbers of persons are making substantial changes in the nature of their careers during middle age. (pp. 1–2)

Heddescheimer (1976) reports that another social factor is the pressure on women to "make something of themselves." The feminist viewpoint insists that women should be free to make choices, but too frequently the implication is that if a woman is not employed in a responsible position she is "not accomplishing much with her life." As a result, an increasing number of former housewives are being confronted with subtle pressures both from the media and from friends to enter the job market. Furthermore, society is becoming more receptive to women and men who combine child-rearing and homemaking with a job in the community.

Internal Pressures.   Pressures from the self can be equally potent motivators for career changes, especially during the middle years (Heddescheimer, 1976). Rogers (1973) believes that during this time changes may occur in individuals' relations to themselves and their external environment:

> Among those who reflect upon the human condition in our Western society, it is increasingly recognized that the decade from 35 to 45 is a time of crucial importance for the development of the individual. It is a period when new possibilities emerge and new patterns of living are explored.
>
> (p. 37)

Among the issues middle-agers should critically examine is their quest for career satisfaction. While most Americans seemingly have a high level of tolerance for their work (Rosow, 1974), many middle-aged workers develop a questioning spirit and consequently think more about themselves and the work they are performing. Such internalizing and questioning usually result in greater growth and maturity.

More specific motivators may be grouped under the term *satisfaction.* In pursuing career changes, some people take into account new interests or long-standing ones that could not be pursued earlier because of financial or family obligations. Others who are dissatisfied with their present line of work begin a quest for something more personally challenging or rewarding. Some may strive to upgrade their social status and income; others may be interested in working with different people who have new interests (Heddescheimer, 1976).

In conclusion, it is important to note that many middle-agers appear to be developing new attitudes about themselves (Hiestand, 1971). Changes in job requirements, the early completion of families, the ability to work and study at the same time, and perhaps most significantly, the desire of both men and women to lead more satisfying and productive lives have encouraged the "recycling" of both life-styles and careers (Hoenninger, 1974).

THE MIDLIFE CAREER EXPERIENCE

After reviewing the literature, Brown (1972) proposed a number of "working hypotheses" about the middle-life career experience. The following discussion contains the more salient features of Brown's research.

As we have already mentioned, the middle-life experience for many today is an experience of *reestablishment* rather than of maintenance. The processes of change in our culture contribute to a search by many for a new sense of establishment in life and work. People feel *disestablished* and look for certainty and confirmation, for ways to realign themselves comfortably and meaningfully within the same occupational milieu if not the same job.

Vocational decision-making is far more complex, "soul-rending", and fearsome in midlife than it is at the earlier (adolescent) or later (retirement) phases of life. The realities of life are not as flexible, idealistic assumptions are not as energizing, and anxiety, depression, and confusion are less readily rationalized as growth phenomena. There is an unavoidable sense that time is short; for most, there will not be enough time for another fantasy or trial period, nor is there likely to be a future period when another shift can be considered. The ability to say, "I can always change when I'm 30 or 40," may make decisions easier for the 18- or 20-year-old; the 40- or 50-year-old is able to say, "Well, it will only last till retirement"—but that is not a very helpful "out". Thus, a sense of crucial importance attaches to the career decisions of midlife.

The individual who fails to develop an adequate, effective life planning process before middle age arrives may be seriously hampered in his capacity to deal with the stresses of middle life. The major task of the early adult years (25 to 34), then, may be not so much establishment as the development, implementation, and refinement of a process that helps keep the whole of life in perspective. Such a method of planning can still be learned in middle life, when failure to have developed it earlier is apt to become suddenly and painfully clear.

The economic and social successes that were so eagerly sought earlier in life are likely to be found lacking in fulfillment during the middle years. "I have done my thing here; I want new horizons, new challenges" is a common feeling. Those who achieve economic and social success often have a sense of "success without meaning". Helping such a person to do more of the same may leave the core of his problem untouched.

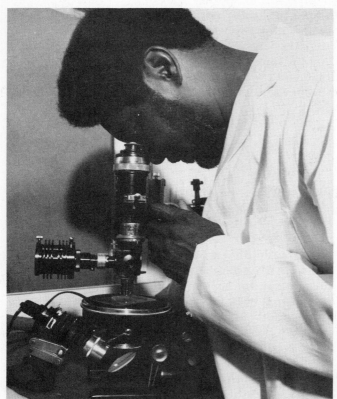

Figure 10–3. The middle years may become a time of career maintenance or realignment.

U.S. Geological Survey
Department of the Interior

Middle life brings a full-scale reorientation of major values. The person who has spent a major part of life searching for power (or responsibility) may now strongly desire to search for pleasure or inner meaning; one who has concentrated on finding pleasure may feel a strong need to focus upon responsibility or meaning. Such reappraisal raises havoc with life-styles, interpersonal relationships, family life, and work.

The problems of unemployment are likely to be more significant in later middle life than in earlier middle life. Mobility is likely to be a greater concern in the forties, unemployment in the fifties.

WOMEN IN THE WORK WORLD

We mentioned earlier that an increasingly large number of women, single and married, are active in the nation's labor force. Many married women simultaneously fulfill the traditional role of mother and the less traditional role of wage-earner (Clayton, 1975). Many women today work for a few years after they complete their schooling, then devote themselves to marriage and parenthood before returning to the labor force. Returning to a career at midlife appears to renew the quality of life for many women (Vriend, 1977).

At midlife, the average woman of the 1970's can expect to spend 30 to 35 years actively working. This represents quite a change from

TABLE 10–1 PROPORTION OF WOMEN IN THE LABOR FORCE, 1960–1971, WITH PROJECTION TO 1985

Age	1960	1971	Projected 1985
16–19	39.1	43.2	41.0
20–24	46.1	57.1	57.7
25–34	35.8	45.5	46.5
35–44	43.1	51.3	53.3
45–54	49.3	53.8	55.2
55–64	36.7	42.4	45.0

Adapted from U.S. Bureau of the Census, *Statistical Abstract of the United States, 1972* (Washington, D.C.: U.S. Government Printing Office, 1972), p. 217.

TABLE 10–2 OCCUPATIONS OF EMPLOYED WOMEN IN THE UNITED STATES, 1900–1971

Occupation	Women Working							
	1900	1910	1920	1930 (Per Cent)	1940	1950	1960	1971
Professional, technical, and kindred workers	8.1	9.7	11.6	13.4	12.7	12.2	13.3	14.8
Farmers and farm managers	5.8	3.7	3.2	2.4	1.2	0.7	0.4	a
Managers, officials, and proprietors, excluding farm	1.4	2.0	2.2	2.7	3.2	4.3	4.6	4.9
Clerical and kindred workers	4.0	9.2	18.6	20.8	21.4	27.4	30.0	34.0
Sales workers	4.3	5.1	6.2	6.8	7.3	8.6	7.2	7.2
Craftsmen, foremen, and kindred workers	1.4	1.4	1.2	1.0	1.1	1.5	0.9	1.3
Operatives and kindred workers	23.8	22.9	20.2	17.4	19.5	19.9	16.1	12.9
Private household workers	28.7	24.0	15.7	17.8	18.1	8.8	9.8	22.3b
Service workers, excluding private household	6.7	8.4	8.1	9.7	11.3	12.6	15.4	
Farm laborers and foremen	13.1	12.0	10.3	5.9	2.7	2.9	2.0	1.7
Laborers, excluding farm and mine	2.6	1.4	2.3	1.5	1.1	0.8	0.3	0.8
TOTAL	99.9	99.9	100.0	100.0	100.0	99.9	100.0	99.9

a Data not available.

b In this enumeration, private household is combined with service workers. The total proportion in the two categories declined by about 10 per cent for the period 1960–1971.

1920, when less than one of every five women 35 to 64 years of age was in the labor force (Suelzle, 1970). From 1950 to 1975, labor force participation rates for women between the ages of 25 and 54 increased from 38 per cent to 55 per cent (Entine, 1976).

There are several explanations for the greater number of American working women. More women are college graduates, which enables them to be more competitive as they search for jobs. Women in contemporary society apparently can go to work without creating the impression that their husbands are inadequate providers. There are now more job opportunities with better pay for women. Finally, census reports indicate that fewer women are having children (Suelzle, 1970).

Midlife Career Development for Women

According to Vriend (1977), many individuals who experience midcareer changes are women. Quite frequently, they "don't like

---

UNEMPLOYMENT DURING THE MIDDLE YEARS

Unemployment is one of the major threats feared by adults of all ages. This fear may be centered not on unsatisfying work or even on temporary loss of work, but rather on the possibility that there will be no work at all (Sykes, 1971). The unemployment rates created by recession have more serious consequences for older adults. Middle-aged and older adults, once unemployed, are likely to stay unemployed for up to 70 per cent longer than younger workers (Entine, 1976). Unemployment during midlife can have serious psychological consequences as well:

> For workers in their middle years, unemployment can be tragic. Family responsibilities are likely to be at their height and the need to accumulate social security credits for adequate benefits upon retirement and to build up savings for old age are most urgent. Unemployment during these years undermines not only the worker's morale but the security of his dependents as well.
>
> (Report of President's Council on Aging, 1961, p. 36)

According to Troll (1975), at least three factors combine to make the plight of the older unemployed worker serious: (1) the rapid pace of technology, (2) the more advanced education of younger workers, which makes them appear more qualified, and (3) the tendency of failing or retrenching companies to be older (consequently having a large proportion of older workers) and to be located in declining parts of the country where the risks of unemployment are high.

In a thought-provoking study, Powell and Driscoll (1973) described four psychological stages the unemployed adult experiences over a prolonged period of joblessness. The first stage, *relaxation and relief,* occurs after the initial shock, frustration, and anger recede. It is characterized by general contentment in being with one's family. At this point many individuals are confident that they will find new positions, so their job-seeking efforts are, at best, only casual. During the second stage, unemployed persons launch a *concerted effort.* After a month, most are becoming bored with their leisure time. They are still optimistic, however, as they make more organized attempts to find work. The third stage, *vacillation and doubt,* usually develops when efforts to find new lines of work are continually unproductive. Job-seeking efforts become sporadic, self-doubts may begin, and some individuals may contemplate a change of vocation. Furthermore, relations with family members and friends become strained. By the time individuals reach the stage of *malaise and cynicism,* apathy and listlessness are apparent. Many of the persons studied reported feelings of helplessness and extremely limited social relationships. Sadly, some claimed that they had difficulty in envisioning themselves as working again.

what they're doing, don't know what they want to do, and think they can't do anything" (p. 329). Like their male counterparts, many women are trapped in low-paying, tedious jobs where they haven't even the modest job satisfaction of the middle manager (Schlossberg, 1977).

Hiestand (as reported by Dullea, 1977) notices a number of trends in regard to midcareer changes for women. Some women in their thirties, typically called "administrative assistants", are being sent to graduate schools by their employers, who are being pressured to hire more female managers. Once in school, the management students may find their interests straying to other fields such as marketing or finance. The result is some "turmoil and changing directions".

Other professional middle-aged women are opting for what Hiestand describes as a "45-degree turn". Individuals in this category move into different but related fields, like the public health nurse who becomes a social worker. A smaller number of women who are highly motivated opt for a "90-degree turn". This kind of career change involves the selection of an entirely new profession. Examples would be the newspaper editor entering law school or an interior designer becoming a child psychologist.

Summary

The middle years are frequently viewed as a period of career realignment. While many workers report varying degrees of job satisfaction, relatively recent research indicates that a sizeable portion of middle-agers are disillusioned and disenchanted with their present jobs. In the pursuit of happiness and occupational satisfaction, some workers are making midlife career changes.

According to Kimmel's concept of a "career clock", middle-agers seem to develop an acute sense of the number of years left before retirement and of the speed with which they are reaching their career goals. If they sense that they are "behind time", readjustment is necessary.

Midcareer changes may be the result of environmental as well as internal pressures. Environmental pressures include family events, changes in job situations, and societal trends. Pressures from the self usually involve desires for job satisfaction, increased social status and income, broader career horizons, and more challenging types of work.

Unemployment is a problem for adults of all ages. Among older adults, however, the effect can be more devastating, since workers in this age group remain unemployed for longer periods than their younger counterparts. It has been suggested that the unemployed individual progresses in time through four fairly distinct psychological stages: (1) relaxation and relief, (2) concerted effort, (3) vacillation and doubt, and (4) malaise and cynicism.

Suggested Readings

1. Hiestand, D. L.: *Changing Careers After 35: New Horizons Through Professional and Graduate Study.* New York: Columbia University Press, 1971.

   A study focusing on the dynamics of career changes after the age of 35. Chapters explore such issues as the nature of middle age, the role of higher education, and the fields in which career changes are found.

2. Holmstrom, L. L.: *The Two-Career Family.* Cambridge, Massachusetts: Schenkman Publishing Company, 1972.

   A most comprehensive and detailed examination of the contemporary two-career family.

3. Osipow, S. H.: "Vocational behavior and career development, 1975, a review." *Journal of Vocational Behavior,* 9:129–145, 1976.

   An excellent review of recent literature concerning career and vocational development. Topics include sex roles and career development, women's careers, and life-span aspects of vocational development.

4. *The Vocational Guidance Quarterly,* June, 1977, Vol. 25, No. 4.

   This special issue is totally devoted to midlife career change.

Section C   The Retirement Years

Holt, Rinehart and Winston

UNIT 11

PHYSICAL AND INTELLECTUAL DEVELOPMENT

Introduction

Never in the history of Western civilization have so many lived for so long. Whereas at the turn of the century the average life expectancy was 47 years, today it is 70.4 years. More than 10 per cent of Americans are over 65, while at the turn of the century only 3 per cent reached this age. Over 4000 Americans are retiring daily. Furthermore, the aged population is growing faster than any other population segment. Since 1960, the elderly population has increased by 35.3 per cent while the overall population has grown by 19 per cent. In 1975, people between the ages of 65 and 74 accounted for 61.9 per cent of the elderly population; those between the ages of 75 and 84 years, 29.7 per cent; and those 85 years and over, 8.4 per cent (Myers and Soldo, 1977). Commenting on this "elderly population explosion", Butler (1975) writes:

> Every day 1000 people reach 65; each year 365,000. More than 70 per cent of the 65 and over age group in 1970 entered that category after 1959. With new medical discoveries, an improved health care delivery system and the presently declining birth rate, it is possible that the elderly will make up one quarter of the total population by the year 2000. Major medical advances in the control of cancer or heart and vascular diseases could increase the average life expectancy by 10 or even 15 years. Discovery of deterrents to the basic causes of aging would cause even more profound repurcussions. The presence of so many elderly, and the potential of so many more, has been a puzzlement to gerontologists, public health experts and demographers, who don't know whether to regard it as "the aging problem" or a human triumph over disease. What is clear is that it will result in enormous changes in every part of our society.
>
> (pp. 16–17)

Old age is the last portion of the life span, and the discussion of old age concludes our analysis of contemporary adulthood. (The technical name for the scientific study of the elderly is *gerontology*). We have elected to call this last section "The Retirement Years" to suggest that some ambiguity and uncertainty exist in charting this stage of life. For example, when exactly does one become "elderly"? What are characteristics of old people? The Social Security Act of 1935 established 65 as the arbitrary age for retirement, and 65 has been widely accepted as the age that separates middle-aged adults from the so-called "elderly".

In an effort to remove the ambiguity that frequently surrounds the definition of old age, some gerontologists distinguish between "early" and "advanced" old age. The former occurs between the ages of 65 and 74 and the latter from 75 on (Butler and Lewis, 1973). Barrett (1972) goes a step further and distinguishes among three gerontological periods: "later maturity" (58 to 68), the "early longevous" stage (68 to 78), and the "later longevous" period (78 and over).

Of course, old age is distinguishable by the physical changes that take place in the body, the result of degenerative processes. Since the metabolic processes are slower in older people, the cells, tissues, and organs function at slower rates. Yet, physical and mental

TABLE 11-1   NUMBER AND PROPORTION OF UNITED STATES POPULATION BY AGE CATEGORIES 65 YEARS OF AGE AND OVER

Age	Population			Per cent Change			Proportion of Aged Population		
	1960	1970	1975[a]	1960-70	1970-75	1960-75	1960	1970	1975
65-69	6,257,910	6,991,625	8,099,000	11.7	15.8	29.4	37.8	34.8	36.2
70-74	4,738,932	5,443,831	5,775,000	14.9	6.1	21.9	28.6	27.1	25.8
75-79	3,053,559	3,834,834	4,001,000	25.6	4.3	31.0	18.4	19.1	17.9
80-84	1,579,927	2,284,311	2,649,000	44.6	16.0	67.7	9.5	11.4	11.8
85+	929,252	1,510,901	1,877,000	62.6	24.2	102.0	5.6	7.5	8.4

[a]Population Estimates and Projections, P-25, No. 614 (Washington, D.C., 1975), p. 11, Table 1.
From: "1970 Census of Population, General Population Characteristics," PC(1)-B1, U.S. Summary (Washington, D.C., 1972), p. 269.

changes in old age vary greatly with the individual (probably more than at any other time in the life span). Consequently, some people may appear very old, while others do not show their age nearly as much.

Chronological age is *not* physical age and is thus a poor criterion for determining when old age begins. Unfortunately, the myth of chronological aging is believed by many (Butler, 1975). Many people envision old age as a time of helplessness and dependency, loss of physical mobility and mental alertness, and general lack of interest in life. One study (Kastenbaum, 1971) indicates that 25 per cent of Americans hold a negative view of old age. Furthermore, many respondents said they would prefer to die before growing old. Perhaps society needs to see more of the Lucille Balls, Bob Hopes, and George Burnses, who are still "going strong" in their sixties, seventies, and eighties, to become more aware that living a long time and becoming "old" are not necessarily synonymous.

AGING AMONG THE ELDERLY

The aging process is lifelong. We readily accept this process up through young adulthood because it signals our physical readiness to enter the adult world (something most of us have dreamed of doing since early childhood). We soon discover, however, that being a "grown-up" entails a bit more responsibility than we were initially prepared to assume. By the time reality catches up with our earlier fantasies about what it means to be labeled an "adult", most of us are rapidly approaching middle age. Suddenly, we become acutely, if not painfully, aware of our own aging process. Many individuals caught up in the later stages of this process begin to experience a good deal of anxiety (perhaps out of fear of losing their membership in one of the most exclusive clubs in the world: "youth").

A major factor in the aging process is genetic make-up. It appears that many humans have the potential of living more than 70 years, but their lives may be shortened by external factors. These causes may be direct (lethal agents) or indirect (the organism is weakened and is consequently more susceptible to such influences as malnutrition, addictions, and stress). The "wear and tear" theory of aging assumes that one simply wears out (much like a machine) over the course of the life cycle. By the time of old age, the body is exhausted and susceptible to some extraneous factor that eventually destroys the organism.

As the degenerative processes of aging set in, the internal organs (heart, lungs, kidneys, nervous system) operate less efficiently. By age 75, for example, the cardiac output at rest for the average individual is approximately 70 per cent of that for the 30-year-old. Breathing capacity at age 75 is about 43 per cent of the age 30 value (Leaf, 1973). As time progresses, the organs, although fully functional during an individual's "resting phase", are unable to regain full efficiency after disease, shock, or other stress (Comfort, 1970;

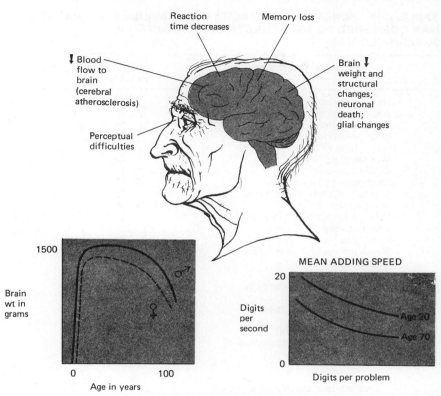

Figure 11–1. Aging and the central nervous system. (*From: Shepro, D., Belamarich, F., and Levy, C.: Human Anatomy and Physiology: A Cellular Approach.* New York: Holt, Rinehart and Winston, 1974.)

Shock, 1960; Timiras, 1972). This explains why older people can die because they lose their resistance—and why the loss of a loved one can so shock the system of an aged person as to cause death (Selye, 1956).

The superficial symptoms of senescence, many of which begin to appear in middle age, are easy to recognize. Skin wrinkles from increasing dryness, hair usually turns gray and sometimes falls out, and there is a tendency to gain weight. Many people need brighter lights to read and require stronger reading glasses, some may begin to notice (or perhaps worse, fail to notice) a loss of hearing ability, and many feel stiff after relatively little exercise. These signs are merely the more obvious manifestations of changes that affect the smallest cells as well as the most complex organs.

During the retirement years, muscle strength and mobility diminish, causing stooping of the shoulders, loss of agility, and finally unsteadiness of the limbs (Vincent and Martin, 1961). Typically, a reduction in height accompanies the stooped posture of the elderly person (Kart, 1976).

Aging is a complex degenerative physiological process. Although no single mechanism can as yet be said to be the primary chemical factor responsible for aging, one important chemical agent

TABLE 11–2   FUNCTIONAL CAPACITY OF AN AVERAGE 75-YEAR-OLD MAN COMPARED TO 100% FUNCTIONAL CAPACITY OF A 30-YEAR-OLD MAN

Physical Characteristic	Comparative Percentage
Nerve conduction velocity	90
Body weight for males	88
Basal metabolic rate	84
Body water content	82
Blood flow to brain	80
Maximum work rate	70
Cardiac output (at rest)	70
Glomerular filtration rate	69
Number of nerve trunk fibers	63
Brain weight	56
Number of glomeruli in kidney	56
Vital capacity	56
Hand grip	55
Maximum ventilation volume (during exercise)	53
Kidney plasma flow	50
Maximum breathing capacity (voluntary)	43
Maximum oxygen uptake (during exercise)	40
Number of taste buds	36
Speed of return to equilibrium of blood acidity	17

Also:
   Less adrenal and gonadal activity
   Slower speed of response
   Some memory loss

has been identified. *Collagen*, a fibrous protein, is the basic structural component of connective tissue. It consists of large, fibrous, elastic molecules, and it is found in all body organs. For example, it is found in its pure form in tendons; it is also found in bones, between cells, in muscle fibers, and in the walls of blood vessels (Timiras, 1972). Collagen is flexible, and it also offers great resistance to pulling forces. In its flexibility and strength, collagen is analogous to a cable that ties a ship to a wharf. Although it is sufficiently pliable to be coiled when not in use, the cable will not allow movement of the ship while at anchor. In much the same manner, fibrous collagen allows skin, tendons, or blood vessels to transmit tension and compression without becoming deformed (Verzar, 1964). These fibers are exceedingly strong, capable of being stretched and then returning to their natural length. However, if they are stretched for a long enough period of time, the stretched length gradually becomes their basic length, a process known as "creeping" (Guyton, 1976).

As collagen loses its elastic properties, organs become less resilient. For example, the bones of the elderly are fragile because of a change in bone mineralization, which makes them more porous and brittle (Timiras, 1972). Decrease in the quality of collagen also allows calcium salts to be deposited in this now degenerating tissue. Calcium salts, which are normally inhibited from accumulating in tissue other than bone, are deposited in arterial walls, causing arteries to become "bone-like tubes" (arteriosclerosis).

Degenerative changes in collagen in capillaries reduce the efficiency of the kidneys as well as the flexibility of the lungs, which in turn can lead to such pulmonary disorders as emphysema. The collagen content of the heart increases, causing the heart muscle itself as well as the valves to become more rigid with age. As a result, the heart cannot bounce back from stress or strain as it once did (Timiras, 1972).

There are other effects of aging collagen in the body. Osteoarthritis, a joint disorder characterized by the breakdown of lubricating fluid (synovial fluid), and the sagging, less resilient skin of old age are just two more examples of the influence collagen has during this period (Timiras, 1972).

DISEASE AND OLD AGE

Old people are susceptible to much the same diseases as anyone else. In preventive medicine, the surgical procedures and drugs used on the elderly are the same as those used on the young. Pneumonia is treated with antibiotics whether the person is 18 or 80 years old. The difference is that while the young have a natural tendency to recover, the elderly tend to deteriorate even further (Timiras, 1972).

Autopsies performed on the aged (especially those in the 70 to 90 age group) reveal a number of internal lesions: structural or functional change in body tissue produced by disease or injury. Because all the organs of the body are deteriorating at this time and because there are so many such lesions, it becomes difficult to pinpoint the actual cause of death.

According to the National Center for Health Statistics (1971), the

TABLE 11-3   CAUSES OF DEATH IN MIDDLE AND OLD AGE

Causes of Death Age 45–64	Rank	Causes of Death Over Age 65	65+ Male to Female Ratio
Diseases of heart	1	Disease of heart	1.408
Malignant neoplasms	2	Malignant neoplasms	1.688
Cerebrovascular diseases	3	Cerebrovascular diseases	1.046
Accidents	4	Influenza/pneumonia	1.468
Cirrhosis of liver	5	Arteriosclerosis	.998
Influenza/pneumonia	6	Accidents	1.439
Diabetes mellitus	7	Diabetes mellitus	.809
Upper respiratory diseases	8	Upper respiratory diseases	6.273
Suicide	9	Cirrhosis of liver	1.819
Homicide	10	Kidney infections	.934

Source: National Center for Health Statistics, Department of Health, Education and Welfare: *Health in the Later Years.* Washington, D. C.: U. S. Government Printing Office, 1971.

major causes of death for older Americans are diseases of the heart, malignant neoplasms (cancer), and cerebrovascular diseases (mainly strokes). In 1968, these three conditions combined accounted for nearly 70 per cent of the 1.7 million deaths of people aged 45 and over. Heart disease is easily the leader, accounting for over 40 per cent of these deaths. Influenza and pneumonia are the fourth leading cause of death among the elderly, while other major causes include bronchitis, emphysema, asthma, arteriosclerosis, diabetes, and cirrhosis of the liver.

Heart disease, hypertension, diabetes, and arthritis are chronic diseases that occur more frequently in older people. Approximately one-sixth of white men and women between the ages of 45 and 64 are afflicted with heart disease, whereas over one-third of black men and women have this condition. For older age groups, these percentages increase significantly. Approximately 80 per cent of the elderly population report some degree of osteoarthritis. Diabetes occurs roughly ten times as frequently in people over 65 as it does in younger people, although the proportion of older people with known diabetes is relatively small in comparison with heart disease, hypertension, and arthritis (National Center for Health Statistics, 1971).

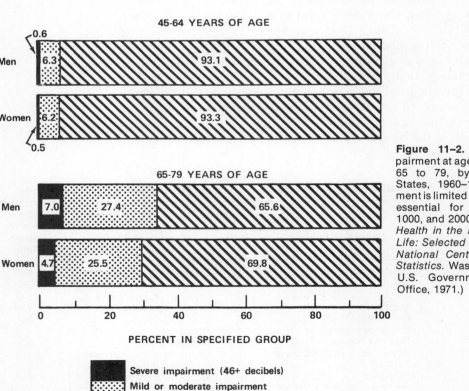

Figure 11–2. Hearing impairment at ages 45 to 64 and 65 to 79, by sex: United States, 1960–1962. (Impairment is limited to frequencies essential for speech—500, 1000, and 2000 hertz.) (*From Health in the Later Years of Life: Selected Data from the National Center for Health Statistics.* Washington, D C.: U.S. Government Printing Office, 1971.)

SENSORY CAPACITIES IN OLD AGE

Sensory abilities decline significantly in old age. Hearing impairment becomes quite dramatic by the mid-sixties, especially for high frequencies (Shock, 1952). Hearing impairment is five times as common in persons aged 65 to 79 as it is in individuals between the ages of 45 and 64 years (see Fig. 11–2). Fortunately, many cases of hearing impairment can be improved with the use of a hearing aid.

Statistically there is also a decline in the visual acuity of elderly people (Kart, 1976) (see Fig. 11–3). After age 60, few people see well without glasses. The components of sight especially susceptible to deterioration are the cornea, retina and lens of the eye, and the optic nerve (Botwinick, 1970; Shock, 1952). Aging also causes a decline in the ability of the eye to adjust rapidly to variations in light, making night driving difficult for the elderly.

Other senses also show a slow deterioration. Smell and taste are on the decline (Kart, 1976), causing some old people to complain that foods have very little taste (Corso, 1971). Consequently, elderly people may exhibit a preference for spicier foods.

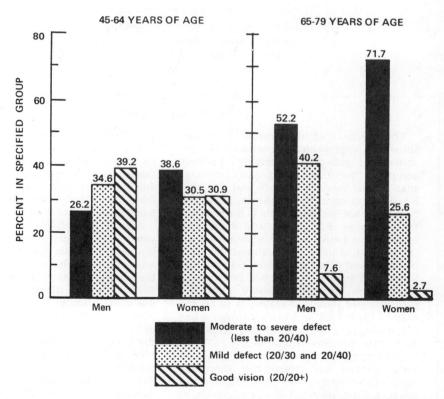

Figure 11–3.   Visual acuity, uncorrected, at ages 45 to 64 and 65 to 79, by sex: United States, 1960–1962. (*From: Health in the Later Years of Life: Selected Data from the National Center for Health Statistics.* Washington, D. C.: U.S. Government Printing Office, 1971.)

MENTAL FUNCTION IN OLD AGE

Many of us regard the elderly as forgetful, unable to think clearly, repetitive in their storytelling, and even senile (see box). As we explained earlier, many of our impressions of old age originate from inaccurate knowledge or social stereotypes. While it is true that sensory and motor abilities decline with age, judgment and accumulated knowledge can compensate for these losses. A majority of older people are capable of functioning satisfactorily, the most practical criterion of adaptive ability (Aiken, 1977). Thus, it is unfair to say that all elderly persons experience a decline in all phases of mental ability.

How do the elderly perform on IQ tests? For this information to be at all meaningful, we must first understand what it is that the standard intelligence test is measuring (see Unit 7). Research findings indicate that there is a general decline in the capacity to successfully complete tasks requiring physical performance (e.g., the subject is asked to arrange blocks) and speed (for certain tasks, the quicker a task is accomplished, the higher the score). Thus, lower scores on IQ tests may be due not to a decline in intellectual functions but, in part, to slower reaction times (Bischof, 1976; Kimmel, 1974). Indeed, it is postulated by some (Baltes and Schaie, 1974; Botwinick, 1967) that many individuals can improve, or at the very least maintain, certain intellectual abilities well into old age. Tasks requiring coordination between visual and motor functions seem to pose the most difficulties for the elderly.

SENILITY: MYTH AND FACT

The notion that old people are senile, showing forgetfulness, confusional episodes and reduced attention, is widely accepted. "Senility" is a popularized layman's term used by doctors and the public alike to categorize the behavior of the old. Some of what is called senile is the result of brain damage. But anxiety and depression are also frequently lumped within the same category of senility, even though they are treatable and often reversible. Old people, like young people, experience a full range of emotions, including anxiety, grief, depression and paranoid states. It is all too easy to blame age and brain damage when accounting for the mental problems and emotional concerns of later life.

Drug tranquilization is another frequent, misdiagnosed and potentially reversible cause of so-called senility. Malnutrition and unrecognized physical illnesses, such as congestive heart failure, may produce "senile behavior" by reducing the supply of blood, oxygen and food to the brain. Alcoholism, often associated with bereavement, is another cause. Because it has been so convenient to dismiss all these manifestations by lumping them together under an improper and inaccurate diagnostic label, the elderly often do not receive the benefits of decent diagnosis and treatment.

Actual irreversible brain damage, of course, is not a myth, and two major conditions create mental disorders. One is cerebral arteriosclerosis (hardening of the arteries of the brain); the other, unfortunately referred to as senile brain disease, is due to a mysterious dissolution of brain cells. Such conditions account for some 50 percent of the cases of major mental disorders in old age, and the symptoms connected with these conditions are the ones that form the basis for what has come to be known as senility. But. . . similar symptoms can be found in a number of other conditions which *are* reversible through proper treatment.

(Butler, 1975, pp. 9–10)

Reed and Reitan (1963) state that problem-solving ability declines with age, but general knowledge does not. Also, it should be noted that scores on verbal subtests (e.g., vocabulary) occasionally decline slightly with age but generally remain constant. For more intelligent individuals, it is not uncommon to find an actual increase in certain verbal abilities. Thus, among the elderly, we often find reduced abilities for complex decision-making, diminished speed of performance, and a decline in some forms of perception. We find few losses or none in verbal comprehension, social awareness, and the application of experience (Kalish, 1975).

Another factor to consider regarding intellectual functioning and old age is general state of health. Riegel and Riegel (1972) found that healthy aged people showed little or no loss of intellectual abilities, whereas those who were approaching death or combating disease exhibited a marked decline in intellectual function. Thinking processes may be altered by a decrease in the blood supply to the brain or by extensive hardening of the arteries. Older people may also respond at slower rates because of general disinterest in the subject area being tested or because they prefer deliberation and accuracy over speed of response in problem-solving situations. Thus, the elderly are slower, but also more accurate in their responses (Botwinick, 1967).

Short-Term and Long-Term Memory

Of the two types of memory storage systems, there appears to be little doubt that short-term memory declines during old age. Short-term store involves remembering recent events or new information that is to be used for only a brief period of time. Among older people, the inefficiency of the short-term memory store may not only lead to frustration and irritation but may also interfere with any type of learning that must pass from short-term to long-term storage (Welford, 1965).

Long-term memory includes accumulated experiences and knowledge of a lifetime and does not appear to disintegrate greatly with age except when disease strikes. As Hendricks and Hendricks (1977) suggest, however, the character of long-term memories needs to be critically examined before any definitive conclusions can be made. "It may well be," they state, "that only 'practical' long-term memories, those which are frequently recalled, can be readily remembered. Do unrehearsed memories also resist dissolution? The answer certainly has practical significance for all levels of mental functioning" (p. 139). In virtually every instance, well-educated and mentally active people do not exhibit the same memory decline as their age peers who do not have similar opportunities to flex their minds. Nevertheless, with few exceptions, the time required for memory scanning for both recent and remote recall is longer among the elderly, more likely the result of social and health factors than of any irreversible effects of age (Hendricks and Hendricks, 1977).

Summary

The retirement years have begun to attract the interest of a number of researchers largely because more and more people are living longer lives. Presently, 4000 people are retiring daily; 1000 reach age 65 every day. Thus, retirees and elderly people make up a substantial portion of the population (over 10 per cent).

Aging is the result of many metabolic changes that slow down physiological and physical processes and some mental ones. Internal organs such as the heart and lungs, which no longer operate at full potential, now lack the ability to regain full efficiency after disease or stress. Collagen, a fibrous protein, is a flexible connective tissue that resides between all cells in the body. It acts like a rubber band—stretching and regaining its original shape—at least in younger people. One major aspect of the aging process is the gradual loss of this elasticity, which has an adverse effect on bones, muscles, organs, and skin.

Elderly people suffer from the same diseases as younger ones, but younger persons have a natural tendency to recover, whereas the elderly have a tendency toward further deterioration. Four leading causes of death among the elderly are diseases of the heart, cancer, hypertension, and diabetes.

Intellectual functions do change in old age, but not to the extent that our cultural myths would have us believe. Very few actually lose intellectual abilities, except for the minority of elderly people who are senile or are actually close to death. Although many aged individuals exhibit a decline in sensory abilities and reaction times, general knowledge and vocabulary tend to remain constant over time and, for superior people, verbal abilities may even increase. Long-term memory remains fairly constant at this time, but there is a noticeable decline in short-term memory.

Suggested Readings

1. Hendricks, J., and Hendricks, C. D.: *Aging in Mass Society: Myths and Realities.* Cambridge, Massachusetts: Winthrop Publishers, 1977.

   An excellent account of the physical and health factors of old age is presented in Chapters 4, 6, and 7.

2. Kalish, R. A., (Ed.): *The Later Years: Social Applications of Gerontology.* Monterey, California: Brooks/Cole, 1977.

   Health and illness among the elderly are afforded separate treatment in Part 5 of this reader.

3. Timiras, P. S.: *Developmental Physiology and Aging.* New York: Macmillan, Inc., 1972.

   An in-depth account of the biochemical changes occurring throughout the life span. Part II of this book deals with the degenerative processes occurring in old age.

Florida State News Bureau

UNIT 12

PERSONALITY AND SOCIAL LEARNING

Introduction

Personality changes of the retirement years are frequently portrayed by poets, dramatists, and novelists. Depending on the writer's purpose and outlook, the elderly may be either caricatured or idealized. Psychologists also view personality changes during old age from differing perspectives. Some stress decline and deterioration while others assert that personality growth continues to occur, in some cases transcending levels reached during earlier maturity (Post, 1973).

Researchers have identified the principal developmental tasks of old age, and several noteworthy theories have been proposed to explain the dynamics of personality growth in later life. Fairly recently, attempts have also been made to define and measure psychological well-being among the elderly, especially in relation to patterns of successful aging.

ADJUSTING TO THE RETIREMENT YEARS

Old age, like early and middle adulthood, has its share of developmental work (see box). In many respects, these complex life tasks may pose more of a challenge than those faced during any other stage of the life cycle. Financial adjustments are especially difficult to make, particularly for those who only have a social security check or a modest pension to depend upon. (These adjustments may be especially hard for a retired couple who were earlier accustomed to a higher standard of living). Financial difficulties may disrupt not only the older couple's retirement life-style but also their marital harmony. Old age is also a critical period of self-assessment, a time to reevaluate one's successes and failures. And, while evaluating the past and attempting to deal with the present, the older person is faced with preparing for the future.

Maintaining self-acceptance and self-esteem is also important for the aged. According to Aiken (1978), reflected evaluations from significant people as well as successes and failures in dealing with the environment will affect the manner in which individuals view themselves. The resulting self-concept

> . . . includes not only the person's evaluations of his own body and behavior, but the overall value that he places on himself as a personality. Biological factors such as physical appearance, health, innate abilities, and certain aspects of temperament are important in determining the frequency and kinds of social experiences that a person has and the degree of social acceptance that he attains. But these biological factors interact in complex ways, and they always operate in a social context. Therefore, the social evaluations placed on the physical and behavioral characteristics of an individual who possesses a particular biological makeup—and consequently his evaluation of himself—depend on the specific sociocultural group to which the person belongs.
>
> (p. 109)

Investigators are not in agreement as to what effect the aging process in general and retirement in particular have on self-esteem.

DEVELOPMENTAL TASKS OF THE RETIREMENT YEARS

1. Adjusting to declining physical strength and health.

2. Adjusting to retirement and reduced income.

3. Adjusting to death of spouse.

4. Establishing an explicit affiliation with one's age group.

5. Adopting and adapting social roles in a flexible way.

6. Establishing satisfactory physical living arrangements.

Adapted from Havighurst (1972)

Some indicate that self-esteem reaches its peak during the middle years and then begins to taper off (Bloom, 1961). Another view is offered by Kaplan and Pokorny (1970), who believe that self-esteem increases with age provided that the individual does not encounter disruptive life experiences such as death in the family; that standards of living are not below the individual's level of aspiration; and that the individual is not faced with the fear of being alone or isolated. Newman and Newman (1975) believe that fluctuations in self-esteem reflect the individual's conscious awareness of new life tasks that pose formidable challenges to his or her abilities. In the later years of life, the person's capacity to maintain a feeling of worth depends on the existence of a supportive social environment and the ability to integrate past life events. It seems likely that self-esteem does not change simply as a function of aging but rather continues to fluctuate in accordance with the personality of the individuals involved as well as the potential crises that confront them.

In summarizing the developmental tasks of the retirement years, Havighurst (1972) writes that in the physical, mental, and economic spheres limitations become especially evident—older people must work hard to maintain what they already have. In the social sphere, there is a fair chance of offsetting the narrowing of some social contacts by broadening others. Successful resolution of the developmental tasks of the retirement years as well as the maintenance of psychological well-being may depend on the success experienced with earlier developmental challenges (Neugarten, 1971).

THEORIES OF PERSONALITY DEVELOPMENT

Erik Erikson's Theory

According to Erikson (1963), the key to harmonious personality development in the later years of life is the ability to resolve the psychosocial crisis known as *integrity versus despair*. Ego integrity implies a full unification of the personality, and the manner in which this crisis is met depends on a number of other factors, including the relevance of social roles, the life-style led, and physical health.

Ego integration enables individuals to view their lives with satisfaction and contentment. Having had satisfying social relationships and a productive life promotes a feeling of well-being. Integrity also implies a sense of purposiveness. In Erikson's own words:

> Although aware of the relativity of all the various life styles which have given meaning to human striving, the possessor of integrity is ready to defend the dignity of his own lifestyle against all physical and economic threats. For he knows that an individual life is the accidental coincidence of but one life cycle with but one segment of history; and that for him all human integrity stands or falls with the one style of integrity which he partakes. The style of integrity developed by his culture or civilization thus becomes the . . . seal of his moral paternity of himself . . . . In such final consolidation, death loses its sting.
>
> (p. 268)

The lack of this accrued ego integration is frequently signaled by a fear of death and the feeling that life is too short. Individuals experiencing despair feel that time is running out and that it is too late to start another life or try out alternate roads to integrity. Consequently, they view their lives with regret and disappointment. Many wish that they had made fuller use of their potential to attain goals established earlier in life. Thus, the stage of integrity versus despair has psychological as well as social relevance to development in the retirement years.

Robert Peck's Theory

Peck (1968) maintains that psychological growth during the retirement years is characterized by three primary psychological adjustments: ego differentiation versus work-role preoccupation, body transcendence versus body preoccupation, and ego transcendence versus ego preoccupation.

Ego Differentiation Versus Work-Role Preoccupation. The central issue here is the impact of vocational retirement. This represents a crucial shift in individual value systems. Personal worth must be reappraised and redefined so that the retiree can take satisfaction in activities that extend beyond his or her long-time specific work role. The salient adjustment issue is related to the question, "Am I a worthwhile person only insofar as I can do a full-time job; or can I be worthwhile in other, different ways—as a performer of several other roles, and also because of the kind of person I am?" (Peck, 1968, p. 90). Peck believes that ego-differentiation is a centrally important issue at the time of retirement. A sense of self-worth derived from activities beyond one's career is apparently crucial to establishing a continued, vital interest in living instead of a despairing loss of meaning in life. Consequently, establishing a variety of valued self-attributes so that any one of several alternatives can be pursued with satisfaction may be a critical prerequisite for successful aging.

Body Transcendence Versus Body Preoccupation. The retirement years bring most people a marked decline in resistance to illness, a decline in recuperative powers, and an increase in bodily aches and pains. For those who equate comfort and pleasure with physical well-being, this decline in health may represent the gravest of insults. There are many retired people whose lives seem to move

Figure 12–1. Satisfying social relationships and a productive life promotes a sense of well-being.

The Bettmann Archive, Inc.

in a decreasing spiral because of their growing concern with the state of their bodies. Many experience a state referred to as "inner preoccupation" (Neugarten and Gutmann, 1964). There are other older people, however, who experience declining health yet enjoy life greatly. This has lead some researchers to believe that the elderly person's bodily concerns are not related to age per se, but rather reflect special life circumstances (Plutchik et al., 1971). Peck suggests that some people may have learned to define "happiness" and "comfort" in terms of satisfying human relationships or creative mental activities, which only sheer physical destruction could seriously interfere with. "In their value system," he writes, "social and mental sources of pleasure and self respect may transcend physical comfort alone" (p. 91). This kind of value system may well have to be developed by early adulthood, if it is to be achieved at all, and the retirement years may bring the most critical test of whether or not such a value system has indeed been internalized.

Ego Transcendence Versus Ego Preoccupation. One of the crucial tasks of elderly people is coming to the realization that they will die. In earlier years, death often comes unexpectedly, but in old age its inevitability is recognized. As Henry Wadsworth Longfellow wrote, "The young may die, but the old must." Buddhist, Confucian, and Hindu philosophers, as well as Western thinkers, have suggested that a positive adaptation even to this most unwelcome of prospects is possible. Peck (1968) suggests that the constructive lifestyle might be defined accordingly:

> To live so generously and unselfishly that the prospect of personal death—the night of the ego, it might be called—looks and feels less important than the secure knowledge that one has built for a broader, longer future than any one ego ever could encompass. Through children, through contributions to the culture, through friendships—these are ways in which human beings can achieve enduring significance for their actions which goes beyond the limit of their own skins and their own lives. It may, indeed, be the only *knowable* kind of self-perpetuation after death.
>
> (p. 91)

Peck cautions that such an adaptation is not a stage of passive resignation or ego denial. To the contrary, it requires a deep, active effort to make life more secure and meaningful, or happier, for those who will go on living after one dies. Adaptation to the prospect of death may well be the crucial achievement of later life. The "successful ager" is the person who is purposefully active as an ego-transcending perpetuation of that culture which, more than anything else, differentiates human life from animal life. Such people are experiencing a vital, gratifying absorption in the future, and they are doing all they can to make it a good world for their familial or cultural descendents. This might be interpreted as vicarious satisfaction, but it actually represents an active and significant involvement with daily life as long as one lives. It might also be viewed as the most complete kind of ego-realization, even as it is focused on people and issues that go far beyond immediate self-gratification in the narrow sense.

Else Frenkel-Brunswik's Theory

Frenkel-Brunswik (1968) provides us with further knowledge about the personality dynamics of the elderly. Like other researchers, she too states that retirement, declining health, and death among family members and close associates affect personality and consequently require considerable adjustment and adaptation.

The scope of social life is obviously reduced in old age, whereas hobbies, like stamp collecting or gardening, assume greater importance. Social interactions are more likely to involve helpfulness, advice, and consolation.

Older people frequently reflect upon their past life and considerations about oncoming death. Loneliness and a preoccupation with religious questions are fairly common. "The balance-sheet of life," as Frenkel-Brunswik calls it, is drawn up, often through the writing of memoirs and autobiographies. In some ways, these activities resemble those of adolescents, who often keep diaries to help themselves in resolving conflicts and frustrations of a period of transition.

PATTERNS OF SUCCESSFUL AGING

Successful aging is difficult to define, and frequently the description merely reflects the values of the person doing the defining (Kalish, 1975). According to Birren (1964), successful aging has two important aspects. One is life satisfaction on the part of the older people themselves: Are they content with their lives? Do they have positive self-regarding attitudes? (Of course, an individual's belief that he or she is growing old gracefully may not be shared by friends and relatives.) The second aspect of successful aging has to do with social roles or interpersonal obligations and responsibilities. In other words, Birren believes that successful aging has an inner, or psychological, criterion and an outer, or social, one. It is expected that these two aspects of the personality will be somewhat consistent, but a one-to-one relationship between the psychological and the social aspect of aging does not necessarily exist.

At present, two theories of successful aging are prevalent: the *theory of disengagement* and the *activity theory*. Although some support can be found for both positions, most experts agree that neither theory fully explains the phenomenon of successful adjustment (Havighurst, 1968).

The Disengagement Theory

The theory of disengagement (Cumming, 1963; Cumming and Henry, 1961) views aging as a mutual withdrawal process between aging persons and the social system to which they belong. Contrary to popular impression, such a gradual withdrawal from society is not a negative experience for the elderly. On the contrary, the aged frequently view disengagement in a positive light, since this is an age of increased reflection, preoccupation with the self, and decreased emotional investment in people and events. Because of this, disengagement is viewed as a natural rather than an imposed process (Cumming and Henry, 1961).

The disengagement theory was developed in Kansas during a five-year investigation of a sample of 275 elderly persons aged between 50 and 90 years. Cumming and Henry (1961) noted that disengagement was generally initiated by the individuals themselves or by the social system. Retirement, for example, is an event that releases older people from specific social roles and enables them to become disengaged to some extent. Loss of a spouse serves as another example. In time, when disengagement is complete, the balance that existed between the person and society in the middle years has shifted to an equilibrium characterized by greater psychological distance, altered types of relationships, and decreased social interaction (Cumming, 1963; Havighurst, 1968).

Figure 12–2. Old age is a critical period of self-assessment.

John C. Goodwin

The disengagement theory has generated considerable controversy among gerontologists. Some researchers agree with the general theme of disengagement, but many have found it to be theoretically unjustified (Carp, 1968; Maddox, 1964, 1968). Rose (1968) offers three major criticisms of the disengagement theory. First, he believes that disengagement in later life is not a new adjustment process in later life but most likely represents a continuation of an earlier life-style. Second, Rose stresses that adults who remain active in their social environment are essentially happier than those who have withdrawn from their social system. Seven years after the original study by Cummings and Henry (1961), Havighurst, Neugarten, and Tobin (1968) initiated a follow-up. (Because of such factors as deaths and geographical moves, the follow-up sample contained only 55 per cent of the people in the original study.) This second study showed that although increasing age is accompanied by increasing disengagement from common social roles, some elderly people who remained active and engaged reported relatively high degrees of contentment. On the whole, those who were most active were happiest (Havighurst, 1968).

Finally, Rose (1968) argues that many of the societal conditions that have forced the elderly into restricted environments are likely to change in the future (e.g., people are retiring earlier; improved health care will enable more older people to remain more physically active; higher social security benefits may increase the economic security of the retired and enable them to engage in more active life-styles). Consequently, disengagement may be discouraged and more active lives encouraged.

CHALLENGING THE DISENGAGEMENT THEORY: TOWARD A MORE ACTIVE LIFE-STYLE AMONG THE ELDERLY

Americans, says gerontologist Robert Butler, take an unhealthy and often unrealistic attitude toward aging, assuming that old people have no further contributions to make to society and should be excluded from it. Many of the elderly share this view, occasionally attempting to conceal evidence of their advancing years and withdrawing from an active life. Butler and others believe that attitudes must change if the aged are ever to be treated fairly in the U.S. They urge society to recognize the basic rights of old people to independence and security. Gerontologists also urge society to make better use of the elderly, drawing on their experience and talents and giving them a greater voice in matters that concern them. It is ridiculous, they agree, to have panels of 35-year-olds determining the wishes of and setting policy for the aged when the aged are better equipped to do the job.

Improvements in these areas are on the way. Congress has moved—albeit not very far—to tap the reservoir of talents the elderly have accumulated during their lives. It has approved $45 million for a variety of projects, including the Foster Grandparent Program, which pays oldsters for supervising dependent and neglected youngsters; $17.5 million for the Retired Senior Volunteer Program (RSVP), which pays out-of-pocket expenses to 100,000 involved in such community activities as entertaining the handicapped and visiting homebound patients; and a skimpy $400,000 for the Senior Corps of Retired Executives (SCORE), which reimburses some 4,500 retired executives for expenses incurred while counseling small businesses and community organizations. . . .

This urge to change things has been inspired in large part by the realization that other countries have done so much more than the U.S. in caring for the elderly. Sweden, Denmark and Norway have used part of the mountain of taxes collected from their citizens (as high as 50% of most salaries in Sweden) to ease many of the burdens of aging. In Sweden, city governments run housing developments where the aged can live close to transportation and recreational activities. Denmark, with a population of 5 million, houses many of its more than 600,000 elderly in subsidized houses or apartments and helps those who want to remain in their own homes by providing them with day helpers and meals. Those who need nursing homes find them a considerable cut above most of their American counterparts: with their excellent design, many look like modern hotels.

Another force behind the new impetus for change is the growing political power and militancy of the elderly themselves. Many groups—blacks, young people, women— have realized how much political muscle their numbers provide and organized in recent years to demand and get attention and help from federal, state and local officials. The aged are following their lead. No longer content to pass their days playing checkers or weaving potholders at senior citizens' centers, a growing number of elderly Americans are banding together to make their wishes known. Several thousand of them have joined a five-year-old group known informally as the Gray Panthers, whose leader, a retired Philadelphia social worker named Maggie Kuhn, 69, is dedicated to altering U.S. attitudes toward the aged. The Panthers have agitated for better housing and medical care and more employment opportunities for the elderly. "Most organizations tried to adjust old people to the system," says Miss Kuhn, "and we want none of that. The system is what needs changing."

The system is changing, and it is likely to change even further. Politicians, aware that the elderly are more likely to register and vote than the young, are listening when senior citizens speak. So are younger people. The new interest is encouraging. Americans have for too long turned their backs on their old people. Now many are seeing them for the first time, recognizing their plight and moving to help them. The interest and action are both humane and pragmatic. Today, millions of Americans are wondering what to do about their parents. Tomorrow, their children will be wondering what to do about them.

(*TIME,* June 2, 1975, p. 51 © 1975 by TIME: The Weekly Newsmagazine.)

The Activity Theory

The activity theory of successful aging suggests that retired individuals prefer to remain productive and active. In contrast to the theory of disengagement, this viewpoint suggests that the aged prefer to resist preoccupation with the self and psychological distance from society. Happiness and satisfaction originate from involvement and the older person's ability to adjust to changing life events (Maddox, 1968).

Finding substitute activities for those roles that have terminated is a key feature of this kind of adjustment. Blau (1973) believes old age offers numerous "role exits" in old age that can prove to be psychologically devastating if no substitute activities are found. Thus, the greater the number of role resources with which individuals enter old age, the better off they will be in adjusting to the demoralizing effects of role exits.

According to Streib (1977), there are four main role changes that must be dealt with by the elderly. Each requires realignment of some kind. First, the work role that may have been the major object of activity and attention throughout the course of one's life is lost. The loss of gainful employment affects both marital partners, who usually must adapt to a changed domestic situation.

The second, related, loss is the loss of income. The elderly may not be able to afford some kinds of activities.

Third, retirement coincides with declining health for many people, although many are automatically retired while they are still in good health. Either way, the elderly discover that as they age, their physical condition deteriorates, and they may have to give up some activities and moderate others.

Finally, changes in the family often require role realignment. As children leave the home, the role behavior and expectations of both parents change. By the retirement years, help and assistance patterns have shifted, sometimes with assistance flowing from child to parent instead of the reverse. Severe illness or death of a spouse also calls for significant adjustment in the partner's role.

In summarizing these role changes, Streib (1977) writes:

> The reduction in role activity as worker and as parent, combined with declining health and usually reduced income, constitute the realistic framework within which most older persons enact their many roles in later life. Many persons—old, young, persons of influence, and the man in the street—must be aware of the role losses and the necessary role realignments which are an integral part of later life. There must be, however, a clear recognition that old age can be a period of new role opportunities. Public and private organizations can aid in reaching broad goals of spending the new leisure time of later life constructively, and achieving positive and well-integrated roles within the family, the community and in a broad spectrum of groups and organizations.
>
> (p. 77)

How valid is the activity theory of successful aging? The fact that not all activities provide sustenance for one's self-concept has long been recognized, but little attention has yet been given to the differences among kinds of activities or the person's ability to exert any

significant control over either the roles themselves or the performance of those roles (Hendricks and Hendricks, 1977). Consequently,
the activity theory has received limited empirical support and has
been criticized as an oversimplification of the questions involved. As
Hendricks and Hendricks (1977) state, "It may hardly be appropriate
merely to substitute pastimes, geared to what is thought to be older
persons' interests and abilities, for those roles they surrendered as
they moved beyond middle age. Busying oneself with enterprises
meaningless in terms of dominant cultural values, presumably still
subscribed to by older people, may not in itself contribute to adjustment" (p. 111). Nevertheless, after reviewing the relevant literature,
these authors conclude that there is an association between morale,
personality adjustment, and activity levels.

Personality Make-up and Successful Aging

Since some individuals are satisfied with disengagement while
others prefer to maintain a high level of social engagement, it is
evident that a broader perspective is needed to provide gerontologists with a useful theory of successful aging. Many agree that a
theory of the relationship of *personality* to successful aging is
needed (Havighurst, 1968).

One such thoery has been developed by Reichard, Livson, and
Peterson (1962). In an analysis of 87 men ranging in age from 55 to 84,
these researchers identified five personality types: *mature* (constructive), *rocking-chair type* (dependent), *armored* (defensive),
angry (hostile), and *self-haters. Mature* men seemed to be ideally
adjusted. They accepted themselves (strengths as well as weaknesses) and their past lives. Most were relatively free of neurotic
conflicts and maintained close personal relationships. The *rocking-
chair type* also had a high level of self-acceptance, although this
acceptance was frequently passive. Individuals in this category are
dependent on others and perceive old age as freedom from responsibility. The *armored* relied considerably on defense mechanisms to
cope with whatever negative emotions arise. Typically well-
adjusted, the armored are fairly rigid individuals who maintain active life-styles, presumably as a means of demonstrating their independent character. The *angry* are not well-adjusted and make a habit
of expressing their bitterness, often in an aggressive manner. They
openly blame others for their troubles and are easily frustrated. The
self-haters are similar to the angry but blame themselves for their
difficulties and failures. They are characteristically depressed and
view old age as a demoralizing stage of life. The mature, the
rocking-chair type, and the armored were successful at aging. The
angry and the self-haters were less adaptive.

A similar classification of personality types and their implication
for successful aging is apparent in another study (Neugarten,
Havighurst, and Tobin, 1968). Investigating elderly subjects between the ages of 70 to 79, these researchers viewed personality and
role activity as critical determinants of life satisfaction. They iden-

TABLE 12-1 PERSONALITY PATTERNS IN AGING

Personality type	Role activity	Life satisfaction	Number
A. Integrated (reorganizers)	High	High	9
B. Integrated (focused)	Medium	High	5
C. Integrated (disengaged)	Low	High	3
D. Armored-defended (holding on)	High or medium	High	11
E. Armored-defended (constricted)	Low or medium	High or medium	4
F. Passive-dependent (succorance-seeking)	High or medium	High or medium	6
G. Passive-dependent (apathetic)	Low	Medium or low	5
H. Unintegrated (disorganized)	Low	Medium or low	7

(*From* Havighurst, 1968)

OLD AGE AND PSYCHOLOGICAL MALADJUSTMENT

The retirement years are not always characterized by successful adjustment. On the contrary, the stresses associated with aging may cause some individuals to become maladjusted. Such maladjustment can be principally psychological, in which case we say the individual has a *psychogenic disor-* der. Other aged persons may become maladjusted owing to actual brain damage arising from physical deterioration due to stress or disease. Individuals in this latter category suffer from any one of a number of disorders called *organic brain syndromes.* An estimated 700,000 elderly persons were in-

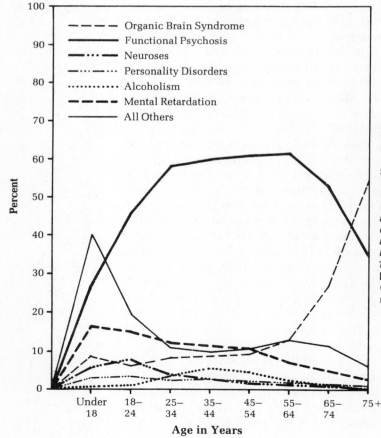

Figure 12-3. Per cent distribution of resident patients in mental hospitals (state and county) by diagnosis, United States, 1970. *Source:* U.S. Department of Health, Education, and Welfare, Public Health Service: *"Age, Sex and Diagnostic Composition of Resident Patients in State and County Mental Hospitals—United States, 1961–1970."* Washington, D.C.: Government Printing Office, 1972. (Converted from numeric data.)

stitutionalized in mental hospitals in 1970, and this figure is expected to rise above the million mark in 1980 (Ford, 1970).

The *psychogenic disorders* of old age, Verwoerdt (1969) states, are related to psychological causes and interpersonal factors that may persist from youth into old age or may appear for the first time in the aged person. Psychogenic disorders include psychotic reactions, neuroses, and personality disorders. In *psychotic reactions* the disorganization of the personality is extensive, the failure to evaluate reality correctly being the cardinal feature. Those suffering from *neurosis* experience considerable anxiety but do not grossly distort reality or exhibit profound personality disorganization. Typical of *personality disorders* (or behavior disorders) is the absence of any internal discomfort, whereas anxiety plays an important role in the neuroses. Disturbing and/or maladaptive behavior patterns and interactions with the environment are prominent instead of neurotic or somatic symptoms.

Individuals with *organic brain syndromes* constitute the largest group of institutionalized elderly mental patients. These disorders afflict 5 to 10 per cent of people between the ages of 65 and 75 and a steadily rising proportion in older age groups. Organic brain syndromes are primarily the result of massive loss of brain cells in the cerebral cortex. They produce such symptoms as disorientation, loss of memory for both recent and distant events, and the inability to perform routine tasks (Clark and Gosnell, 1977). Kisker (1972) categorizes organic brain syndromes into *presenile* and *senile* disorders and *cerebral arteriosclerosis*. *Presenile* disorders are conditions that appear at an earlier age than would ordinarily be expected. *Senile brain* disease is a progressive disorder characterized by increasing mental and physical deterioration. Unfortunately, other ailments of the elderly sometimes mimic senility and lead to misdiagnosis. Chief among these is depression—by all odds the most common psychological problem of the retirement years. Depressed individuals frequently display confusion and forgetfulness as well as apathy, helplessness, hypochondria, low motivation, and an inability to concentrate (Clark and Gosnell, 1977).

In *cerebral arteriosclerosis,* or hardening of the arteries of the brain, the involvement of the cerebral blood vessels interferes with the exchange of essential substances between the bloodstream and the brain tissue. Frequently, the individual afflicted with this disorder experiences dizziness, headaches, and general confusion (Kisker, 1972).

tified personality types similar to those devised by Reichard and associates, (1962), namely, *integrated, armored-defended, passive-dependent,* and *unintegrated* (Table 12–1). However, unlike the Reichard group, Neugarten and associates categorized specific types of role activities within these major types.

The integrated type of personality includes the *reorganizers,* the *focused,* and the *successfully disengaged.* The *reorganizers* are involved in a wide range of activities and, as the title suggests, they reorganize their lives to substitute new activities for lost ones. The *focused* engage in moderate levels of activity. They are more selective about their activities than the reorganizers, and they tend to devote their energy to one or two role areas. The *disengaged* have low activity levels and high life satisfaction (thus supporting the disengagement theory of successful aging). With age they have voluntarily moved away from role commitments.

The armored-defended category includes *holding-on* and *constricted* personality patterns. *Holding-on* individuals attempt to cling as long as possible to activities of middle age. As long as they succeed in doing this, they attain high levels of life satisfaction. The *constricted* reduce their role activities and involvements with other people, presumably as a defense against aging. They differ from the focused group in that they have less integrated personalities.

The passive-dependent personality category consists of two types, *succorance-seeking* and *apathetic*. The *succorance seekers* are dependent on others and frequently seek emotional support. They maintain a medium level of role activity and life satisfaction. *Apathetic* individuals are characteristically passive and have little or no interest in their surroundings.

The last category consists of *disorganized* persons. Many have poor control over their emotions and have deteriorated thought processes. They barely maintain themselves in the community and have low or at best medium levels of life satisfaction.

These two studies indicate that personality is the pivotal factor in determining whether an individual will age successfully, and that the activity and disengagement theories, alone, are inadequate to explain successful aging. As Havighurst (1968) concludes, the relationships between levels of activities and life satisfaction are influenced by personality make-up, and particularly by the extent to which the individual remains able to integrate emotional and rational elements of the personality. People with well-integrated personalities appear to handle the adjustments of old age effectively.

Summary

Like other phases of the life cycle, the retirement years are characterized by numerous developmental tasks. Particularly significant tasks include coping with declining physical health, establishing satisfactory financial and living arrangements, adjusting to the death of a spouse, maintaining self-esteem, and adapting to a reduced income. Most experts agree that old age is also a time to reevaluate past successes and failures.

Personality theories concerning the retirement years have been developed by Erik Erikson, Robert Peck, and Else Frenkel-Brunswik. Erikson believes the key to harmonious personality growth is the successful resolution of the psychosocial crisis known as "*integrity versus despair*". Peck provides a detailed account of three adjustments required by individuals in their retirement years, referred to as *ego differentiation versus work-role preoccupation, body transcendence versus body preoccupation,* and *ego transcendence versus ego preoccupation.* Frenkel-Brunswik emphasizes the retrospective quality of the older person's personality and the nature of social interactions in old age.

Successful aging is difficult to define, although it appears that satisfactory adjustment has an inner, or psychological, aspect and an outer, socially oriented, aspect. Two theories of successful aging have been proposed, but neither fully explains successful adjustment. The *disengagement theory,* which views aging as a mutual withdrawal process between aging persons and society, is by far the more controversial. The *activity theory* directly contradicts the disengagement theory, proposing that retired people adjust successfully when they remain productive and active.

Since some retired people are satisfied with disengagement, whereas others prefer to remain active, it is evident that the dynamics of successful aging involve an additional factor, namely, personality. Three personality types ideal for successful adjustment have been identified: *mature* (constructive), *rocking-chair type* (dependent), and *armored* (defensive). Unsuccessful personality types are the *angry* (hostile) and the *self-haters*. A study by Neugarten and her associates identified similar personality types but placed more of an emphasis on role activities and the resulting levels of life satisfaction within each type. These studies indicate that personality may well be the pivotal factor in determining patterns of aging and in predicting relationships between activity levels and life satisfaction.

Not all retired persons age successfully. Some may react negatively to the pressures of later life and develop *psychogenic disorders:* psychotic reactions, neuroses, or personality disorders. Other aged persons suffer from actual brain damage, known technically as *organic brain syndrome.* Organic brain syndromes include presenile and senile disorders as well as cerebral arteriosclerosis.

Suggested Readings

1. Boyd, R. R., and Oakes, C. G., (Eds.): *Foundations of Practical Gerontology.* Columbia, South Carolina: University of South Carolina Press, 1969.

   A fairly extensive treatment of psychological and psychiatric aspects of aging can be found in Chapters 8 and 9.

2. Hendricks, J., and Hendricks, C. D.: *Aging in Mass Society: Myths and Realities.* Cambridge, Massachusetts: Winthrop Publishers, Inc., 1977.

   The psychological processes of the aged, including a description of psychological disorders, are dealt with in Chapter 6 of this text.

3. Kart, C. S., and Manard, B. B., (Eds.): *Aging in America: Readings in Social Gerontology.* New York: Alfred Publishing Co., Inc., 1976.

   Part 3 of this reader focuses on biological and psychological aspects of aging. Contributors, among others, include Robert Havighurst and James Birren.

4. Neugarten, B. L.: "Personality and the Aging Process." *The Gerontologist, 12*:9–15, 1972.

   The dynamics of personality during the later years of life are explored by this widely recognized authority on aging.

H. Armstrong-Roberts

UNIT 13
THE FAMILY

Introduction

The final stage of the family life cycle typically begins with retirement. Then comes the loss of one spouse, and the cycle concludes with the death of the other. During this stage, the aging couple continue to be "family" to their grown children, grandchildren, and in some cases, great-grandchildren. Together, husband and wife face their developmental tasks and seek to maintain family harmony (Duvall, 1977).

According to Streib (1977), people are inclined to paint a bleak and pathetic picture of aged couples as being rejected, lonely, and isolated—forgotten by their children and other relatives. To be sure, there are people who have never married, have never had children, or have outlived their kin and hence are lonely in old age. In other instances, parent-child relations have been strained for a lifetime, a situation that makes it unrealistic to expect a reconciliation when the parent is old and needs assistance. For the most part, however, the image of socially isolated aged parents is inaccurate and misleading (Nye and Berardo, 1973).

Like any other period in the family cycle, old age requires that certain adjustments be made. Of particular importance are adjustments associated with marital relations, living arrangements, kin relations, grandparenthood, and loss of a spouse.

MARITAL RELATIONS

According to one writer (Adams, 1975), the shift of focus away from children and the incorporation of the husband into the home give married life among the elderly its particular character. Physical, economic, social, and emotional factors will affect marital relations at this time. However, how successfully the husband adapts to the retirement role seems to be especially important.

Research evidence supports the idea that most marriages are characterized by satisfaction and not disenchantment during the retirement years. Stinnett and his associates (1972) interviewed 408 husbands and wives belonging to senior citizens clubs and found that most couples had extremely favorable perceptions of their marriages. A majority (54.9 per cent) felt the current phase of their marriage was the happiest they had experienced. Nearly half the respondents believed that most marriages improve over time and that companionship and honesty towards one another enhance a couple's relationship. Other important qualities of marriage mentioned by the respondents included respect, sharing common interests, and love. The belief that shared interests enhance marital relations during the retirement years is also stressed by Peterson (1973).

Another study (Rollins and Feldman, 1970) supports the claim that marriages among the elderly are quite satisfactory. Ninety-four per cent of the husbands and 88 per cent of the wives studied felt that their relationships were harmonious most of the time. Relatively few

Figure 13–1. Most retired couples report considerable marital satisfaction rather than disenchantment.

Annon Photo Features
© Marcel Cognac

(6 per cent of the husbands and 10 per cent of the wives) said they had negative feelings about their relationship more often than once or twice a month. Furthermore, 66 per cent of the husbands and 82 per cent of the wives reported that they found the present stage of the family life cycle "very satisfying".

Yet, while these and other findings suggest that marriage is satisfying during the retirement years, it is important to realize that the couples interviewed may have had a previous history of harmonious family relations. In this sense, marital adjustment in later years is a reflection of the adjustments worked out earlier (Nye and

Berardo, 1973). For those who had marital difficulties earlier in life, problems may be compounded by retirement. Blacks and couples with inadequate incomes, low education, and physical disabilities are most susceptible to marital dissatisfaction during old age (Duvall, 1977).

It is important for the couple to adjust to new household routines during the final stage of the marriage cycle. When the husband retires and spends most of his time in the household, he frequently becomes aware of new responsibilities and expectations. For example, husband and wife become coequals in authority and share certain tasks. Also, the objective of family living is no longer economic productivity but rather the personal development and happiness of its members (Burgess et al., 1971). The husband's involvement in household chores may necessitate a change in the wife's domestic orientation as well as her self-image:

> Since her husband's new activities have blurred the traditional distinction between the male and female roles, the woman can no longer view her major role primarily as good housekeeper and homemaker. Both men and women who had clearly and rigidly defined their preretirement role in a predominantly instrumental fashion that strongly differentiated husband's and wife's activities, now move toward a common area of identity in role activities—an area that emphasizes sharing and cooperation, where similar expressive qualities such as love, understanding, companionship, and compatibility become the most important things they can both give in marriage. These non-sex-differentiated supportive roles that demand expressive, rather than instrumental qualities, appear well adapted for the personality system of both the husband and wife in retirement.
>
> (Lipman, 1962, pp. 484–485)

According to Duvall (1977), household responsibilities during the retirement years are assumed on the basis of interest, ability, and strength. The husband routinely tackles some chores, the wife others, and both assume those tasks they enjoy doing as a team. In the case of illness, or when one of the partners is away, the other typically takes over because of the familiarity with the routines established. Decisions are usually jointly made and the couple collectively assumes authority. Husband and wife are accountable to each other and to the realities of the situation at hand.

As far as sexual activity is concerned, it is fairly well recognized that there is a decline with advanced years (Jacobson, 1974). However, many elderly persons enjoy sex on a regular basis. Decreases in sexual activity appear to originate not so much from the aging process as from social and emotional problems (Young, 1975), although physical illness, the side effects of certain medications, and other health problems also have an adverse effect on the sex drive (Butler and Lewis, 1973).

Some members of our society regard the elderly as asexual, while others have developed a number of cruel misconceptions concerning the sex lives of older people. For example, old men are thought of as being either impotent or "dirty old men", and post-menopausal women who are interested in sex are viewed as "frustrated old women". Those elderly people who claim to be sexually active may be seen as either morally perverse or boastful and deceptive (Aiken, 1978; Leaf, 1975).

Among both men and women, those who have enjoyed long and recurrent sex lives without lengthy interruptions are more likely to remain sexually active longer than those whose history is different (Hendricks and Hendricks, 1977). On the average, the rate of coitus for married couples decreases from 1.8 times per week at 50 years to 1.3 times per week at age 60 and 0.7 times per week at age 70 (Kinsey et al., 1948).

Most research indicates that elderly men are more sexually active than elderly women (Pfeiffer et al., 1970). Approximately 70 per cent are still sexually active at age 70, and 50 per cent are active at age 75 (Feigenbaum, 1977). As we learned in Unit 7, men, as they grow older, fear impotency, a condition that may be caused by anxiety or fatigue. By age 70, there are many men who believe they are impotent because they expect to be by this time; this belief in itself may lead to impotency. The rate of impotency increases from approximately 18 per cent at age 60 to 27 per cent at age 70 (Kinsey et al., 1948). Impotency, as Masters and Johnson (1966) point out, presents its share of stress and frustration to the male. "Once impotent under any circumstances, many males withdraw voluntarily from any coital activity rather than face the ego-shattering experience of repeated episodes of sexual inadequacy" (pp. 269–270).

It is reported that older women are less sexually active than older men, but this may be the result of factors other than differences in sex drive. For example, a large percentage of women are widows. Also, since there are more older women than older men, the male has

TABLE 13–1 FREQUENCY (IN PER CENT) OF SEXUAL INTERCOURSE IN LATER LIFE

Group	Number	None	Once a month	Once a week	2–3 Times a week	More than 3 times a week
Men						
46–50	43	0	5	62	26	7
51–55	41	5	29	49	17	0
56–60	61	7	38	44	11	0
61–65	54	20	43	30	7	0
66–71	62	24	48	26	2	0
Total	**261**	**12**	**34**	**41**	**12**	**1**
Women						
46–50	43	14	26	39	21	0
51–55	41	20	41	32	5	2
56–60	48	42	27	25	4	2
61–65	44	61	29	5	5	0
66–71	55	73	16	11	0	0
Total	**231**	**44**	**27**	**22**	**6**	**1**

From: Pfeiffer, E., Verwoerdt, A., and Davis, G. C.: "Sexual behavior in middle life." Amer. J. Psychiatry *128*, 10:1264, 1972.

a wider range of choice, and a widow may be less able to find a suitable partner than a widower. Furthermore, it is considered more socially acceptable for an older man to marry a younger woman than for an older woman to marry a younger man. Society also frowns on a woman's extramarital sexual activity more than on a man's (Aiken, 1977).

In one study of the sexual lives of older women (Christenson and Gagnon, 1965), it was found that by age 60, 70 per cent of the respondents were still sexually active; by age 65, 50 per cent engaged in sexual activities. Twenty-five per cent of the 65-year-olds also reported that they frequently masturbated.

These findings suggest that although sexual activity declines during the retirement years, it by no means ceases. Most elderly people are capable of enjoying sexual pleasure, and in some cases, the pleasure may actually increase (Lobsenz, 1975). Sexual relations can serve as a cohesive force in older marriages, and their continuation is considered desirable. When sex terminates, the reasons should be thoroughly evaluated just as they are with younger couples. Some forms of sexual dysfunction among the elderly are responsive to treatment and counseling, and the aged can usually benefit from both. Gratifying numbers of elderly people have been restored to some level of sexual activity, and others have been assisted in adjusting to their limitations (Jacobson, 1974).

LIVING ARRANGEMENTS

One of the more difficult decisions confronting the elderly couple is whether to remain in the home in which children were reared or to move. Suitable living arrangements, whether they be existing residences or new locations, are quite important to the elderly because they spend so much time at home. It is estimated that people over age 65 spend 80 to 90 per cent of their lives in their homes (Hansen, 1971).

Judging from the statistics, retired couples prefer not to move. In 1974, the U.S. Bureau of the Census reported that approximately four out of every five Americans 65 years or older remained in the same residence. Montgomery (1965) conducted a study to analyze why older couples prefer not to move. The reasons cited by the 512 respondents included an unwillingness to face adjustment problems brought on by moving, declining health, and a limited income. Eighty-one per cent of the people had lived in their present home for ten or more years, 78 per cent had positive feelings toward their neighborhood, and 76 per cent liked their homes a great deal. Thus, unlike younger couples, who are rather mobile, elderly couples are affected by numerous anchoring variables.

Today, approximately a quarter of the elderly live in rural areas, a third live in inner cities, and another 40 per cent reside in older working-class neighborhoods on the fringes of central cities (Hendricks and Hendricks, 1977). While almost 70 per cent of all heads of households over age 65 own their own homes (Brotman, 1972), these

---

LIFE AFTER 65: TO MOVE OR NOT TO MOVE?

Two-thirds of Americans over age 65 own their own homes, but with the family gone, the house may be too large, too expensive, and too difficult to maintain.

Therefore, the question, "to move or not to move," looms large. Especially when you consider that a major share of retirement income goes into housing costs.

Most older people prefer not to live with their child's family, and studies have shown that you may well stay healthier and live longer and happier if you maintain your own home, whatever it may be. . .

Think twice about tearing up your roots; selling an old house can be a devastating emotional experience. . . .

If you are serious about making a change, spend some time researching the possibilities open to you. Don't be hasty. Visit the areas you think you might want to live in, get the feel for the new community. . .

Also, think through the specific type of housing you would prefer: a small house, a co-op apartment, a condominium, a mobile home, or a "retirement" community. . .

Questions to ask before deciding to move (add up the pluses and minuses):

Do my present home and community suit my notion of a good life in the future?

Do I now have convenient access to transportation, shopping, medical care, church, entertainment and recreation, educational and cultural facilities of interest to me?

Will I be embarrassed to live in my present home on retirement income?

Does the old house impose too much of a workload on me?

Should I move for health reasons?

Would I be able to adjust to a new situation at my age?

How much will I really miss my old friends?

Will I make new friends as easily as I used to?

What can I gain by moving—socially, economically, or otherwise?

What could I lose by making the change?

If the move doesn't work out, can I afford to relocate again?

Jack Gourlay: "Life After 65: To Move or Not to Move?" *Wisconsin State Journal*, March 6, 1974.

---

residences are mostly older and some are run-down. Butler (1975) stresses that the elderly homeowner does not necessarily enjoy the advantages associated with home ownership, such as substantial equity, low housing costs in relation to income, and sufficient capital assets to move to a new residence if desired. On the contrary, the elderly couple may face a number of problems, including low equity, rising property taxes, and excessive utility and maintenance costs. Those who live in deteriorating neighborhoods are often trapped there because declining property values make it financially impossible to sell and move elsewhere—even if a buyer could be found.

Some retired couples decide to move to new locations. For those who do want to move yet do not wish to own or rent a house, several alternatives exist: mobile homes, senior citizen hotels, and retirement communities.

Mobile homes are becoming quite popular among the elderly; it is estimated that over half the residents at some trailer courts are retired (Kalish, 1975). Living quarters are cramped, but many enjoy the independent living mobile homes offer, not to mention the low cost. Contrary to the belief of many, mobile-home owners move no more frequently than the rest of the population. In 1970, mobile-

INSTITUTIONAL CARE FOR THE ELDERLY

When older people are disabled or can no longer take care of themselves, institutional care may be required. Although only 5 per cent of the aged are institutionalized (approximately one million people), the population of these facilities is disproportionately old. Eighty-eight per cent of nursing home patients and virtually all residents of homes for the aged are over 65, the average age being 82. Most of the residents of nursing homes will die there (Gottesman, 1977; Whitworth, 1975).

According to Kalish (1977), institutions for care of the elderly can be grouped into three categories of ownership or control. One type is public ownership, in which the institution is owned and operated by a city, county, or state government. Another type is ownership by a voluntary organization such as a social or fraternal organization (Masonic Order, Moose Lodge), a religious group, or a union or professional group (facilities for retired teachers, actors, and so forth). A third type is private ownership, often referred to as proprietary. Proprietary nursing homes are run for a profit; increasingly, they are under corporate, rather than individual, ownership. Of the three types, the private institution serves the largest number of elderly people.

In the traditional nursing home, the aged are patients as well as residents. Typically, rooms are shared, preventing their occupants from having much privacy or doing much personal decorating. Many nursing homes have a recreation room for those not confined to bed, and some offer social activities, but most residents occupy their time by watching television or reading. The majority of residents in nursing homes are single, their spouses having died before them (Leslie and Leslie, 1977).

In the past, nursing homes have received a fair amount of criticism, most of which was focused on administrative inefficiency and depersonalized treatment of the residents. Another criticism is that few long-term care facilities provide any intellectual or sensory stimulation for those who live in them (Kalish, 1975). Gottesman (1977) believes that nursing homes are replaying the tragedy that mental hospitals have been trying to overcome—the tragedy of people with years filled with nothing to do. He suggests that nursing care, which only fills small parts of each day, be distributed so that more individual and group activities can be planned for the aged. Such activities can bring life back to the residents and also tie the nursing home more closely into the larger community.

Concerned parties have combined forces to improve standards of living in nursing homes. Increased professionalism, accreditation, and certification have upgraded many institutions and closed down those deemed inadequate in meeting the needs of the elderly. Licensing laws have begun to include standards for nursing as well as other care and to require that certain minimum qualifications for personnel be met. In 1972, states were required by the Federal government to establish minimum standards of training and experience for nursing home administrators (Lenzer, 1977). In order that the elderly receive the best possible care and living arrangements, continued investigation and reform is needed. At the very least, the overall operation of nursing homes needs to be made more accountable (Gottesman and Bourestom, 1974).

home firms were manufacturing 450,000 units a year, approximately four times the number produced in the early 1960s (Butler, 1975).

Senior citizen hotels are usually older hotels or apartment houses located in an urban setting. Among the reasons for the popularity of the senior citizen hotel are the low cost, the accessibility to the city, the independent life-style offered, and the fact that such an establishment does not carry the stigma of a home for the aged. The buildings and their management are not supervised by any state authority. Consequently, health codes and fire regulations for senior citizen hotels are more lax than those for nursing homes operating under state laws, a fact that does not always work to the best interests of the elderly who reside there (Knopf, 1975).

Retirement communities, originally established in Florida, California, and other states with warm climates, are also increasing in popularity. Although an appreciable number of retired couples are moving into these communities, many cannot financially afford to do so (Golant, 1975). People under 50 are not allowed to purchase homes in the average retirement community (homes are typically purchased on a long-term payment plan), although rules vary from community to community (Kalish, 1975). In many villages, there are swimming pools, golf courses, and tennis courts as well as organized social programs. The economic and physical segregation of retirement communities protects retired couples from street crime and other hazards of city life (Leslie and Leslie, 1977). In 1973, it cost a minimum of $6000 a year for a single person and $8000 for a couple to live in an average retirement community (Butler, 1975).

KIN RELATIONS

Retired persons are likely to keep in touch with whatever kin they have. While for some this may mean considerable contact with aging brothers and sisters, more often than not the focus of kin relations is on children and grandchildren. It seems as though "separate but near" is the rule of residence during the retirement years (Adams, 1975).

Relations with children may be influenced by whatever care the aging parent needs. Through a great portion of the life cycle, help flowed mainly from parents to children. This flow gradually reverses itself as parents begin to get old and feeble. Even if they are financially independent, they may need a great deal of attention and care.

Retired people tend to live near their children, although this is more true in urban environments than in rural settings (Adams, 1967; Sussman, 1965). Research reveals that many retired couples live within a half-hour's drive of at least one child and see their offspring fairly regularly (Shanas et al., 1968), although the actual extent of interaction between the elderly and their adult children may be influenced by social class. In an exhaustive study of 2500 elderly individuals in the United States, Britain, and Denmark (Shanas et al., 1968), the following observations were made:

> Middle class, white collar persons in both Britain and the United States are more likely than working class persons to have only a few children and to live at a greater distance from their children. The married children of middle-class families, both sons and daughters, tend to live apart from their parents, not only in separate households, but also at a greater distance from them. In some degree this physical separation of parents and children is compensated for by more overnight visiting on the part of white collar families. The average old person of white collar background maintains strong relationships with his children. He is more likely than his blue collar counterpart, however, to see his children infrequently or not at all. In the case of white collar parents, the patterns of help in old age flow from parents to children; in the case of blue collar parents, they flow from children to parents.
>
> (Shanas et al., 1968, p. 256)

Hendricks and Hendricks (1977) add that there is a tendency for kin relationships to be focused more closely on the female side of the family. Daughters, more than sons, appear to be willing to suppress their value conflicts with their aged parents so that participation in activities and the sharing of resources can take place. Interestingly, there seems to be a trend among middle-aged couples to establish closer ties to the wife's family than to the husband's (Troll, 1971).

The emotional support given to aged parents is more critical to their psychological wellbeing than financial support (Streib, 1965). Furthermore, a large percentage of retired persons refuse to accept financial assistance from their children:

> Older people want to be financially independent. A majority of them feel that if an older person has been unable to save enough to make such independence possible in later life, the government should assume responsibility for his support through various income maintenance programs. A substantial group of sons and daughters (about two of every five) feel that the support of older people is their duty. What older people seem to want most from their children is love and affection.

HARMONIOUS THREE-GENERATIONAL LIVING

Approximately 8 per cent of American families are true three-generational households (Troll, 1971). Although such a living arrangement may bring disharmony and confusion, numerous husbands and wives have discovered ways to promote intergenerational happiness and stability. The following suggestions are offered by Duvall (1954):

1. Develop together a clear understanding of financial, household, and other responsibilities so that each one may know just what is expected of him or her.

2. Be reasonable in your expectations of one another. No one is perfect. Everyone makes mistakes from time to time. Perfectionists are hard to live with in any family.

3. Make some provision for protecting the personal property of each member of the family. It may be little more than a closet or a bureau of his or her own, but everyone welcomes some place for his things that will be respected as his alone.

4. Respect each person's need for privacy. It is not only the great who need their "islands of solitude," as Adlai Stevenson suggested. The elderly, the adolescent, and all the rest of us from time to time desire undisturbed privacy. We have the right to open our own mail, answer our own phone calls, and make our own friends with some sense of privacy.

5. Encourage each member of the household to develop his own talents and to pursue his own interests in his own way. This means you, too.

6. Jointly plan for whole-family activities so that each may have a share in deciding what is to be done and what part he or she will play in the affair.

7. As disagreements arise, and they will from time to time, take the time to hear the other(s) out. Listen well enough to grasp what the situation means to those who differ from you. Respond to their feelings as well as to the "sense" of the situation.

8. Unify the larger family unit, sharing the household's hospitality by celebrations and rituals that bring the family closer together in its own most meaningful ways.

9. Take a positive attitude toward your joint living arrangement by being appreciative of the benefits derived from sharing the household, instead of merely bemoaning the sacrifices involved.

10. Gain some perspective by realizing that through the ages families have lived more often together than in the little separate family units more popular today.

(pp. 323–324)

Apparently many older people feel that to ask their sons or daughters for financial support would threaten the affectional relationship between the generations.

(Shanas, 1961, p. 38)

Some aged couples live with their children, especially when independent living in a separate location is no longer feasible. Statistics tell us that approximately one third of all people who have living children reside with them, although such joint households are usually without grandchildren. The proportion of elderly persons sharing households is higher for women than men, and significantly higher for widowed, divorced, and separated parents than for married parents (Bell, 1975; Robins, 1962).

According to Blood (1969), the decision of whether to bring an aged parent into the home rests on both practical and personal factors, including how satisfactory the alternative facilities are and what spare living arrangements are available in the home. Of course, the relationships that exist between the aged parent and each family member deserve critical examination. The daughter or daughter-in-law faces an especially formidable task, since she is called upon to provide most of the attention, care, and sociability. For both generations, the merging of households requires careful planning, cooperation, and understanding.

GRANDPARENTHOOD

An important family role that many retired couples assume is grandparenthood. The increased life expectancy of the aged, combined with the earlier age of marriage of their children and a shorter child-rearing period, have exposed more middle-aged and retired couples than ever before to the role of grandparent (Nye and Berardo, 1973; Troll, 1971).

The grandchild typically establishes a bond of common interest between the grandparents and the younger couple (Burgess et al., 1971). Becoming a grandparent also adds a new dimension to the lives of retirees, and, in most instances, this dimension is a positive one. When intergenerational differences develop over such issues as child discipline, or when grandparents are exploited for babysitting services, some negativism may be reported (Lopata, 1973; Neugarten and Weinstein, 1968).

The role of grandparent seems to have special significance for the grandmother. Cavan (1962) goes so far as to describe grandparenthood as primarily a maternal experience, largely because of the woman's dominant role in child-rearing. Although most men enjoy grandparenthood, grandmothers assume a more active role right from the very beginning:

Grandmothers frequently care for the new mother, her baby, and her family during the immediate postnatal period, making the grandmother the person who first diapers, bathes, and otherwise cares for the baby outside the brief intervals while the mother does so. After she returns to her own home, she is permitted and, indeed, is expected to continue a grandmotherly concern for the mother's well-being and the grandchild's care. . . . The adjustments made by grandmothers do not change appreciably as they grow older. Unlike their husbands, they do not have to cope with the threat of retirement. They continue essentially the same roles right on into old age. Their care of grandchildren usually is welcomed, and they can slow the pace down gradually as their own physical and emotional needs dictate.

(Leslie, 1973, pp. 674–675)

Grandfathers appear to become more involved with their grand-children after retirement. Without jobs to claim most of their energy, many are able to identify with their grandchildren, and some want to spend more time with them. They begin to visit with them more, take them for walks, buy them gifts, and participate in their overall care (Leslie, 1973).

One of the more comprehensive investigations of grandparent-hood was undertaken by Neugarten and Weinstein (1968). Studying 70 sets of middle-class grandparents (46 were maternal grandparents and 24 were paternal), the researchers discovered that a sizeable number expressed comfort, satisfaction, and pleasure over their role (see Table 13–2). One third of the couples had difficulty adjusting

TABLE 13–2   EASE OF ROLE PERFORMANCE, SIGNIFICANCE OF ROLE, AND STYLE OF GRANDPARENTING IN 70 GRANDMOTHERS AND 70 GRANDFATHERS

	Grandmothers (N = 70) N	Grandfathers (N = 70) N
A. *Ease of role performance:*		
1. Comfortable—pleasant	41	43
2. Difficulty—discomfort	25	20
(Insufficient data)	4	7
Total	**70**	**70**
B. *Significance of the grandparent role:*		
1. Biological renewal and/or continuity	29[a]	16[a]
2. Emotional self-fulfillment	13	19
3. Resource person to child	3	8
4. Vicarious achievement through child	3	3
5. Remote; little effect on the self	19	20
(Insufficient data)	3	4
Total	**70**	**70**
C. *Style of grandparenting:*		
1. The Formal	22	23
2. The Fun-Seeking	20	17
3. The Parent Surrogate	10[a]	0[a]
4. The Reservoir of Family Wisdom	1	4
5. The Distant Figure	13	20
(Insufficient data)	4	6
Total	**70**	**70**

[a]The difference between grandmothers and grandfathers in this category is reliable at or beyond the .05 level (frequencies were tested for differences of proportions, using the Yates correction for continuity).

From: Neugarten, B. L., and Weinstein, K. K.: "The changing American grandparent." *In* B. L. Neugarten (Ed.): *Middle Age and Aging: A Reader in Social Psychology.* Chicago: University of Chicago Press, 1968.

to grandparenthood; most of this group reported negative feelings such as resentment over babysitting.

Although the role of grandparent has multiple meanings for each person, Neugarten and Weinstein (1968) were able to group the meanings given by their subjects into five principal categories. First, grandparenthood may be a source of *biological renewal* or *biological continuity* with the future. Statements such as "It's through my grandchildren that I feel young again" or "It's through these children that I see my life going on into the future" embody this frame of mind. Second, grandparenthood affords individuals the opportunity to succeed in a new emotional role, with the implication that they feel themselves to be better grandparents than they were parents. In this sense, grandparenthood offers a certain vindication of the life history by providing *emotional self-fulfillment* in ways parenthood had not. As one grandfather remarked, "I can be, and I can do for my grandchildren things I could never do for my own kids. I was too busy with my business to enjoy my kids, but my grandchildren are different. Now I have the time to be with them." (pp. 282–283)

A third meaning of grandparenthood is that it provides the individual with a new role of teacher or *resource person*. Grandparents gain satisfaction by contributing to the grandchild's welfare, either through financial aid or by the grandparents' unique life experience.

Figure 13–2. Grandparenthood adds a new dimension to the lives of retirees. (Photo courtesy of Nancy G. Turner.)

Fourth, grandparenthood may represent an extension of the self in that the grandchild will *accomplish vicariously* that which neither the grandparents nor their first generation offspring could achieve.

Finally, grandparenthood for some may imply a sense of *remoteness* or psychological distance from their kin. Individuals who reported this feeling acknowledged that grandparenthood had relatively little effect on their lives. The causes for this feeling of remoteness varied among the men and women studied. Some of the grandfathers stated that the young age of their grandchildren had something to do with their feelings of psychological distance. For instance, one stated, "My grand-daughter is just a baby, and I don't even feel like a grandfather yet. Wait until she's older—maybe I'll feel different then." (p. 283) Most of the grandmothers reporting remoteness were working or were active in community affairs and reported not having much time to devote to grandparenthood. Other grandmothers who felt remote from their grandchildren attempted to explain the feeling by referring to strained relations with their adult children.

STYLES OF GRANDPARENTING

Somewhat independent of the significance of grandparenthood is the issue of *style* in enacting the role of grandmother or grandfather. Neugarten and Weinstein (1968) have identified five major styles of grandparenting:

1. The *Formal* are those who follow what they regard as the proper and prescribed role for grandparents. Although they like to provide special treats and indulgences for the grandchild, and although they may occasionally take on a minor service such as baby-sitting, they maintain clearly demarcated lines between parenting and grandparenting, and they leave parenting strictly to the parent. They maintain a constant interest in the grandchild but are careful not to offer advice on childrearing.

2. The *Fun Seeker* is the grandparent whose relation to the grandchild is characterized by informality and playfulness. He joins the child in specific activities for the specific purpose of having fun, somewhat as if he were the child's playmate. Grandchildren are viewed as a source of leisure activity, as an item of "consumption" rather than "production," or as a source of self-indulgence. The relationship is one in which authority lines—either with the grandchild or with the parent—are irrelevant. The emphasis here is on mutuality of satisfaction rather than on providing treats for the grandchild. Mutuality imposes a latent demand that both parties derive fun from the relationship.

3. The *Surrogate Parent* occurs only, as might have been anticipated, for grandmothers in this group. It comes about by initiation on the part of the younger generation, that is, when the young mother works and the grandmother assumes the actual caretaking responsibility for the child.

4. The *Reservoir of Family Wisdom* represents a distinctly authoritarian patricentered relationship in which the grandparent—in the rare occasions on which it occurs in this sample, it is the grandfather—is the dispenser of special skills or resources. Lines of authority are distinct, and the young parents maintain and emphasize their subordinate positions, sometimes with and sometimes without resentment.

5. The *Distant Figure* is the grandparent who emerges from the shadows on holidays and on special ritual occasions such as Christmas and birthdays. Contact with the grandchild is fleeting and infrequent, a fact which distinguishes this style from *Formal*. This grandparent is benevolent in stance but essentially distant and remote from the child's life, a somewhat intermittent St. Nicholas.

(pp. 283–284)

In the minds of many, grandparenthood is pictured as a unique generational relationship that exists primarily between very young grandchildren and their grandparents. Unfortunately, very little research has concentrated on the relationship between adolescent grandchildren and their grandparents. Kalish (1975), however, suggests that a closeness or affinity frequently exists between the two and hypothesizes circumstances shared in common that might promote such an affinity. First, both are age groups adjacent to the age group that dominates society, yet often neither has much power over or influence on the decision-makers. Second, both tend to be reminded of their nonproductive roles (at least the retired elderly and the adolescents who are not yet employed), and both may perceive themselves as "taking from society without putting anything back in" (although the potential of the adolescent to be productive in the future is denied the elderly). Third, both are viewed as having a leisurely life: education and retirement are seen as pleasure, not as work or boredom. Fourth, both live with their time quite unstructured. The time structure that does exist for the two is seldom perceived by middle-agers. Fifth, both are frequently viewed as being inadequately educated, the adolescents not yet educated by experience and the elderly lacking more formal education. Finally, both are seen as relatively poor and consequently vulnerable and weak. Yet, in spite of these similarities, Kalish (1975) notes, there are tensions between the young and the old, largely based on the differing needs and values of the two age groups.

DEATH OF THE MARRIAGE PARTNER

The death of a spouse is an especially severe crisis during the retirement years. Although the loss of a beloved marriage partner can occur at any age, the shock is devastating for the elderly person. For the surviving spouse, the remaining years of life are usually spent alone, or at least without a marriage partner (Burgess, et al., 1971). Of course, the emotional aftermath of a spouse's death will depend on the state of the marriage before the loss (Hendricks and Hendricks, 1977).

Statistically speaking, there are more widows than widowers in the United States, and the discrepancy is continually growing greater (see Table 13–3). According to the Bureau of the Census, widows in the United States outnumbered widowers by approximately four to one in 1970. There are approximately 10 million widows in the United States, and it is estimated that this number will increase by more than 100,000 each year. Widows live, on the average, 18.5 years after their husbands die, whereas widowers, on the average, survive 13.5 years after the death of their wives (Carter and Glick, 1970).

At least two reasons account for the growing number of widows in the United States. First, mortality rates are lower for women than for men; consequently more women survive to advanced years. Second, wives are typically younger than their husbands at marriage

TABLE 13–3   NUMBER OF WIDOWERS AND WIDOWS IN THE UNITED STATES, 1890–1970

Year	Widowers	Widows
1890	815,000	2,155,000
1900	1,178,000	2,718,000
1910	1,471,000	3,176,000
1920	1,758,000	3,918,000
1930	2,025,000	4,734,000
1940	2,144,000	5,700,000
1950	2,296,000	6,967,000
1960	2,112,000	8,064,000
1970	2,103,000	9,625,000

Source: U. S. Bureau of the Census: *Statistical Abstract of the United States: 1970.* Washington, D. C.: U. S. Government Printing Office.

and thus are likely to outlive their husbands (Nye and Berardo, 1973).

Since bereavement and its adjustments are discussed in detail in Unit 15, only a few remarks on the subject are made here. Adjustment to life without one's spouse places great demands on both widowers and widows, but widows may have the greater problem. Because women are less likely to remarry, they may become more socially isolated than men and consequently more depressed (Blau, 1973). Their financial status is affected in varying degrees by the loss of at least some of their husbands' retirement income (Harvey and Bahr, 1974), and many widows are forced to live on incomes well below the national average (Berardo, 1968).

It appears that those who adjust most successfully to loss of a marriage partner are fairly autonomous, enjoy continuing personal interests, are economically secure, possess a comforting philosophy of life, maintain concern for others, and have meaningful friendships that have lasted over the years (Duvall, 1977).

Summary

The family life cycle of old age typically begins with retirement, is followed by the loss of one spouse, and ends with the death of the other. Most experts agree that the keys to successful aging among retired couples are harmonious family relations, continued activity, and comfortable disengagement.

Most retired couples report considerable satisfaction with their marriages. After retirement, the husband frequently assumes new domestic responsibilities, and the involvement in household chores brings about changes in his domestic orientation and self-image as well as his wife's.

It is generally recognized that sexual activity declines with age but by no means ceases. Decreased sexual activity appears to originate not so much from the aging process as from social and emotional difficulties. Those couples who have had active sex lives in the past are likely to remain sexually active during the retirement years.

Generally speaking, older men are more sexually active than older women, although we learned that his may be owing to factors other than differences in the sex drive.

Most retired couples do not want to change their residence, primarily because they do not wish to face adjustment difficulties associated with moving. Declining health and limited incomes are other anchoring variables. Alternative living arrangements for the elderly include mobile homes, senior citizen hotels, and retirement communities. When the elderly are afflicted with a disability or can no longer care for themselves, institutional care may be required.

Kin relations for most retired couples focus on their children and grandchildren. Many aged people live near their children and interact rather frequently, although this is more true in urban environments than in rural settings. As far as family relationships are concerned, the emotional support given to aged parents is especially important.

Grandchildren add a new dimension to the lives of middle-aged and retired couples, although grandparenthood is frequently seen as a maternal experience. Granfathers typically become more involved with their grandchildren after retirement. Grandparenthood may have numerous meanings to the individual, such as a sense of biological renewal or continuity, emotional self-fulfillment, the chance to serve as a resource person, vicarious experience, or a sense of remoteness. Five styles of grandparent have been identified: formal, fun-seeker, surrogate parent, reservoir of family wisdom, and distant figure.

Adjusting to death of the marriage partner is an especially difficult task during the retirement years. There are more widows than widowers in the United States, owing to lower mortality rates among women and the fact that wives are typically younger than their husbands at marriage. While both widows and widowers have to make numerous adjustments, it is generally agreed that widows face a greater complexity of tasks.

Suggested Readings

1. Kalish, R. A., (Ed.): *The Later Years: Social Applications of Gerontology.* Monterey, California: Brooks/Cole Publishing Company, 1977.

   Social institutions and the elderly is the focal point in Part 7 of this book, while Part 10 concentrates on institutional living.

2. Kart, C. S., and Manard, B. B., (Eds.): *Aging in America: Readings in Social Gerontology.* New York: Alfred Publishers, 1976.

   Discussion of the retired couple's living environment represents a strength in this reader. The editors have also collected a diverse selection of articles on institutional care.

3. Neugarten, B. L., (Ed.): *Middle Age and Aging: A Reader in Social Psychology.* Chicago: University of Chicago Press, 1968.

   Part 5 of this reader is devoted to family relationships and includes treatment of such topics as aging and sexual behavior, grandparenthood, and multi-generational families.

4. Puner, M.: *To the Good Long Life: What We Know About Growing Old.* New York: Universe Books, 1974.

> *A highly readable account of the retirement years and the adjustments needed to attain life satisfaction. Puner devotes considerable attention to the retired couple's lifestyle and the nature of changing kin relationships, among other topics.*

Horst Schäfer
Photo Trends

UNIT 14
RETIREMENT

Introduction

Retirement (generally in the sixties) from the world of work is a developmental task that can be viewed in a variety of ways—as a process, as a social role, or as a phase of life. Regardless of the perspective from which it is viewed, however, one thing is certain—retirement is a complex social phenomenon that touches the life of almost everyone (Atchley, 1976; Epstein and Murray, 1968).

Few issues in the field of gerontology arouse so much emotion, so much disagreement, and so strong a sense of injustice as the issue of retirement (Kalish, 1977). Some perceive compulsory retirement as a curtailment of an individual's rights. Requiring people to leave their jobs, relinquish what is often a meaningful and important role, and accept a lowered income, all because they have reached the age of 65, may constitute one of the greatest injustices of our time. When this happens, the retired person is covertly categorized as a second-class citizen, regardless of individual abilities. Paradoxically, federal laws that prohibit age discrimination do not offer protection to people who are 65 or older. For many, retirement is the first "insult" of aging and represents tangible evidence that one is publicly recognized as "elderly" (Manion, 1976).

Yet, there are those who look forward to retirement eagerly, having waited years to be free to do the things they have always wanted to do, without having to go to work each day (Leslie and Leslie, 1977). These individuals would be most upset if the option of retirement were removed (Kalish, 1977).

According to Manion (1976), retirement is a phenomenon of modern industrial society. At present, there are more than 21 million Americans over the age of 65 who are classified as retired. The proportion of retirees in the general population will steadily increase. If present trends continue, there will be approximately 33 million retired Americans in the year 2000 (Aiken, 1978). Yet, at the beginning of this century, work filled almost the whole of the individual's adult life. By the 1950s, however, most people were in retirement after the age of 65 (Irelan and Bond, 1974). It has been estimated that in 1900 the labor force participation rate of men 65 years of age and older was 68.4 per cent; in 1960 this figure had dropped to 30.5 per cent and by 1970 it had fallen to 25.0 per cent. Now, as we approach the 1980s, the age of retirement is edging downward toward 60 (Jaffe, 1972).

Thus, the retirement period for most people is growing longer. Presently, the average life expectancy after retirement is 15.3 years (Ullmann, 1976). However, by the turn of the century, it is expected that this figure will rise to 25 years (Entine, 1976). Thompson and Streib (1969), acknowledging the fact that life expectancy after retirement is increasing, have divided the retirement years into two stages, early and later retirement. Early retirement lasts from age 65 to age 74, and later retirement is the period from age 75 onward.

THE SCOPE OF RETIREMENT

Retirement has numerous dimensions and consequently can be defined in several ways (Carp, 1972). The most inclusive definition of a retired person is, "an individual who is not employed full time annually and who receives some kind of retirement pension from previous years of job service" (Epstein and Murray, 1968). Atchley (1976) points out, however, that some individuals—such as career military personnel—finish their terms of employment, only to begin another full-time job. Thus, even though such individuals draw pensions and are likely to receive other retirement benefits, they cannot be classified as being retired. Similarly, numerous older workers lose their jobs and cannot find another. Until they reach the minimum age, they are unable to draw retirement pensions and consequently are classified as unemployed rather than retired.

To stop working in a work-oriented society is a milestone event, and it may be a sensitive process (Bischof, 1976). Many view retirement as a turning point in adult development, since it marks the shift from the middle years to old age. Retirement may be seen as a transition point, similar in many respects to the transition point at puberty but reflecting the fact that social factors are more important in adulthood than the biological factors that are so critical in the younger years (Kimmel, 1974).

Simpson (1969) also refers to retirement as the concluding stage of the occupational cycle. Retirement is a stage of life, likely to be experienced by most employed individuals. In past decades, workers who were self-employed could establish their own age of retirement, although ceasing to work was usually a luxury only the wealthy could enjoy. Workers of yesteryear also had more options available to them when they retired. For example, older workers could alternate from full-time to part-time employment and could turn over some responsibility for the shop or farm to a relative or a younger associate. They were also able to slow their work pace or switch to less demanding types of work. Yet these work-related options are normally not open to people such as a factory worker, civil-service employee, school-teacher, or executive, who must abide by organizational regulations that render retirement inescapable for most workers (Kalish, 1975; Simpson, 1969).

THE DECISION TO RETIRE

It is true that some individuals retire from work voluntarily, whether because of a desire for greater leisure, being needed at home, poor health, or job dissatisfaction. For many others, retirement is not a voluntary matter but rather the decision of employers, who often make retirement policies on the basis of consultation with labor unions. For most occupations, the mandatory retirement age is 65 (Aiken, 1978; Sykes, 1971), although employers may soon be forced to raise that age to 68 or 70. In some instances, however, the retirement age may range as high as age 70, and some workers may remain employed on a year-to-year basis if they are shown to be nonexpendable (Kalish, 1975).

Mandatory retirement is frequently justified on several grounds. Its supporters claim that it is simple and easy to administer (whereas retirement "for cause" would require complicated decisions), that it eliminates bias or discrimination in the phase-out process, and that it opens channels of promotion for younger employees (Atchley, 1976).

The concept of a mandatory retirement age has been widely criticized, however. Many elderly people and their supporters argue that compulsory retirement is discriminatory in nature and should be abolished. Margaret Kuhn (1975), leader of the Gray Panthers, be-

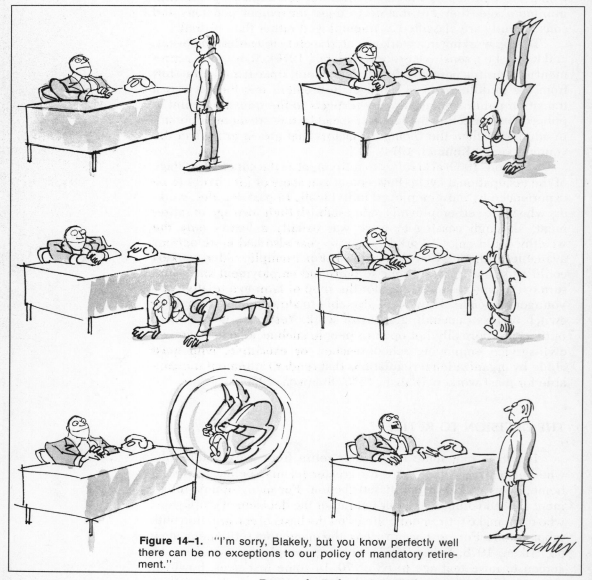

Figure 14–1. "I'm sorry, Blakely, but you know perfectly well there can be no exceptions to our policy of mandatory retirement."

Drawing by Richter: © 1977 The New Yorker Magazine, Inc.

lieves it is the responsibility of management, labor, and consumers to reverse the trend of forced **retirement** and abolish age-discrimination laws. Palmore (1972) **and Butler** (1975) go even further, stating that mandatory retirement wastes talent and productive potential.

Research indicates that an appreciable number of employees over 65 desire to continue working. A 1974 Harris Poll found that a third of the nation's retirees said they would return to work if they could. In 1971, 105,000 federal workers who could have retired chose not to do so (Butler, 1975). As one might expect, however, those who most vigorously oppose retirement are usually employed in high-level occupations (Hepner, 1969).

In response to the expressed desire of their older employees to continue working, some major firms have modified their retirement policies to allow individuals to stay on the job past their 65th birthday. United States Steel, for example, has no mandatory retirement age for more than 153,000 nonoffice employees. They are allowed to continue working as long as they can do their jobs and pass annual medical exams.

Those less fortunate older and still active workers who are forced out of their jobs because of a compulsory retirement age may develop negative self-images and lowered self-esteem. Kastenbaum (1971) feels that being old and white in our society are serious disadvantages that diminish what few hopes the aged have of finding re-employment. Sykes (1971) believes that the educational level of the elderly is likely to be lower than that of their younger counterparts in the labor market, particularly since they grew up at a time when mass education was just emerging, and the schooling that they did receive was likely to be loosely linked to the technical demands of today's jobs. The occupational distribution of older workers in many respects resembles the work world of the past—a remnant of a different economy, with more farmers, small businessmen, and craftsmen, and fewer professionals and factory operatives. Yet unfortunately, the size of this earlier work world is shrinking at the same time that the number of older workers is growing. Consequently, it is especially difficult for older workers to find jobs once they have reached a mandatory retirement age or when they face unemployment.

EARLY RETIREMENT

Ironically, while many workers are saddened by retirement at age 65, an increasing number of individuals are starting a trend toward early retirement (Jaffe, 1971). Many of these early retirees are military personnel and civil servants, but this occupational phenomenon is becoming widespread in a diversity of industries and companies (Pyron and Manion, 1970).

Many of today's workers opt for early retirement when they anticipate a comfortable income. Others retire early because of pressures generated by technological obsolescence among workers in their fifties and sixties, and by increasing relocation of major firms, cyclical unemployment, and stagnation of certain sectors of the economy (Binstock, 1977). To this list, Bischof (1976) adds the following reasons for early retirement: status (the image of the early retiree is becoming more positive), support (fellow workers, friends, and family may encourage early retirement), and future concern (the desire for early retirement may be promoted by the individual's awareness of "time left to live").

Additional research has given us further insight into the nature of early retirement. In studies of auto workers (Barfield and Morgan, 1969; Katona et al., 1969; Orbach, 1969), it was found that early retirement planning is often associated with : (1) a favorable financial outlook and a suitable standard of living for the retiree, (2) declining health, (3) the desire to assume a lighter work load, (4) difficulty in keeping up with one's work, (5) having discussed the issue of retirement with persons outside the immediate family, and (6) having attended at least one program focusing on retirement preparation.

While the drift toward early retirement has a positive side for many people, it also poses questions of both immediate and long-term significance (Kreps, 1971). Binstock (1977) addresses himself to some of these issues by stating:

> . . . millions of persons in their 50's may face problems now associated with the chronologically aged, such as the economic dependency that comes from living on a reduced, fixed income in an inflationary economy. Inadequate housing, lack of access to transportation, and other problems stemming from inadequate purchasing power may emerge. If they choose to re-enter the labor force they may find it extremely difficult to obtain employment. And they will no longer have the social roles and the various forms of status that work provides. At the same time, the retirement status of these younger retirees may lead the rest of society to assign to them the stereotypes of aging. For along with images of physical aging and the infirmities associated with old age, retirement status is one of the chief means of identifying the aging in American society.
>
> (p. 195)

ADJUSTING TO RETIREMENT

When retirement takes place, functions must be reintegrated if life is to continue fruitfully and harmoniously. Since retirement as a period of life is such a new developmental phenomenon, however, our culture has yet to prescribe suitable behavior for this time. Consequently, each of us may react differently (Rayner, 1971; Spence, 1975).

Today's retired people, particularly those who decide to retire early, are healthier than retirees of past generations and will be actively investigating more varied life options. Some will be looking for new paid or volunteer work, and most will be exploring leisure activities. Many experts say that harmonious retirement depends to a considerable extent on past adjustment patterns (Entine, 1976; Lowenthal, 1972). As Reichard (1962) puts it, those who adjust well to retirement are able to develop a life-style that provides continuity

WHY THE BIG SWING TO EARLY RETIREMENT

The idea of quitting the job before the traditional age of 65 is getting wider acceptance among American workers—spurred along by bigger and bigger pension benefits.

The trend would be speeding up even faster, a survey shows, if inflation were not rampant and cutting the purchasing power of pension dollars.

One after another, union-negotiated plans are boosting the amounts of the benefit checks for those retiring in their late 50s or early 60s.

Many employer-established pension plans, following suit, also are aiding early retirees.

An auto worker, for example, regardless of age, can collect a pension of $550 a month after he has spent 30 years in the shop. On October 1, that will rise to $625, and by 1978 it will amount to $700 a month.

Upward trend. Latest reports from the Social Security Administration reflect the trend toward early retirement.

At the start of 1974 more than 8 million workers had retired before age 65. That is 52.6 per cent of those on Social Security rolls, and triple the number on early retirement a decade earlier.

Employes of the Federal Government are one large group showing a tendency toward earlier retirement. One reason is a special cost-of-living bonus that will be paid to all federal retirees this summer. It will mean a boost in benefits of at least 5.8 per cent, based on rising living costs.

Defense Department employes have an extra incentive this year to retire early. During the summer, a civilian Pentagon employe can retire at a reduced benefit at age 50 if he or she has 20 years' service. An employe can quit at any age after 25 years' service.

The normal retirement rules for Civil Service employes allow a worker to draw a full pension at age 55 with 30 years' experience; at 60 with 20 years' experience or at the age of 62 with 5 years' experience.

One official estimated that 10,000 to 15,000 employes at Defense will retire this summer. . . .

"30 and out." Early retirement in the auto industry is being promoted by the "30 and out" plan demanded of companies by the United Auto Workers. Many persons are able to qualify for the 30 years of service required for a full pension at 47 or 48—or even younger. Fears of auto-company officials that the early-retirement plan would bring massive numbers of retirees, however, have failed to materialize. Observers list several reasons for this, including the prom-

ise of larger benefits coming later, and fear of inflation.

Asked about those who do retire early, a UAW spokesman put it this way:

"Thirty years in the plant is enough. It's really as simple as that."

The quit-early plan of the UAW has spread to agricultural-implement firms and to many of the auto-parts suppliers.

International Harvester Company is one of the farm-implement firms under the UAW's quit-early plan. A company official reports that up to one half of its eligible employes are opting to retire before age 65.

Nonunion employes of the firm are covered by an identical plan, allowing full pensions for those with 30 years on the job.

Growing weary. Why do employees decide to take the early retirement? Ray Stevenson, company pensions director, says:

"Many are tired of working. Things get to be a grind. These new pension levels, as a result, get to looking better than they actually are."

At another Midwestern company, Zenith Radio Corporation, officials see no increasing trend to early retirement. Frank DeLay, director of retirement planning, believes that this is because of the current high rate of inflation and the desire to earn larger retirement benefits by working longer.

Other pension experts, looking at the national picture, confirm the earlier departures from jobs.

Martin E. Segal Company, of New York, a consulting and actuarial firm in the employe-benefit field, reports:

"An analysis of recent collective-bargaining agreements shows that age 62 is becoming increasingly the normal retirement age for American workers."

Preston C. Bassett, of the actuarial firm of Towers, Perrin, Forster & Crosby, Inc., Philadelphia, finds this:

"The idea of early retirement started basically with unions pressing for earlier and earlier retirements. It has proved to be a good way for a company to cut back on employment when it wants to, by simply urging employes to go out earlier with special supplements."

So far, the early-retirement push is mainly among the larger companies, according to Edward Boynton, an actuary at the Wyatt Company, of Washington, D.C. He adds, however:

"Usually, the trend eventually sifts down to the smaller companies because of the competition for talent."

with the past and meets their long-term needs. Successful adjustment is also characterized by the harmonious resolution of demands and tasks throughout the course of one's life.

What are the primary adjustments required of most people during retirement? In a review of the literature, Leslie and Leslie (1977) have identified at least five factors that must be dealt with. First, as already mentioned, there is a *loss of finances*. For most retired people, income drops drastically. Only about 10 per cent of retired American households report annual incomes of $5000 or more, and 65 per cent have annual incomes under $3000. Social Security retirement pensions are the sole source of income for approximately 80 per cent of retired Americans. Two-thirds of our nation's retirees are struggling to live on incomes at or below the minimum required to meet basic necessities (Atchley, 1976). Second, withdrawal from the labor force may cause a major *loss of self esteem*. In most cases, replacement activities must be found to regain a sense of self-worth. Third, retirement may cause the *loss of work-oriented social contacts*, although many retirees compensate for this by establishing new friendships. Fourth, individuals may have difficulty in adjusting to the *loss of meaningful tasks* associated with employment (although it is possible to shift the locus of task achievement from the place of work to the home). Finally, *loss of a reference group* may affect people's self-images. Since individuals have perceived themselves not only as citizens but also as members of their businesses or professions, retirement may imply the realignment or reassessment of identity.

To understand the adjustments required of elderly persons, it is helpful to develop an awareness of the various phases of retirement. Atchley (1976) views retirement not only as a process but also as a social role that unfolds through a series of six phases. Furthermore, he believes that various adjustments must be made by the retiree as these stages are encountered. Because the retirement period is an individual phenomenon that varies in duration, relating these six phases to chronological ages is impossible. Also, individuals may not experience all the phases or encounter them in the order proposed.

1. Preretirement.   This period can be further divided into two substages, remote and near. In the *remote* phase, retirement is perceived as an event that is a reasonable distance in the future. This phase can begin before a person takes his or her first job; it ends when retirement nears. Anticipatory socialization and adjustment for retirement at this point are usually informal and unsystematic. The individual may also become exposed to negative stereotypes concerning retirement. (Of course, an individual's positive or negative reaction depends in part on the prevalent view of retirement on the part of relatives, friends, and co-workers.) The *near* phase emerges when workers become aware that they will take up the retirement role very soon and that adjustments are necessary for a successful transition. This phase may be initiated by a company's preretirement program or by the retirement of slightly older friends. Some workers may develop negative attitudes at this time because the realities of retirement are much clearer and financial prerequisites for the retirement role may not have been met. Many workers also fantasize about retirement and attempt to imagine what their life-styles might entail after work stops. Preretirement programs appear to be successful in reducing anxious feelings about the subject.

2. The honeymoon phase.   This period, immediately following the actual retirement event, is frequently characterized by a sense of euphoria that is partly the result of one's newfound freedom. It is a busy period for many people, filled with such activities as fishing, sewing, visiting family members, and traveling, although these activities will be influenced by numerous factors including finances, life-style, health, and family situation. The honeymoon period may be short or long, depending on the resources available to people and their imaginativeness in using them. Ingraham (1974) reports the happiness of a married 61-year-old man in the midst of this stage:

> "I can now do the many things I've wanted to do but couldn't find time to while working. My job came first and I worked at it 70 hours per week if necessary. I like retirement so much that I even hate to go back to the office when they call me for help. I can fish, hunt, go canoeing, boating, hiking, bird watching, do a lot of photography work, catch up on my stamp and coin collection, find time to do some carving and lathe work, read the things I've saved up for 25 years, etc., etc. We can visit our children in Texas and New Mexico when we choose, go camping anytime we like, sleep late if we desire (but we never do—not even on Sundays: There are so many things to do!) . . .."
>
> (p. 79)

3. The disenchantment phase.   After the honeymoon phase is over and life begins to slow down, some retirees become disenchanted and feel let-down or even depressed. The depth of this emotional let-down is related to a variety of factors such as declining health, limited finances, or being unaccustomed to such an independent lifestyle. In some cases, eagerly anticipated post-retirement activities (i.e., extensive traveling) may have lost their original appeal. Unrealistic preretirement fantasies as well as inadequate anticipatory socialization for retirement may also promote disenchantment. As one retired teacher remarked, "I had not realized how seriously I would miss daily contacts with students and others. An unexpected silence descended on my world." A retired woman described her disenchantment by saying, "I miss so much being a part of the mainstream. Sometimes I wonder if the one who wrote 'grow old along with me, the best is yet to be' had arrived at that point" (Ingraham, 1974, pp. 107, 110).

4. The reorientation phase.   For those whose retirements either never got off the ground or landed with a loud crash, a reorientation phase of adjustment is necessary. At this time, one's experience as a retired person is used to develop a more realistic view of life alternatives. Reorientation may also involve exploring new avenues of involvement, sometimes with the assistance of groups in the community. Many seek to become actively involved in jobs especially designed for the retiree, either on a volunteer basis or for pay. One 95-year-old woman reflects on the rewards she received through various aspects of civic involvement:

> "I moved into a strange community but I was living with a sister and had lots of time on my hands so I joined the League of Women Voters and it was not long before I was Chairman of the Foreign Relations Committee. Through that I became very much interested in the United Nations Organization. I joined several groups who were working with the Red Cross. Next thing I got into was working with the Girl Scouts and I was Juliette Low Chairman of the Girl Scouts in Wilmette. At the same time I was trapping and banding birds for the Fish and Wildlife Service of the United States Department of the Interior."
> (Ingraham, 1974, p. 70)

5. The stability phase. Stability, as defined by Atchley, does not refer to the absence of change but rather to the routinization of criteria for dealing with change. People who reach this stage have established a well-developed set of criteria for making choices, which allow them to deal with life in a fairly comfortable and orderly fashion. They know what is expected of them and know what they have to work with, strengths as well as weaknesses. In the stability phase, the individual has mastered the retirement role.

6. The termination phase. Although death may end retirement in any phase, the role itself is most often cancelled out by the illness and disability that sometimes accompany old age. When people are no longer capable of housework or self-care, they are transferred from the retirement role to the sick and disabled role. This role transfer is based on the loss of able-bodied status and autonomy, both of which are instrumental for carrying out the retirement role. Retired status is also lost, of course, if a full-time job is taken.

THE NEED FOR PRERETIREMENT PLANNING

Recently, a variety of tax-financed and private preretirement programs designed to assist the individual leaving the work world have evolved. Many leaders of business and industry have come to

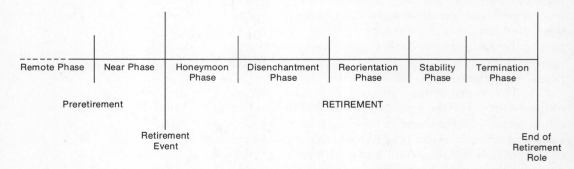

Figure 14–2. Phases of retirement. (*From* Atchley, R. C.: *The Sociology of Retirement.* Cambridge, Massachusetts: Schenkman Publishing Company, 1976.)

EMPLOYMENT OPPORTUNITIES FOR THE NATION'S RETIREES

Where can an older American turn to find a job?

A few communities have set up free employment referral services for older persons. One of these, in Jackson, Miss., has placed a hundred or so persons in jobs in hospitals, stores and clerical positions.

Jim Smith, personnel director of Jackson's Day Detectives, says he will hire as many older workers as the registry can provide.

"You really can't count on the young ones," he says. "But nine times out of 10 the older person will come through."

Some older Americans are employed in federally-funded community service jobs and public works and economic development projects.

The New York City Department for the Aging placed 1,300 older persons in a variety of jobs. A western Kentucky community has a federally-funded project in which older persons are hired as homemakers and home repairers.

MODEST PAY

Elizabeth Brooks, 74, and Bessie Brown, 73, are Foster Grandparents, a program sponsored by Action. Five days a week, they spend four to six hours caring for children at St. Christopher's Hospital for Children in Philadelphia.

Both are widows. Both had limited incomes. And both love their jobs.

"Believe me, I'm needed," said Mrs. Brooks. "Besides this keeps me out of mischief."

"If I didn't have this job, I'd be bored to death and climbing the walls," said Mrs. Brown.

The two women and some 14,000 other Foster Grandparents serving in hospitals, orphanages, day care centers, and correctional institutions across the nation receive only a small salary, $32 a week, the same amount as when the program was begun

more than a decade ago. They also receive carfare and one hot meal each working day.

In Jersey Ctiy, N. J., 71-year-old Catherine Hanley is employed as a Senior Companion in another federally-funded Action program. A widow who was forced to retire from her post with the Western Electric Co. when she was 65, she soon became bored.

"I had nothing to do," she said, "I'm not a bingo-player and I'm not much for the bus rides to the country. For about three years I was climbing the walls looking for something that I could do part time. That's just the way I am."

Today, she is Senior Companion to two elderly women, dividing her time between the two, preparing their lunches and just sitting with them.

There are about 2,600 Senior Companions in 46 localities in the nation, working in hospitals, nursing homes and private homes. They, too, receive $32 a week, plus travel expenses.

MANY VOLUNTEER

By far the largest of the federally-sponsored action programs for older Americans is the R.S.V.P. (Retired Senior Volunteer Program.) As of last fall, 205,000 volunteers were serving, without pay, in schools, courts, libraries, museums, hospitals, nursing homes, and daycare centers.

Mrs. Minnie Fitzgerald, 83, found a volunteer job on her own. A former teacher, she spends three days a week as an unpaid teacher's aide in second-grade classes in Boise, Idaho.

She pays her own bus fare to the school and even pays for her own lunches.

Does she feel older persons anxious to work are being ignored?

"I don't know, " she says. "I'm too busy working."

(Hunter: M., "What Happens After Retirement?" New York Times News Service. August 2, 1977)

realize the difficulty of the transition from regular working hours to a life of retirement, and they have begun to take measures to help facilitate the later-life adjustments associated with this change (Knopf, 1975; Manion, 1976; Ullmann, 1976). As Senator Walter Mondale stated in the Federal Employees Preretirement Assistance Act of 1975:

Planning for retirement can help workers make the transition from years of active employment to their leisure time years. Our society is work oriented and youth oriented: retirement can produce a real identity crisis, and often a loss of interest in living. Yet, with adequate advance preparation, retirement from a job does not need to mean retirement from life. By learning to avoid the pitfalls of retirement, and how to get the most from the new opportunities being opened up, preretirement planning can facilitate the vital and necessary continuation of personal growth.

(Mondale, 1975, p.S. 19393)

Since participation in preretirement education programs is voluntary, some workers may avoid them and claim they are not interested (Knopf, 1975). However, for those who do attend such programs, there are several important positive results, of which Atchley (1976) provides an excellent summary. First, uncertainties about retirement are reduced. Second, the tendency to miss one's job during retirement is reduced. Third, there is a decrease in dissatisfaction with retirement and a reduction in negative stereotypes associated with retirement. Fourth, worries about post-retirement health are reduced.

Manion (1976) states that the various, occasionally conflicting, assumptions underlying the purpose and objectives of preretirement education have given rise to a diversity of approaches in program design and delivery. He distinguishes four primary types of preretirement programs: coping, prescriptive, pedagogical, and T-group.

Coping.   Programs such as this emphasize that retirement will have its share of negative dimensions and stress the need for the development of coping mechanisms. Facilitators may suggest how one might cope with the problems of a lowered income, more time, and deteriorating health. Information is typically dispensed in lecture or pamphlet form.

Prescriptive.   This approach, as the title implies, prescribes rather specific retirement life-styles. The content of the program is typically problem-oriented and consists of books, pamphlets, and lectures that offer numerous practical suggestions to the participants but imply that retirement can be a negative experience unless one follows the right formula.

Pedagogical.   This type of program is educationally oriented, the material being delivered by teachers trained in adult education or by expert resource professionals such as lawyers or medical doctors. Topics might include how to estimate income at retirement, pensions and social security, insurance and hospitalization, health and aging, and relationships with family and friends (Knopf, 1975). Programs such as this provide interesting general information for large audiences. Frequently, the format is not conducive to dealing with individual questions and issues, although individual consultation sessions can be arranged in most cases.

T-Group Approach.   This program presents retirement preparation subjectively and is geared to generate relevant questions from the participants about their lives in retirement, including resources, social relationships, personal needs, and aspirations. This type of format encourages peer-group interaction under the direction of trained facilitators.

Figure 14–3. Many retired citizens continue to lead an active life by becoming involved in volunteer work.

Colonial Penn Group, Inc.

Whatever format is employed, retirement preparation should begin early and include the spouse as well as the employee. Too often, the role of the retiree's spouse is overlooked. Although retirement is a different experience for the wife than for the husband, and although she may feel less deeply involved, her attitudes will influence the satisfactions both partners derive during the retirement years (Heyman and Polansky, 1977; Knopf, 1975).

At least some preretirement programs should be tax-supported and available to everyone, especially to those who are employed in small businesses or in service occupations where formal programs run by the employer are rare (Atchley, 1976). Tax support and wider availability, together with additional research and experience in designing the most effective preretirement programs possible, will better prepare older employees to embark on a new lifestyle (Manion, 1976).

Summary

Retirement, the departure from the world of work, is a phenomenon that can be viewed as a process, an event, a social role, or a phase of life. Few issues in the field of social gerontology have aroused as much controversy as the issue of retirement. Some view compulsory retirement as an abridgement of the individual's right to work, but others look forward to retiring as a time of full-time freedom and relaxation.

In the United States, there are approximately 21 million retirees, and this figure is expected to reach 33 million by the year 2000. While work filled almost the entirety of adult lives at the beginning of the twentieth century, by midcentury, retirement characterized most people's lives after age 65. Today, the age of retirement is edging downward toward 60, a trend that will lengthen the retirement period for most people. Today, the average life expectancy after retirement is 15.3 years.

Retirement for most workers is not a voluntary matter but rather rests in the hands of employers. Although the usual retirement age is 65, in some instances it may range as high as age 70, and some older workers may remain employed on a year-to-year basis if they are shown to be "nonexpendable".

Polls indicate that a significant number of employees over 65 would continue working if they were given the opportunity. In response to such attitudes, some companies have modified their retirement policies to allow employees to remain on the job past their 65th birthday. However, for those older and still active workers who are forced out of their work because of compulsory retirement, reemployment possibilities are poor.

Our society has witnessed a fairly recent trend toward early retirement. Workers opt for early retirement for a number of reasons, including, among others, anticipation of a comfortable income, the relatively high rate of technological obsolescence among older workers, increasing relocation of major firms, cyclical unemployment, and stagnation of certain sectors of the economy. Yet, while the drift toward early retirement has a positive side for many people, it also poses questions of both immediate and long-term significance.

Adjustment to retirement is a difficult task for most people. Five particular problems of adjustment have been identified, namely, loss of finances, loss of self-esteem, loss of work-oriented social contacts, loss of meaningful tasks associated with employment, and a loss of a reference group. Robert Atchley has described six phases of retirement and the adjustments required at each stage. These phases are (1) preretirement, (2) the honeymoon phase, (3) the disenchantment phase, (4) the reorientation phase, (5) the stability phase, and (6) the termination phase.

Preretirement programs have become more widespread in recent years and have yielded numerous positive results. Four types of preretirement programs can be distinguished: coping, prescriptive, pedagogical, and T-group. Effective programs, whatever the design, usually begin early and include the spouse as well as the employee.

Suggested Readings

1. Atchley, R. C.: *The Sociology of Retirement*. Cambridge, Massachusetts: Schenkman Publishing Company, 1976.

   Atchley defines retirement from a historical perspective and brings it into focus as it affects the individual socially, biologically, psychologically, and financially. An excellent resource text.

2. Butler, R. N.: *Why Survive? Being Old in America*. New York: Harper and Row, 1975.

   In Chapter 4 of this book, Butler critically examines the older employee's right to work and the issue of compulsory retirement.

3. Irelan, L. M., and Bond, K.: "Retirees of the 1970's." *In* C. Osterbird (Ed.): *Migration, Mobility and Aging*. Gainesville, Florida: University of Florida Press, 1974, pp. 42–63.

   A well-researched examination of the quality of life of those approaching retirement. Areas of interest include socioeconomic status, health, social relations, and retirement expectations.

4. Sheldon, A., McEwan, J. M., and Ryser, C. P.: *Retirement: Patterns and Predictions*. Washington, D. C.: National Institute of Mental Health, 1975.

   An outstanding feature of this publication is an excellent summary of the literature related to retirement.

Holt, Rinehart and Winston

UNIT 15

DEATH AND BEREAVEMENT

Introduction

Accepting the inevitability of one's own death and preparing for
it represent life's final developmental tasks. Many terms can be used
to describe the individual's emotional reactions to dying: fear, sorrow, anger, despair, resentment, resignation, defiance, pity, tri-
umph, or helplessness. To be sure, each of us will probably have
different reactions to death (Aiken, 1978; Hinton, 1967).

In western culture, the subject of death seems to be taboo (Pattison, 1977a). For most, it is a sensitive topic, one that is avoided and
frequently repressed. Some people flatly refuse to acknowledge or
discuss their feelings about death, while others employ a common
defense mechanism: "It's not going to happen to me" (Kimmel,
1974). Even medical specialists, trained to save lives and to view
death as an enemy, are frequently uncomfortable with the subject
and do not like to be present when their patients die (Aiken, 1978).

To many, death is not a real part of the human experience. Yet
paradoxically, the thoughts of death that are denied by the culture
reemerge in perverse forms as large segments of the population are
preoccupied with violence, killing, and war. Multitudes are drawn to
newspaper and television accounts of death and react with a mixture
of fascination, curiosity, and excitement. Others are attracted to
violent movies and paperback novels that depict death in countless
ways. We deny death, but we are also obsessed by it.

Ironically, the increase in life expectancy in the United States
during the past few decades may have indirectly made death less
familiar (Pattison, 1977a). Whereas in 1900 most people had a life
expectancy of 40 years and many children were thus orphaned,
parents today typically live to age 70 or more and see their grandchildren and in some cases, great-grandchildren. However, while
many elderly Americans live with their families or at least nearby,
many others are sequestered in retirement colonies, decaying neighborhoods, or nursing homes. Consequently, we give the impression
that we are living in a culture of youth, one that removes death and
dying from the midst of everyday life.

In many instances, the dying are kept hidden or isolated from all
but close relatives, doctors, and nurses. We frequently give hospitals
the responsibility of caring for the dying, yet many are ill-equipped
to deal with such a task (Krant, 1974; Taylor, 1973). It goes without
saying that death is disturbing to virtually everyone, but the facility
with which it can be hidden makes it possible to deny its presence
(Rayner, 1971). Rollo May (1969) makes some especially poignant
remarks concerning this:

> We dress death up in grotesquely colorful caskets in the same way
> Victorian women camouflaged their bodies by means of voluminous
> dresses. We throw flowers on the casket to make death smell better.
> With make-believe funerals and burial ceremonies and fancy tombs we
> act as though the deceased had somehow not died; and we preach a
> psycho-religious gospel that says the less grief the better . . . .
>   (p. 106)

Partly because of this isolation and denial, death, like other
disturbing events, arouses awe and dread. Death has been made

more difficult to comprehend and accept. Younger people have had little direct experience with death and the sense of humility that it can bring (Rayner, 1971). For those who experience the loss of someone, understanding death becomes a formidable and frequently painful task (Stein, 1974).

According to Puner (1974), death used to be a less hidden and more intimate family affair:

> An old man would die in bed, at home, as a patriarch surrounded by his family. Most likely his body would be prepared for burial there, too. Today, death is "bureaucratized", and an old man is more likely to die in an institution, a curtain around his bed, few if any members of his family with him at the final moments. More than 55 per cent of all deaths now occur in hospitals which manage "the crisis of dying". The mortuary industry—the term "funeral parlor" or "funeral home" nods to tradition—prepares the body and makes most of the arrangements. In urban centers, more than 90 per cent of funerals start out from a mortuary, not a home. Thus the dying and the dead are segregated, placed in the hands of relatively impersonal specialists . . . .
>
> (pp. 228–229)

What influence might such attitudes have on the individual's life-style and quest for meaning in life?

Most authorities agree that the denial or repression of death results in limited self-growth. Seeking to comprehend it, on the

Figure 15–1. Accepting the reality of death represents one of life's final developmental tasks.

Holt photo by John King

other hand, may add a new and healthy dimension to our existence (Sheidman, 1974). Kimmel (1974) contends that if we try to humanize the dying process and come to deal with our own fears of death, we may well arrive at more "fully humanized living". Speaking from an existentialist's standpoint, he writes that the reality of death is necessary for life to be meaningful. In other words, if death is denied, life is also denied.

Kübler-Ross (1975) concurs with this belief and adds a further dimension. As she explains, death always has been and always will be with us. Because it is an integral part of human existence, it will always loom as a subject of deep concern. It is our task to learn to view death, not as a dreaded stranger, but rather as an expected companion to life. If this can be accomplished, we can also learn to live our lives with more meaning—with full appreciation of our finiteness, and of the limits on our time here.

DEATH AS AN ENCOUNTER

Understanding death becomes especially difficult when people think about the ending of their own particular lives. Consequently, adults often avoid the mention of death when it has a personal connotation (Hinton, 1967; Sheidman, 1971). It is impossible for us to picture an ending to our own life, and such an end is usually attributed to a malicious intervention from the outside by another party. To put it another way, in our unconscious, we can only be killed; we cannot die of old age or a natural cause. Death in itself, therefore, is associated with a bad act or a frightening happening, something that calls for retribution and punishment (Kübler-Ross, 1969).

While death can—and does—occur at any age, elderly people are more aware of its imminence. And even though death preoccupies them more than it does younger people, the elderly seem less afraid of it (Kalish, 1975; Kalish and Reynolds, 1976). It appears as though they fear the *process* of dying more than death itself (Kimmel, 1974). Some older people may even perceive death as an acceptable alternative to a life that has become devoid of meaning (DeBeauvoir, 1972).

Through fairly recent research we have been able to learn more about the personality dynamics of the dying person. One of the most significant findings is that dying people are usually willing to talk about their impending death; moreover, many appear to need and welcome such discussions (Epstein, 1975; Rayner, 1971; Smith, 1973). In one study (Feifel, 1963), over 80 per cent of terminally ill patients wanted to know about—and discuss—their personal situation.

Unfortunately, the dying person is sometimes trapped in a conspiracy of silence by relatives or medical staff members. Frequently, the situation is discussed but the patient is excluded. Some relatives and friends may avoid any discussion whatsoever because they are too uncomfortable with the topic (Weisman, 1972).

When told about impending death, most dying people are thankful to have learned the truth and to have been able to discuss it (Puner, 1974). Furthermore, Rayner (1971) suggests that those who break through the barrier of silence and talk to dying people rarely regret it. "They feel they have contributed something to a person in his last days that is very intimate, and have been enriched themselves by the unforgettable, humbling experience of being with a person who has forsaken defenses and illusions" (p. 249).

Among older people, it is fairly common to reminisce about the past as death draws nearer. According to Butler (1968, 1971) this *life review* allows the individual to relive past experiences and deal with persisting conflicts. The concept of a period of life review is strikingly similar to Erikson's psychosocial stage of *integrity vs. despair*. It may culminate in wisdom, serenity, and peace, or it may produce depression, guilt, or anger.

According to Butler (1968), reviewing past life is especially important for the aged. Faced with isolation, the loss of loved ones, and the nearness of death, the elderly frequently seek to escape into the past. Some memories will produce nostalgia, others mild regret, and others despair. In extreme cases, the older person's preoccupation with the past may cause panic, terror, or even suicide.

Butler (1968) believes that the life review serves as a major step in overall personality development. It is his contention that memory serves our sense of identity and provides continuity and wisdom. The act of recall is capable of renewing our awareness of the present and restoring our sense of wonder. By engaging in a life review, the individual is able to survey, observe, and reflect upon the past. In so doing, new insight into life's experiences is often achieved.

Figure 15–2. The life review is especially prominent among the aged. (Photo courtesy of Melissa Engel.)

LOOKING BACKWARD THROUGH TIME: THE LIFE REVIEW

The life review, described by Butler (1968) as "a looking-back process that has been set in motion by looking forward to death", may first consist of stray and seemingly insignificant thoughts about oneself and one's life history. These thoughts may persist in brief intermittent spurts or may become continuous. Some thought patterns may undergo continual reorganization and reintegration at various levels of awareness. Consider the dialogue of a 76-year old man:

"My life is in the background of my mind much of the time; it cannot be any other way. Thoughts of the past play upon me; sometimes I play with them, encourage and savor them; at other times I dismiss them." (p. 489)

The existence of the life review is also evident in dreams and thoughts. The elderly frequently report dreams and nightmares that focus on the past and death. Furthermore, images of past events and symbols of death appear frequently in waking life as well, indicating that the life review is a highly visual process.

Perhaps the most common manifestation of the life review is mirror-gazing. The following quotation illustrates this phenomenon:

"I was passing by my mirror. I noticed how old I was. My appearance, well, it prompted me to think of death—and of my past—what I hadn't done, what I had done wrong." (p. 489)

Butler describes one hospitalized 80-year-old woman whose husband had died five years before her admission. Her family had discovered her berating her mirror image for past deeds and shaking her fist at herself. A nurse recorded the following, which indicates how preoccupied the woman was with past deeds and omissions in her personal relationships:

"Patient in depths of gloom this morning—looking too unhappy for anything. Patient looked angry. I asked her with whom. She replied, 'Myself.' I asked, 'What have you done that merits so much self-anger so much of the time?' She replied, 'Haven't you ever looked yourself over?' In the course of conversation I suggested she might be too harsh with herself. At this she gave a bitter laugh and stuck out her chin again." (p. 489)

Interestingly, the woman purposely avoided all mirrors later in her hospitalization.

PSYCHOLOGICAL STAGES IN THE DYING PROCESS

Few researchers have contributed more toward understanding the dying process than Elisabeth Kübler-Ross. Described by herself as a "country doctor", Kübler-Ross is a psychiatrist who joined the faculty at the University of Chicago in 1965. Shortly afterward, she served as an advisor to a group of theological graduate students who were investigating various aspects of death. To gather more complete information and to increase her own knowledge of death, Kübler-Ross began interviewing dying patients. It was from these interviews, hundreds in number, as well as from her seminars, workshops, and lectures, that several books emerged. These widely cited texts include: *On Death and Dying* (1969), *Questions and Answers on Death and Dying* (1974), and *Death: The Final Stage of Growth* (1975).

At the heart of Kübler-Ross's research is the concept of the dying process as consisting of five interrelated stages. All individuals, she maintains, will pass through these five stages as death draws nearer. Although some stages may overlap, all are usually identifiable. The following discussion is based on the work of Kübler-Ross (1969).

Denial

The first stage of the dying process is called *denial*. When informed of impending death, most people react with shock and the general feeling of, "No, not me, it cannot be true." Because in our unconscious minds we are all immortal, it is inconceivable for us to acknowledge that we have to face death. When first told that they are going to die, some patients may demand more tests or change doctors with the hope of receiving a more favorable prognosis. In essence, the stark reality of the situation is denied.

One terminally ill patient described by Kübler-Ross (1969) was convinced her x-rays were "mixed-up" by the hospital and could not possibly be back so soon. When none of this could be confirmed, she asked to leave the hospital and began to search for other physicians to get a more satisfactory explanation for her symptoms. Whether these doctors confirmed the original diagnosis or not, she reacted in a similar fashion each time; she requested examination and reexamination, partially aware that the original diagnosis was accurate, but also wanting additional opinions in the hope that the first conclusion was an error. At the same time, she wanted to stay in contact with these doctors so that she could have their help "at all times".

Denial, or at least partial denial, is employed by virtually all patients and is believed to be a relatively healthy way of initially dealing with this uncomfortable situation. Denial can serve as a "buffer" after unexpected shocking news and enables patients to collect their thoughts and, with time, to utilize other, less radical defenses. The use of these other defenses, however, will depend on several factors, including how patients are told the news and how much time they have to acknowledge the inevitable event gradually.

Anger

The second stage proposed by Kübler-Ross is *anger*. When denial is no longer successful, the patient typically experiences feelings of anger, rage, envy, and resentment. Whereas the patient's reaction to catastrophic news in stage one is "No, it's not true, there must be some mistake," the patient may say in stage two, "Why me? Why not someone else?"

Compared to the period of denial, this stage is difficult for the family and medical staff to handle, largely because the patient's anger is projected and displaced at random. Kübler-Ross illustrates how patients may displace anger. They may complain that:

> the doctors are just no good, they don't know what tests to require and what diet to prescribe. They keep the patients too long in the hospital or don't respect their wishes in regard to special privileges. They allow a miserably sick roommate to be brought into their room when they pay so much money for some privacy and rest, etc. The nurses are even more often a target of their anger. Whatever they touch is not right. The moment they have left the room, the bell rings. The light is on the very

EMOTIONAL REACTIONS OF THE DYING PATIENT

It is not uncommon for the dying patient to experience a number of feelings. The following list represents some of the more specific, as compiled by Pattison (1977b).

Fear of the Unknown. As death draws nearer, dying patients may be afraid because they do not know what lies ahead. They wonder: What is my fate in the hereafter? What will happen to my body after death? How will my family and friends respond to my dying? What will happen to my survivors? Some of these questions can be answered rather quickly, but others will take longer. Some will remain unanswered.

Loneliness. With sickness, there appears to be a sense of isolation from oneself and from others. For the dying person, this feeling becomes even more evident and produces a fear of loneliness—in many cases right from the very beginning. Withdrawal from work or recreational activities, increasing physical debilitation and bed confinement, and perhaps not knowing what to say when friends do visit may contribute to this fear.

Sorrow. The dying face many losses, including loved ones, their jobs, and future plans, to mention but a few. Accepting these losses and learning to tolerate the painful experience of sorrow that accompanies each may produce a state of fear or anxiety.

Loss of Body. Since our bodies represent part of our self-concept, illnesses affect us both physically and psychologically. Patients may react to debilitating conditions with shame and feelings of disgrace, inadequacy, and lowered self-esteem.

Loss of Self-control. As debilitating diseases progress, we become less capable of self-control. Generally speaking, there is less energy, vitality, and responsiveness. Most people think less quickly and accurately, and may fear this loss of mental function.

Suffering and Pain. This fear is not just a physical one, but rather a fear of the unknown and the unmanageable. While senseless pain is intolerable to most people, pain may be accepted and dealt with if it does not involve punishment, being ignored, or not being cared for.

Loss of Identity. The loss of human contact, family and friends, body structure and function, self-control, and total consciousness all threaten one's sense of identity. As Pattison states, "Human contacts affirm who we are, family contacts who we have been, and contact with our body and mind affirms our own being-self" (p. 53). The dying process, to be sure, threatens many facets of one's self-identity.

minute they start their report for the next shift of nurses. When they do shake the pillows and straighten out the bed, they are blamed for never leaving the patients alone. When they do leave the patients alone, the light goes on with the request to have the bed arranged more comfortably. The visiting family is received with little cheerfulness and anticipation, which makes the encounter a painful event. They then either respond with grief and tears, guilt or shame, or avoid future visits, which only increases the patient's discomfort and anger. (pp. 50–51)

Kübler-Ross believes it is important for family members and hospital personnel to empathize with the dying patient and realize why and how anger originates. To be sure, wherever patients look at this stage they will find grievances. Yet patients who are understood and given some time and attention will soon lower their voices and reduce their angry demands. In time, they will come to realize that they are valuable human beings who are cared for and permitted to function at the highest possible level as long as they can.

Bargaining

The third stage of the dying process is termed *bargaining*. While the patient was unable to face the truth in the first stage and was generally angry in the second, he now hopes that death can be postponed or delayed in some way. Some may entertain thoughts of entering into some type of agreement with their creator: "If God has decided to take us from this earth and he did not respond to my angry pleas, he may be more favorable if I ask nicely" (p. 82).

The terminally ill patient may know from past experience (usually from childhood) that good behavior results in a reward, sometimes the granting of a wish for special privileges. Now the patient usually wishes for an extension of life, or for a few days without pain or physical discomfort. An example of bargaining is provided by Kübler-Ross (1969). She describes a patient who was:

> . . . in utmost pain and discomfort, unable to go home because of her dependence on injections for pain relief. She had a son who proceeded with his plans to get married, as the patient had wished. She was very sad to think that she would be unable to attend this big day, for he was her oldest and favorite child. With combined efforts, we were able to teach her self-hypnosis which enabled her to be quite comfortable for several hours. She had made all sorts of promises if she could only live

---

BARGAINING AND DEATH: CAN THE "GRIM REAPER" BE DELAYED?

Folk legends—and many Hollywood epics—are rich with accounts of individuals in the process of dying who somehow "hold on" until the occurrence of some important event. For example, an aged father may cling to life until he can speak a few parting words to a long absent child. Similarly, a mortally wounded soldier may stay grimly at his post until his comrades make good their escape. Incidents of this type make interesting reading or viewing, for they pose an intriguing question: can human beings actually defer their deaths until after the completion of some significant final act? An investigation conducted by David Phillips (1972) suggests that this may be true.

In this study, Phillips reasoned that if individuals can actually postpone their deaths, fewer persons than expected by chance would die in the month preceding their birthday, while more persons than expected would die in the month following this date. In order to examine this hypothesis, he obtained both the date of birth and date of death of 1251 famous Americans. Amazingly, when these dates were compared, evidence for the major prediction was obtained: 17 per cent fewer individuals than expected died in the month preceding their birthday, while 13 per cent more than expected died in the month following this date. Even more dramatic results were obtained when these public figures were divided into three groups on the basis of their

degree of fame. Phillips reasoned that those in the most famous category (e.g., George Washington, Benjamin Franklin, Mark Twain) would have the strongest reasons for deferring death, since their birthdays would probably be the subject of public celebrations and awards. This prediction, too, was confirmed. Among individuals in the most famous group, fully 78 per cent fewer deaths than expected occurred in the crucial period. Among those in the least famous category (e.g., Millard Filmore, H. L. Mencken), deaths were reduced by only 20 per cent.

These findings seem to suggest that human beings can indeed postpone their own deaths, and that the stronger their reasons for doing so, the greater their success in this regard. In addition, they appear to provide one possible explanation for such famous "coincidences" as the fact that both Thomas Jefferson and John Adams died on July 4, 1826—exactly 50 years after the signing of the Declaration of Independence! Although the psychological mechanisms underlying such effects are still something of a mystery, it seems possible that they are related, in some manner, to the ability of human beings to control even their most basic bodily processes. . . . The investigation of such possibilities should make for exciting research in the years ahead.

(Reprinted from Baron, Byrne, and Kantowitz, 1977, p. 268)

long enough to attend the marriage. The day preceding the wedding she left the hospital as an elegant lady. Nobody would have believed her real condition. She was "the happiest person in the whole world" and looked radiant. I wondered what her reaction would be when the time was up for which she had bargained.

I will never forget the moment when she returned to the hospital. She looked tired and somewhat exhausted and—before I could say hello—said, "Now don't forget I have another son!" (p. 83)

Thus, in essence, the bargain is an attempt to postpone. Among its most important features, bargaining includes a prize offered "for good behavior," a self-imposed "deadline" (e.g., the son's wedding), and an implicit promise that the patient will not request more if this one delay is granted. (In regard to the last, however, few if any patients keep their promises.) Interestingly, Kübler-Ross reports that a large number of patients promise "a life dedicated to God" or "a life in the service of the church" in exchange for some additional time. Many also promised to donate parts of their body to science, if, in return, the doctors would use their knowledge of science to extend their lives.

Depression

Depression is the fourth stage identified by Kübler-Ross. When the terminally ill cannot deny their illnesses any longer, when additional surgery or hospitalization is required, when more symptoms develop, they become engulfed with a sense of great loss. To be sure, the terminally ill patient must endure numerous hardships in addition to physical problems, including financial burdens and the loss of employment because of many absences or an inability to function. Instead of reacting with anger or rage at this point as they might have earlier, patients are likely to experience depression.

Kübler-Ross distinguishes between two kinds of depression. The first, called *reactive depression,* results from a loss that has already occurred. The cause of the depression can usually be elicited by an understanding person, and some of the unrealistic guilt or shame that often accompanies this depression can be alleviated. The woman who has had breast surgery and is worried about no longer being a woman can be complimented for some especially feminine feature. In this way she can be reassured that she is still as much a woman as she was before the operation.

The second type of depression, called *preparatory depression,* occurs in response to impending loss. Whereas encouragement and reassurance are useful in helping people suffering from reactive depression, they are not effective in helping those experiencing preparatory depression. Here, depression is a preparation for the impending loss of love objects, a means by which the state of acceptance can be facilitated. For this reason, it would be contradictory for us to tell the patient to look at the sunny side of things and not to be sad, especially since everyone is terribly sad when a loved one is lost.

A better approach would be to allow depressed patients who are terminally ill to express their sorrow so that a final acceptance of their condition will be easier. Such patients frequently express gratitude towards those who can sit nearby during this period of depression and not constantly remind the patient that sadness is to be avoided.

Unlike reactive depression, preparatory depression is frequently a silent response. Many times there is no or little need for words.

> It is much more a feeling that can be mutually expressed and is often done better with a touch of a hand, a stroking of the hair, or just a silent sitting together. This is the time when the patient may just ask for a prayer, when he begins to occupy himself with things ahead rather than behind. It is a time when too much interference from visitors who try to cheer him up hinders his emotional preparation rather than enhances it.
> (Kübler-Ross, 1969, pp. 87–88)

Acceptance

The fifth and final stage of the dying process is called *acceptance*. If patients have had enough time, that is, if the death is not sudden or unexpected, and if they have been given some assistance in working through the four previous stages, they will reach a stage where they are neither depressed nor angry about their "fate".

In most instances patients in the acceptance stage have had the opportunity to express their previous feelings: their envy for the healthy and living and their anger and resentment toward those who do not have to face death so soon. The need to mourn the impending loss of meaningful people and places has usually been met, and patients typically contemplate their approaching death with a certain degree of quiet expectation. Acceptance is a period almost devoid of feeling. For this reason, families usually need more help and support during this time than patients themselves.

Patients prefer to be left alone much of the time, and their interests generally diminish. They also need frequent brief intervals of sleep. Because patients in the acceptance stage are seldom talkative, communication is generally more nonverbal than verbal. As Kübler-Ross (1969) describes this stage, it is as if the pain has disappeared and the struggle is over. It becomes a time for "the final rest before the long journey."

A few patients may struggle right to the very end, fighting to keep alive whatever hopes they can. For these individuals, it is impossible to reach this stage of acceptance. In other words, the harder one fights to avoid the inevitable death and the more one denies it, the more difficult it is to die with peace and dignity.

Considerable interest has been directed toward the patient's "right to die". Many people believe the terminally ill should be given some individual autonomy as death draws nearer. Indeed, accepting and even desiring death may be a rational choice for the hopeless, helpless terminal patient who has no meaningful reason for living (Aiken, 1978). The "Living Will" developed by the Euthanasia Educational Council is supportive of this "right to die" (see Figure 15–3).

CARING FOR THE TERMINALLY ILL: THE HOSPICE CONCEPT

St. Christopher's Hospice, a 54-bed facility in London, England, and St. Luke's Hospice, a 25-bed facility in Sheffield, England, are the prototypes for the Hospice currently being planned for construction in Branford, Connecticut, a suburban New Haven community. Though modified to reflect our particular culture and ethic, America's first Hospice will incorporate many of the principles of care already demonstrated as viable by the English models. These principles include a comprehensive, coordinated program of home care and in-patient care. Particular medical expertise in pain control, the management of nausea and other symptoms, maintenance of alertness and mood will be stressed. Pharmacological consultation and research will be important. Expert nursing care will be given, but in addition, nurses will be specifically trained, and given the time, to attend to the needs of the patient and family. Social work, psychiatric consultation, clergy services, and volunteer activities will be offered to support patients and families and to include them in an ongoing living process designed to maximize their valuable contribution and participation.

These concepts have application in general health care, but nowhere are they more important than in terminal care. In the process of dying and bereavement, it is vital that relationships are lived out and concluded as productively as possible. Families will be included as important members of the Hospice team, whether the patient is at home or in the in-patient facility.

This emphasis means that the patient/family is involved in teaching the staff about their needs, and in the decision-making regarding their treatment. Hospice will assist the patient and family to maintain their own lifestyle and a sense of their own responsibility while receiving supportive services.

One of the supportive services now in operation is the Hospice volunteer program. Volunteers, well-oriented to the Hospice program, are an integral part of the caregiving service, fulfilling a wide variety of needed tasks, including patient care, family support and assistance to the staff in planning and community education.

For the past several years, numerous groups have asked Hospice to provide programs of general information about its work, and to participate in specialized workshops and seminars. We will continue to develop these and other educational aspects of our program for health care professionals, religious groups, students, and the general public. We know that all persons will not be served by Hospice, but what we learn will be shared.

Another shared aspect of [the Hospice] program is in the field of research and program evaluation. Although some research has focused on the terminally ill, this population has never been observed in a comparative controlled environment such as Hospice will provide. Present research has documented the physical and psychological trauma experienced by the dying and given valuable insights into their special needs. Since Hospice will offer a situation where these needs are known and generally met, research can concentrate on comparative modes of care.

Any new part of a health care system does not effectively work in isolation. If it is to be most useful to the person in need, it must be integrated into the total fabric of the health care system of the community. Hospice includes approximately 250 people—health professionals from all disciplines and lay people from the community—on the task forces carrying out its planning and development. Many of these individuals have important primary responsibilities in the acute general hospital, the university teaching hospital, the Veterans Administration Hospital, the Visiting Nurse Association, community medicine, nursing homes, or community agencies in Greater New Haven.

The care that patients will receive in Hospice, although highly personal and specialized, will cost appreciably less than services in an acute care hospital. Care in Hospice is expected to cost approximately 40 per cent less per day than general hospitals in Connecticut. In addition, the Home Care Program enables the patient to remain home for an extended period, shortening the patient's stay in the facility, and further reducing the cost of care.

(Lack, 1977, pp. 352–354)

TO MY FAMILY, MY PHYSICIAN, MY LAWYER, MY CLERGYMAN
TO ANY MEDICAL FACILITY IN WHOSE CARE I HAPPEN TO BE
TO ANY INDIVIDUAL WHO MAY BECOME RESPONSIBLE FOR MY HEALTH, WELFARE OR
AFFAIRS

Death is as much a reality as birth, growth, maturity and old age—it is the one certainty of life. If the time comes when I, _____ can no longer take part in decisions for my own future, let this statement stand as an expression of my wishes, while I am still of sound mind.

If the situation should arise in which there is no reasonable expectation of my recovery from physical or mental disability, I request that I be allowed to die and not be kept alive by artificial means or "heroic measures". I do not fear death itself as much as the indignities of deterioration, dependence and hopeless pain. I, therefore, ask that medication be mercifully administered to me to alleviate suffering even though this may hasten the moment of death.

This request is made after careful consideration. I hope you who care for me will feel morally bound to follow its mandate. I recognize that this appears to place a heavy responsibility upon you, but it is with the intention of relieving you of such responsibility and of placing it upon myself in accordance with my strong convictions, that this statement is made.

Signed _____

Date _____

Witness _____

Witness _____

Copies of this request have been given to _____

_____

_____

_____

Figure 15–3. (Reprinted courtesy of Euthanasia Educational Council, 250 West 57th Street, New York, N.Y. 10019.)

BEREAVEMENT

One of the most painful experiences we undergo in our lifetime is dealing with the death of a loved one. While such an event may be recognized as inevitable, we are seldom prepared for its occurrence. In proportion to the degree of our intimacy with the dying person, we find it hard to imagine life without that person—an emotional emptiness akin to our own death (Insel, 1976).

It is fairly well established that people will react in different ways when death strikes close to home (Hinton, 1967; Insel, 1976). The more common emotional reactions include a mixture of sorrow, misery, emptiness, and loneliness. Some family members report a general feeling of "numbness" and only vague awareness of the events taking place around them (Nye and Berardo, 1973). Among widows, life may not seem worth living any more, and some may even look forward to their own early death (Bock and Webber, 1972).

230   Section D—Epilogue

A PHYSIOLOGICAL EXPLANATION OF DEATH

Death is a process as well as an event, and while there are numerous signs that serve to signal the termination of life, each manifestation in itself does not prove that irreversible extinction has taken place. Research focusing on the nature of death (the study of death is known technically as thanatology) reveals that even after *clinical death* has been pronounced, the body is not *biologically* dead. The hair, for example, continues to grow for several hours; the liver converts glycogen to glucose, and the muscles contract (this is referred to as rigor mortis). Rigor mortis generally begins two hours after death, the muscles remaining contracted for approximately thirty hours.

The criteria for death are not fixed, and only recently has the medical profession attempted to establish guidelines for evaluating this condition. It goes without saying that the heart, lungs, and brain form the trinity upon which the standards for irreversible death are established. More specific criteria include (1) an absence of respiration, (2) the absence of heartbeat, and (3) a flat electroencephalogram. When these signs are coupled with such obvious alterations as the absence of pupillary reflexes, the clouding of the cornea, and an absence of body movement, it can quite certainly be said that death has occurred.

(Shepro, Belamarich, and Levy, 1974)

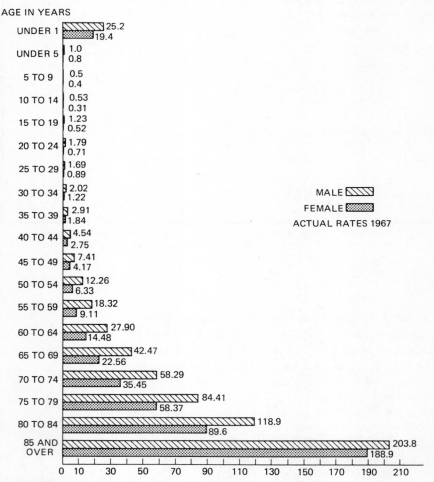

Figure 15–4. Death rates of men and women per 1000 midyear population, by age, United States, 1967. At all age periods male death rates far exceed female. (*From:* U.S. Public Health Service: Vital Statistics Report, Vol. 17, No. 12, Supplement, March 25, 1969.)

One team of researchers (Clayton et al., 1971) has identified the "symptoms" that characterize the mourning process. In this study of 109 widows during their first month of bereavement, the symptoms most frequently reported (by over 80 per cent of the respondents) included crying, depression, and difficulty in sleeping. Nearly half of those interviewed claimed difficulty in concentrating, lack of appetite, and reliance on such medication as sleeping pills or tranquilizers.

How long does the bereavement period typically last? According to Kimmel (1974), it usually has a duration of one to two years. During this time, the individual's ability to function may be somewhat impaired, but this does not always involve overt pathological symptoms, unless previous symptoms were present. In a summary of the literature, Kimmel states that during this time there may be an increase in the risk of a fatal illness, accident, or suicide among

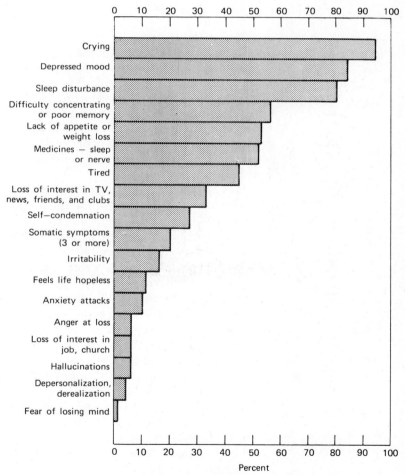

Figure 15–5. Percentage of 109 recently widowed persons reporting symptoms of bereavement. (*From:* Clayton, P. J., Halikes, J. A., and Maurice, W. L.: "The bereavement of the widowed." *Diseases of the Nervous System 32* :(9):597–604, 1971.)

spouses of the deceased, perhaps the result of physical exhaustion, loneliness, and grief itself.

Some investigators have attempted to outline the stages of bereavement. One such researcher was Bowlby (1960), who isolated five fairly distinct stages of mourning:

1. Concentration directed toward the deceased.
2. Anger or hostility toward the deceased or others.
3. Appeals to others for support and help.
4. Despair, withdrawal, and general disorganization.
5. Reorganization and direction of the self toward a new love object.

Another researcher (Kavanaugh, 1974) suggests that there are seven stages involved in the grieving process:

1. Shock.
2. Disorganization.
3. Violent emotions.
4. Guilt.
5. Loss and loneliness.
6. Relief.
7. Reestablishment.

Kimmel (1974) agrees with Kübler-Ross (1969) by stating that "reworking" the events leading up to the loss of a loved one is often helpful in coping with grief and mourning, especially for a grieving person (such as the physician) who knew the deceased right up to the end. The immediate expression of grief also appears to have beneficial value. In one study (Parkes, 1972), widows who had expressed their grief within several days of the death of their spouses exhibited less emotional disturbance several months later than those who repressed their emotions.

It is apparent from the preceding discussion that mourning for the deceased does not end when the funeral is over. On the contrary, the most painful void is felt *after* the funeral, when relatives have departed and the bereaved is alone. Therefore, meaningful communication with family members on a continual basis may help the bereaved over their initial grief and gradually prepare them for acceptance (Kübler-Ross, 1969).

In many instances, the bereaved become preoccupied by memories of the deceased, sometimes even talking to the departed as though they were still alive. These individuals are not only isolating themselves from the living but are making it harder for themselves to face the reality of the person's death. Yet it must be understood that this is their way of coping with the loss of a loved one, and it is inappropriate to confront them daily with the unacceptable reality. A more helpful approach would be to understand this need and to help these individuals detach themselves by drawing them out of their isolation gradually (Kübler-Ross, 1969).

Another fairly common emotional reaction on the part of the bereaved is to be filled with shame, guilt, or self-doubt. For some time after the funeral, family members may blame themselves for not having done enough for the deceased:

TREATMENT OF THE DEAD: A HISTORICAL PERSPECTIVE

Among the more interesting aspects of burial practices are the useful clues they provide about the customs and society of the living (Mitford, 1963). Various civilizations have treated the dead in unique ways. Habenstein and Lamers (1955) provide readers with a thought-provoking analysis of some of these practices.

Upon the death of the head of the house in *Ancient Egypt,* women would "rush frantically through the streets, beating their breasts from time to time and clutching their hair" (p. 19). The body of the deceased was removed as soon as possible to the embalming chambers, where a priest, a surgeon, and a team of assistants proceeded with the embalming operation. (The Egyptians believed in the life beyond; embalming was intended to protect the body for this journey.) While the body was being embalmed, arrangements for the final entombment began. When the mummified corpse was ready for the funeral procession and installation in its final resting place, it was placed on a sledge drawn by oxen or men and accompanied by wailing servants, professional mourners simulating anguished grief, and relatives. It was believed that when the body was placed in an elaborate tomb (family wealth and prestige exerted an obvious influence on tomb size), its elements would depart and later return through a series of ritualistic actions.

Reverence for the dead permeated burial customs during all phases of *Ancient Greek* civilization. Within a day after death the body was washed, anointed, dressed in white, and laid out in state for one to seven days, depending on the social prestige of the deceased. Family and friends could view the corpse during this time. For the funeral procession, the body was placed on a bier carried by friends and relatives and followed by female mourners, fraternity members, and hired dirge singers. Inside the tomb were artistic ornaments, jewels, vases, and articles of play and war. Like the Egyptians, the ancient Greeks prepared their tombs and arranged for subsequent care while they were still alive. About 1000 B.C. the Greeks began to cremate their dead. While earth burial was never entirely superseded, the belief in the power of the flame to free the soul acted as a strong impetus to the practice of cremation. A choice of inhumation (burial) or cremation was available during all late Greek periods.

Generally speaking, the *Romans* envisioned some type of afterlife and, like the Greeks, practiced both cremation and earth burial. When a wealthy person died, the body was dressed in a white toga and placed on a funeral couch, feet to the door, to lie in state for several days. For reasons of sanitation, burial within the walls of Rome was prohibited; consequently, great roads outside the city were lined with elaborate tombs erected for the well-to-do. For the poor, there was no such magnificence; for slaves and aliens, there was a common burial pit outside the city walls.

In *Anglo-Saxon England* (approximately the time when invading Low German tribes conquered the country in the fifth century), the body of the deceased was placed on a bier or in a hearse. On the corpse was laid the book of the Gospels as a symbol of faith and the cross as a symbol of hope. For the journey to the grave, a pall of silk or linen was placed over the corpse. The funeral procession included priests bearing lighted candles and chanting psalms, friends who had been summoned, relatives, and strangers who deemed it their duty as a corporal work of mercy to join the party. Mass was then sung for the dead, the body was solemnly laid in the grave (generally without a coffin), the mortuary fee was paid from the estate of the deceased, and liberal alms were given to the poor.

Burials and funeral practices were models of simplicity and quiet dignity in *eighteenth-century New England.* Upon death, neighbors (or possibly a nurse if the family was well-to-do) would wash and lay out the body. The local carpenter or cabinetmaker would build the coffin, selecting a quality of wood to fit the social position of the deceased. In special cases, metal decorations imported from England were used on the coffin. In church, funeral services consisted of prayers and sermons said over the pall-covered bier. Funeral sermons often were printed (with skull and cross-bones prominently displayed) and circulated among the public. The funeral service at the grave was simple, primarily a brief prayer followed by the ritual commitment of the body to the earth. The filling of the grave, with neighbors frequently supplying the necessary labor because there were no professional gravediggers, marked the formal end of the early colonial funeral ceremony.

Although it may be clear that they have made the correct choices when faced with the difficult decisions involved in the care of the dying person, after the death they often question the standards of their own conduct. Should they have got the patient to the hospital earlier or insisted upon some different plan of treatment? Should they have taken the dying person from the hospital to end his days at home, even though it was patently clear that he could have been looked after adequately only in the hospital? In their grief, people are very apt to produce more and more self-recriminations. They feel they could have behaved better towards the dead person while he was alive, shown him more appreciation, affection, and so on. It is not uncommon for the bereaved even to accuse themselves of having contributed towards the death by their neglect or by the demands they had made on the deceased.

(Hinton, 1967, p. 168)

In time, the bereaved will find new outlets for their energies. If satisfactory adjustment has been made during the mourning period, the person who died is not forgotten. Instead, the immediate experience of the dead person loses force and gives way to the memory of the individual as he was when he was alive. In this sense, the deceased has gained a certain immortality in the memory of loved ones. While the spirit of the deceased cannot be touched, it cannot be destroyed either. In this way, the living are able to carry on their existence and are a little more prepared to die themselves someday, leaving other generations to carry their memory into the future (Rayner, 1971; Stein, 1974).

Summary

One of life's most formidable tasks is learning to understand and accept death. For many people, death is a sensitive topic that is avoided in conversations and often repressed. Our reactions to the subject are varied.

Elderly people appear to be more aware of death's imminence than younger individuals. Research also indicates that older people are seemingly less afraid of death and may even perceive it as an acceptable alternative to a life that has become devoid of meaning.

Contrary to the popular tradition, dying patients usually want to talk openly about their impending death. Unfortunately, well-meaning family members or medical personnel may trap the terminally ill in a shroud of silence and avoid any discussion of the topic whatsoever. Most experts agree that dying patients are often able to sense their impending death and consequently need to verbalize their feelings. Some may spend considerable time reflecting back on various aspects of their lives, a process Robert Butler refers to as the "life review".

The dying process has attracted the attention of numerous researchers, most notably Elisabeth Kübler-Ross. At the heart of her research is a five-stage theory of the dying process. These stages include denial, anger, bargaining, depression, and acceptance.

Most researchers agree that we each act differently when death strikes close to home. The bereavement period, which generally lasts between one and two years, produces a mixture of sorrow, emptiness, and depression. Some of the more commonly reported symptoms of bereavement include crying, difficulty in sleeping, and general lethargy. Some investigators, such as Bowlby and Kavanaugh, have proposed that stages exist in bereavement.

Mourning for the deceased does not end when the funeral is over; rather, the bereaved must deal with intense feelings of emptiness and isolation. Conversations with relatives and friends may assist the bereaved in accepting the loss of a loved one. Becoming preoccupied with memories of the deceased or experiencing guilt or self-doubt over the manner in which the deceased was treated before his death are fairly common reactions among the bereaved. If satisfactory adjustment has been made during the mourning process, the bereaved, in time, will find new distributions for their energies. When this is the case, the deceased has gained a certain immortality in the memory of loved ones.

Suggested Readings

1. Becker, E.: *The Denial of Death.* New York: The Free Press, 1973.

   This Pulitzer Prize winning book examines our struggle against death and how we attempt to transcend it in our culture.

2. Hinton, J.: *Dying.* Baltimore, Maryland: Penguin Books, 1967.

   An authoritative and well-referenced book that offers excellent coverage on the medical and social aspects of death. Specific sections include Attitudes to Death, The Dying, Care of the Dying, and Mourning.

3. Kübler-Ross, E.: *On Death and Dying.* New York: Macmillan Inc., 1969.

   Perhaps the most widely cited current text on death. This book includes captivating interviews with terminally ill patients which add dimension and depth to the author's five-stage theory of dying.

4. Kübler-Ross, E.: *Death: The Final Stage of Growth.* Englewood Cliffs, New Jersey: Prentice-Hall, Inc., 1975.

   A collection of readings designed to cover various aspects of death and dying. Particularly interesting are articles related to the cultural differences that exist in handling death and the manner in which confrontations with death and dying can provide individuals with valuable self-growth and insight.

5. Pattison, E. M.: *The Experience of Dying.* Englewood Cliffs, New Jersey: Prentice-Hall, Inc., 1977.

   A clinically oriented text that provides an in-depth portrayal of the dying process. Incorporating the viewpoints of many of the leading authorities in this area, Pattison also offers the reader an excellent suggested bibliography.

Figure 15–6. Does the matrix of life ever end?

Horst Schäfer
Photo Trends

BIBLIOGRAPHY

Adams, B. N.: "Occupational position, mobility, and the kin or orientation." *American Sociological Review*, June 1967.

Adams, B. N.: *The Family: A Sociological Interpretation*. Chicago: Rand McNally, 1975.

Adelson, J.: "What generation gap?" *New York Times Magazine*, January 18, 1970.

Aiken, L. R.: *The Psychology of Later Life*. Philadelphia: W. B. Saunders Company, 1978.

Albee, G. W.: "The Protestant ethic, sex, and psychotherapy." *American Psychologist* 32(2):150–161, 1977.

Allport, G. W.: Pattern and Growth in Personality. New York: Holt, Rinehart and Winston, 1961.

Aries, P.: *Centuries of Childhood*. New York: Alfred A. Knopf, 1962. (Translated by R. Baldick.)

Atchley, R. C.: *The Sociology of Retirement*. Cambridge, Massachusetts: Schenkman Publishing Company, 1976.

Ausubel, D. B.: *Educational Psychology, A Cognitive View*. New York: Holt, Rinehart and Winston, 1968.

Baley, N.: "Development of mental abilities." *In* P. H. Mussen (Ed.): *Carmichael's Manual of Child Psychology*, Vol. 1. New York: John Wiley and Sons, 1970.

Baltes, P. B., and Schaie, K. W.: "Aging and the IQ: the myth of the twilight years." *Psychology Today* 7:35–40, March 1974.

Bardwick, J. M.: *Psychology of Women*. New York: Harper and Brothers, 1971.

Barfield, R. E., and Morgan, J.: *Early Retirement: The Decision and the Experience*. Ann Arbor, Michigan: Institute of Social Research, 1969.

Baron, R. A., Byrne, D., and Kantowitz, B. H.: *Psychology: Understanding Behavior*. Philadelphia: W. B. Saunders Company, 1977.

Barrett, J. H.: *Gerontological Psychology*. Springfield, Illinois: Charles C Thomas, 1972.

Bart, P. B.: "Mother Portnoy's complaints." *Trans-Action* 8:69–74, November-December, 1970.

Bartell, G. D.: "Group sex among the mid-Americans." *Journal of Sex Research* 6(2):113–130, May 1970.

Belbin, R. M.: "Middle-age: what happens to ability." *In* R. Owen (Ed.): *Middle Age*. London: Cox and Wyman, 1967, pp. 98–106.

Belcher, D.: *Giving Psychology Away*. San Francisco: Canfield Press, 1973.

Bell, R. R.: *Marriage and Family Interaction* (3rd Ed.). Homewood, Illinois: The Dorsey Press, 1975.

Bell, R. R.: *Premarital Sex in a Changing Society*. Englewood Cliffs, New Jersey: Prentice-Hall, 1966.

Bell, R.: *Premarital Sex, Social Deviance*. Homewood, Illinois: The Dorsey Press, 1971.

Bell, R. R., and Chaskes, J. B.: "Premarital sexual experience among coeds, 1958 and 1968." *Journal of Marriage and the Family* 32:81–84, February 1970.

Bender, M.: "Switching careers in mid-stream." *The New York Times*, January 17, 1971.

Benson, L.: *The Family Bond*. New York: Random House, 1971.

Berardo, F. M.: "Widowhood status in the United States: perspective on a neglected aspect of the family life cycle." *Family Coordinator* 17:191–202, July 1968.

Bernard, H. W., and Fullmer, D. W.: *Principles of Guidance* (2nd Ed.). New York: Thomas Y. Crowell Company, 1977.

Binstock, R. H.: "Aging and the future of American politics." *In* R. A. Kalish (Ed.): *The Later Years: Social Applications of Gerontology*. Monterey, California: Brooks/Cole Publishing Company, 1977.

Birren, J. E.: "The experience of aging." *In* R. E. Davis and M. E. Neiswender (Eds.): *Aging: Prospectus and Issues.* Los Angeles: Andrus Gerontology Center, 1973, pp. 1–11.

Birren, J. E.: *The Psychology of Aging.* Englewood Cliffs, New Jersey: Prentice-Hall, Inc., 1964.

Bischof, L. J.: *Adult Psychology.* New York: Harper and Row, 1969.

Bischof, L. J.: *Adult Psychology* (2nd Ed.). New York: Harper and Row, 1976.

Bixby, L. E.: "Income of people age 65 and older: overview from the 1968 survey of the aged." *Social Security Bulletin,* April 1970, 3–34.

Blau, Z. S.: *Old Age in a Changing Society.* New York: Franklin Watts, New Viewpoints, 1973.

Blood, R. O., Jr.: *Marriage* (2nd Ed.). New York: The Free Press, 1969.

Blood, R. O., and Wolfe, D. M.: *Husbands and Wives: The Dynamics of Married Living.* New York: The Free Press, 1960.

Blood, R. O.: *The Family.* New York: The Free Press, 1972.

Bloom, B.: *Stability and Change in Human Characteristics.* New York: John Wiley and Sons, 1964.

Bloom, K. L.: "Age and the self-concept." *American Journal of Psychiatry 118*:534–538, 1961.

Bock, R. W., and Webber, I.: "Suicide among the elderly: isolating widowhood and mitigating alternatives." *Journal of Marriage and the Family 34*:24–31, February, 1972.

Botwinick, J.: *Aging and Behavior: A Comprehensive Integration of Research Findings.* New York: Springer Publishing Company, 1973.

Botwinick, J.: *Cognitive Processes in Maturity and Old Age.* New York: Springer Publishing Company, 1967.

Botwinick, J.: "Geropsychology." *Annual Review of Psychology 21*:239–272, 1970.

Bowlby, J.: "Grief and mourning in infancy and early childhood." *Psychoanalytic Study of the Child 15*:9–52, 1960.

Brammer, L. M., and Shostrum, E. L.: *Therapeutic Psychology* (3rd Ed.). Englewood Cliffs, New Jersey: Prentice-Hall, 1977.

Brayshaw, A. J.: "Middle-age marriage: idealism, realism, and the search for meaning." *Marriage and Family Living 24*(4), 1962.

Breger, E. M.: "Vocational choices in college." *The Personnel and Guidance Journal. 34*(4), May 1968.

Brim, O. G., Jr.: "Theories of the male mid-life crisis." *The Counseling Psychologist 6*(1):2–9, 1976.

Bromley, D. B.: *The Psychology of Human Aging.* Baltimore, Maryland: Penguin Books, 1966.

Brotman, H. B.: *Facts and Figures on Older Americans* (5, An Overview, 1971). Washington, D. C.: Department of Health, Education and Welfare, 1972.

Brown, T. E.: "The search for vocation in middle-life." *Eastern Career Development Newsletter 1*(1):1–2, 1972.

Buhler, C.: "The course of human life as a psychological problem." *In* W. R. Looft (Ed.): *Developmental Psychology: A Book of Readings.* New York: Holt, Rinehart and Winston, 1972.

Burchinal, L. G.: "School policies and school age marriages." *Family Life Coordinator 8*:43–48, 1960.

Burchinal, L. G.: "Trends and prospects for young marriages in the United States." *Journal of Marriage and the Family,* May 1965.

Burg, A.: "Light sensitivity as related to age and sex." *Perceptual and Motor Skills 24*:1279–1288, 1967.

Burgess, E. W., and Locke, H. J.: *The Family: From Institutional to Companionship* (2nd Ed.). New York: American Book, 1953.

Burgess, E. W., Locke, H. J., and Thomes, M. M.: *The Family: From Traditional to Companionship* (4th Ed.). New York: D. Van Nostrand Company, 1971.

Burr, W. R.: *Successful Marriage: A Principles Approach.* Homewood, Illinois: The Dorsey Press, 1976.

Butler, R. N.: "The life review: an interpretation of reminiscence in the aged." *In* B. Neugarten (Ed.): *Middle Age and Aging.* Chicago: University of Chicago Press, 1968.

Butler, R. N.: "Age: the life review." *Psychology Today,* December 1971.

Butler, R. N.: *Why Survive? Being Old in America.* New York: Harper and Row, 1975.

Butler, R. N., and Lewis, M. I.: *Aging and Mental Health: Positive Psychological Approaches.* St. Louis: C. V. Mosby, 1973.

Canestrari, R. E., Jr.: Paced and self-paced learning in young and elderly adults. *Journal of Gerontology 18*:165–168, 1963.

Carp, F. M. (Ed.): *Retirement.* New York: Behavioral Publications, 1972.

Carp, F. M.: "Some components of disengagement." *Journal of Gerontology 23*:382–386, 1968.

Carter, H. D.: "Vocational interests and job orientation." *Applied Psychology Monographs 2*, 1944.

Carter, H., and Glick, P. C.: *Marriage and Divorce: A Social and Economic Study*. Cambridge, Massachusetts: Harvard University Press, 1970.

Cavan, R. S.: "Self and role in adjustment during old age." *In* A. M. Rose (Ed.): *Human Behavior and Social Processes*. Boston: Houghton Mifflin Company, 1962.

Christenson, C., and Gagnon, J. H.: "Sexual behavior in a group of older women." *Journal of Gerontology*, July 1965.

Clark, M., and Gosnell, M.: "The graying of America." *Newsweek*, February 28, 1977.

Clayton, P. J., Halikes, H. A., and Maurice, W. L.: "Bereavement of the widowed." *Diseases of the Nervous System*, 32:597–604, 1971.

Clayton, R. R.: *The Family, Marriage, and Social Change*. Lexington, Massachusetts: D. C. Heath and Company, 1975.

Comfort, A.: Biological theories of aging. *Human Development* 13:127–139, 1970.

Corso, J. F.: "Sensory processes and age effects in normal adults." *Journal of Gerontology* 26:90–105, 1971.

Cortés, J. B., and Gatti, F. H.: "Physique and self-description of temperament." *American Psychology* 19:572, 1964 (abstract).

Cowgill, D. O., and Holmes, L. O. (Eds.): *Aging and Modernization*. New York: Appleton, 1972.

Cox, F.: "Communes: a potpourri of ideas." *In* F. Cox (Ed.): *American marriage: A Changing Scene?* Dubuque, Iowa: Wm. C. Brown Company, 1972.

Cox, F. D.: *Youth, Marriage and the Seductive Society*. Dubuque, Iowa: Wm. C. Brown Company, 1974.

Cumming, E.: "Further thoughts on the theory of disengagement." *International Social Science Journal* 15:377–393, 1963.

Cumming, E., and Henry, W. E.: *Growing Old*. New York: Basic Books, 1961.

Davis, J. L., and Hackman, R. B.: "Vocational adjustment: prevention or correction emphasis?" *In* J. Adams (Ed.): *Human Behavior in a Changing Society*. Boston: Holbrook Press, 1973.

Davis, K.: *The American Family in Relation to Demographic Change*. International Population and Urban Research Institute of International Studies, University of California at Berkeley. Reprint No. 425, 1973.

De Beauvoir, S. D.: *The Coming of Age*. New York: G. P. Putnam's Sons, 1972.

DeCarlo, T. J. (Ed.): "Recreational participation patterns and successful aging." *Journal of Gerontology* 29:416–422, 1974.

Deese, J.: *Psychology as science and art*. New York: Harcourt, Brace, Jovanovich, 1972.

Denfield, D., and Gordon, M.: "The sociology of mate swapping: or, the family that swings together clings together." *Journal of Sex Research* 6(2):85–100, May 1970.

Dennis, W.: "Creative productivity between the ages of twenty and eighty years." *In* B. Neugarten (Ed.): *Middle Age and Aging*. Chicago: University of Chicago Press, 1968.

Deutscher, I.: "Socialization for postparental life." *In* M. E. Lasswell and T. E. Lasswell (Eds.): *Love, Marriage, Family: A Developmental Approach*. Glenville, Illinois: Scott, Foresman, 1973, pp. 510–517.

Deutscher, I.: "The quality of post-parental life: definitions of the situation." *Journal of Marriage and the Family* 26:52–59, 263–268, February 1964.

DiCaprio, N. S.: *Personality Theories: Guides to Living*. Philadelphia: W. B. Saunders Company, 1974.

Dizard, J.: *Social Change and the Family*. Chicago: Community and Family Study Center, 1968.

Dodson, F.: *How to Father*. New York: Signet Books, 1974.

Dreyer, P. H.: "Changes in the meaning of marriage among youth: the impact of the revolution in sex and sex role behavior." *In* R. E. Grinder (Ed.): *Studies in Adolescence* (3rd Ed.). New York: Macmillan, 1975.

Duberman, L.: "Step-kin relationships." *Journal of Marriage and the Family* 35:283–292, 1973.

Duberman, L.: *Marriage and Its Alternatives*. New York: Praeger Publishing Company, 1974.

Dullea, G.: "Women change careers in mid-life now, too." New York Times News Service, 1977.

Duvall, E. M.: *In-Laws: Pro and Con*. New York: Association Press, 1954.

Duvall, E. M.: *Family Development* (4th Ed.). Philadelphia: J. B. Lippincott, 1971.

Duvall, E. M.: *Marriage and Family Development* (5th Ed.). New York: J. B. Lippincott, 1977.

Dyer, E. D.: "Parenthood as crisis: a repeat study." *Marriage and Family Living* 25:196–201, May 1963.

Elkind, D.: "Cognitive and educational psychology. *In* Mussen, P., Rosenzweig, M.

R., et al.: *Psychology, an Introduction.* Lexington, Massachusetts: D. C. Heath and Company, 1977.

Elkind, D.: "Measuring young minds." *Horizon 13*(1):35, 1971.

England, J. L., and Kunz, P. R.: "The application of age specific rates to divorce." *Journal of Marriage and the Family 37*:40–46, February 1975.

Entine, A. D.: "Mid-life counseling: prognosis and potential." *The Personnel and Guidance Journal 55*(3):112–114, November 1976.

Epstein, C.: *Nursing the Dying Patient.* Reston, Virginia: Reston Publishing Company, 1975.

Epstein, J.· *Divorced in America.* New York: E. P. Dutton, 1974.

Epstein, L. A., and Murray, J. H.: "Employment and retirement." *In* B. L. Neugarten (Ed.): *Middle Age and Aging.* Chicago: University of Chicago Press, 1968.

Erikson, E. H.: *Childhood and Society* (2nd Ed.). New York: W. W. Norton, 1963.

Farnsworth, P. R., McNemar, O., and McNemar, Q. (Eds.): *Annual Review of Psychology,* Vol. 16. Palo Alto, California: Annual Reviews, 1965.

Feifel, H., "Death." *In* N. L. Farberow (Ed.): *Taboo Topics.* New York: Atherton Press, 1963.

Feigenbaum, E. M.: "Sexual behavior in the later years." *In* R. A. Kalish (Ed.): *The Later Years: Social Applications of Gerontology.* Monterey, California: Brooks/Cole Publishing Company, 1977.

Feuer, L. S.: *The Conflict of Generations.* New York: Basic Books, 1969.

Fitzsimmons, C.: *The Management of Family Resources.* San Francisco: Freeman, 1950.

Ford, A. B.: "Casualties of our time." *Science 167*:(3196) 256–263, 1970.

Freeman, H. E., and Jones, W. C.: *Social Problems: Causes and Controls.* Chicago: Rand McNally, 1970.

Frenkel-Brunswik, E.: "Adjustments and reorientation in the course of the life span." *In* B. L. Neugarten (Ed.): *Middle Age and Aging.* Chicago: University of Chicago Press, 1968.

Fromm, E.: *Escape From Freedom.* New York: Holt, Rinehart and Winston, 1941.

Fromm, E.: *The Art of Loving.* New York: Harper and Row, 1955.

Gagnon, J. H., and Simon, W.: *Sexual Conduct, The Social Sources of Human Sexuality.* Chicago: Aldine Publishing Company, 1973.

Ginzberg, E.: *Occupational Choice, An Approach to General Theory.* New York: Columbia University Press, 1951.

Ginzberg, E.: "Toward a theory of occupational choice: a restatement." *Vocational Guidance Quarterly 20*(3):169–176, 1972.

Glick, P. C.: *American Families.* New York: John Wiley, 1957. Reprinted in 1974 by Russell.

Glick, P. C.: "A demographer looks at American families." *Journal of Marriage and the Family 37*:15–26, February 1975.

Glick, P. C., and Norton, A. J.: "Frequency, duration, and probability of marriage and divorce." *Journal of Marriage and the Family 33*:307–317, May 1971.

Goethals, G. W., and Klos, D. S.: *Experiencing Youth.* Boston: Little, Brown, and Company, 1970.

Golant, S. M.: "Residential concentrations of the future elderly." *In* B. L. Neugarten (Ed.): "Aging in the year 2000: a look at the future." *The Gerontologist 15*(1):16–23, February 1975.

Gottesman, L. E.: "The institutionalized elderly: a new challenge." *In* R. A. Kalish (Ed.): *The Later Years: Social Applications of Gerontology.* Monterey, California: Brooks/Cole Publishing Company, 1977.

Gottesman, L. E., and Bourestom, N. C.: "Why nursing homes do what they do." *Gerontologist 14*:501–506, 1974.

Gould, R.: "The phases of adult life: a study in developmental psychology." *American Journal of Psychiatry 5*:521–531, 1972.

Gould, R.: "Adult life stages: growth toward self-tolerance." *Psychology Today 8*(9):74–78, February 1975.

Guyton, A. C.: *Textbook of Medical Physiology* (5th Ed.). Philadelphia: W. B. Saunders Company, 1976.

Habenstein, R. W., and Lamers, W. M.: *The History of American Funeral Directing.* Milwaukee, Wisconsin: Bulfin Printers, 1955.

Hansen, G. O.: "Meeting housing challenges: involvement—the elderly." *In Housing Issues.* Proceedings of the Fifth Annual Meeting, American Association of Housing Educators. Lincoln, Nebraska: University of Nebraska Press, 1975.

Harbeson, G. E.: *Choice and Challenge for the American Woman* (Rev. Ed.). Cambridge, Massachusetts: Schenkman Publishing Company, 1971.

Harvey, C. D., and Bahr, H. M.: "Widowhood, morale, and affiliation." *Journal of Marriage and the Family 36*:97–106, February 1974.

Havighurst, R. J.: *Developmental Tasks and Education* (3rd Ed.). New York: David McKay, 1972.

Havighurst, R. J.: *Human Development and Education.* New York: Longmans, 1953.

Havighurst, R. J., Neugarten, B. L., and Tobin. S. S.: "Disengagement and patterns of aging." *In* B. L. Neugarten (Ed.): *Middle Age and Aging.* Chicago: University of Chicago Press, 1968.

Health in the Later Years of Life: Selected Data from the National Center for Health Statistics. Washington, D. C.: U. S. Government Printing Office, 1971.

Heath, D. H.: *Growing Up in College.* San Francisco: Jossey-Bass, Inc., Publishers, 1968.

Heddescheimer, J. C.: "Multiple motivations for mid-career changes." *The Personnel and Guidance Journal* 55(3):109–111, November 1976.

Helms, D. B., and Turner, J. S.: *Exploring Child Behavior.* Philadelphia: W. B. Saunders Company, 1976.

Hendricks, J., and Hendricks, C. D.: *Aging in Mass Society: Myths and Realities.* Cambridge, Massachusetts: Winthrop Publishers, 1977.

Hepner, H. W.: *Retirement–A Time to Live Anew.* New York: McGraw-Hill Book Company, 1969.

Heyman, D. K., and Polansky, G. H.: "Social services in the community." *In* R. A. Kalish (Ed.): *The Later Years: Social Applications of Gerontology.* Monterey, California: Brooks/Cole Publishing Company, 1977.

Hiestand, D. C.: *Changing Careers After Thirty-five.* New York: Columbia University Press, 1971.

Hinton, J.: *Dying.* Baltimore: Penguin Books, 1967.

Hobbs, D. F.: "Parenthood as crisis: a third study." *Journal of Marriage and the Family* 27:367–372, August 1965.

Hodgkins, J.: "Influence of age on the speed of reaction and movement in females." *Journal of Gerontology* 17:385–389, 1962.

Hoenninger, R.: "New careers for midlife: may we help you?" Unpublished paper prepared for the Board of Directors of the National Vocational Guidance Association, 1974.

Holland, J. L.: *The Psychology of Vocational Choice.* Waltham, Massachusetts: Blaisdell Company, 1966.

Horner, M.: "Toward an understanding of achievement related conflicts in women." *Journal of Social Issues* 28:157–176, 1972.

Horrocks, J. E., and Mussman, M. C.: Middlescence: age-related stress periods during the adult years. *Genetic Psychology Monographs* 82:119–159, 1971.

Hunt, M., and Hunt, B.: *The Divorce Experience.* New York: McGraw-Hill, 1977.

Hunter, M.: "What happens after retirement?" New York Times News Service, August 2, 1977.

Ingraham, M.: "My Purpose Holds: Reactions and Experiences in Retirement of TIAA-CREF Annuitants." Educational Research Division, Teacher Insurance and Annuity Association, College Retirement Equities Fund, New York, 1974.

Insel, S. A.: "On counseling the bereaved." *The Personnel and Guidance Journal* 55(3), 1976.

Irelan, L. M., and Bond, K.: "Retirees of the 1970's." *In* C. Osterbird (Ed.): *Migration, Mobility, and Aging.* Gainesville, Florida: University of Florida Press, 1974.

Jacobson, S. B.: "The challenge of aging for marriage partners." *In* W. C. Bier (Ed.): *Aging: Its Challenge to the Individual and to Society.* New York: Fordham University Press, 1974, pp. 187–194.

Jaffe, A. J.: "Has the retreat from the labor force halted? A note on the retirement of men, 1930–1970." *Industrial Gerontology* 9:1–12, 1971.

Jaffe, A. J.: "The retirement dilemma." *Industrial Gerontology* 14(Summer), 1972.

Jersild, A. T.: *The Psychology of Adolescence* (2nd Ed.). New York: The Macmillan Company, 1963.

Kalish, R. A.: "After work: then what?" *In* R. A. Kalish (Ed.): *The Later Years: Social Applications of Gerontology.* Monterey, California: Brooks/Cole Publishing Company, 1977.

Kalish, R. A.: "Institutional living." *In* R. A. Kalish (Ed.): *The Later Years: Scoial Applications of Gerontology.* Monterey, California: Brooks/Cole Publishing Company, 1977.

Kalish, R. A.: *Late Adulthood: Perspectives on Human Development.* Monterey, California: Brooks/Cole Publishing Company, 1975.

Kalish, R. A., and Reynolds, D. K.: *Death and Ethnicity: A Psychocultural Study.* Los Angeles: University of Southern California Press, 1976.

Kantner, J., and Zelnick, M.: "The probability of premarital intercourse." *Social Science Research* 1:335, 1972.

Kaplan, H. B., and Pokorny, A. D.: "Aging and self-attitude: a conditional relationship." *Aging and Human Development* 1:241–250, 1970.

Kart, C. S.: "Some biological aspects of aging." *In* C. S. Kart and B. B. Manard: *Aging in America: Readings in Social Gerontology*. New York: Alfred Publishing Company, 1976.

Kastenbaum, R.: "Age: getting there ahead of time." *Psychology Today*, December 1971, pp. 52–54.

Katona, G., Morgan, J. N., and Barfield, R. E.: "Retirement in prospect and retrospect." *In Occasional Papers in Gerontology, No. 4*. Ann Arbor, Michigan: University of Michigan, Wayne State University Institute of Gerontology, 1969, pp. 27–49.

Kavanaugh, R. E.: *Facing Death*. Baltimore: Penguin Books, 1974.

Kelley, R. K.: *Courtship, Marriage, and the Family* (2nd Ed.). New York: Harcourt Brace Jovanovich, 1974.

Keniston, K.: "Social change and youth in America." *In* E. Erikson (Ed.): *Youth: Change and Challenge*. New York: Basic Books, 1963.

Keniston, K.: "Youth: a new stage of life." *The American Scholar* 39:631–641, Autumn 1970.

Kephart, W. M.: *The Family, Society, and the Individual*. (3rd ed.) Boston: Houghton Mifflin Co., 1972. (4th ed.) Boston: Houghton Mifflin Co., 1977.

Kerckhoff, A. C., and Davis, R. E.: "Value consensus and need complementarity in mate selection." *American Sociological Review* 27:295–303, 1962.

Kimble, G. A., and Garmezy, N.: *Principles of General Psychology* (3rd Ed.). New York: The Ronald Press, 1968.

Kimmel, D. C.: *Adulthood and Aging, An Interdisciplinary View*. New York: John Wiley and Sons, 1974.

Kimmel, D. C.: "Adult Development: Challenges For Counseling." *The Personnel and Guidance Journal* 55 (3):103–105, Nov. 1976.

Kinsey, A. C., Pomeroy, W. B., Martin, C. E., and Gebhard, P. H.: *Sexual Behavior in the Human Female*. Philadelphia: W. B. Saunders Company, 1953.

Kinsey, A. C., Pomeroy, W. B., and Martin, C. E.: *Sexual Behavior in the Human Male*. Philadelphia: W. B. Saunders Company, 1948.

Kirby, I. J.: "Hormone replacement therapy for postmenopausal symptoms." *Lancet* 2:103, 1973.

Kisker, G. W.: *The Disorganized Personality* (2nd Ed.). New York: McGraw-Hill Book Company, 1972.

Knopf, O.: *Successful Aging*. New York: The Viking Press, 1975.

Kowitz, G. T., and Kowitz, N. G.: *An Introduction to School Guidance*. New York: Holt, Rinehart and Winston, 1971.

Krant, M. J.: *Dying and Dignity: The Meaning and Control of a Personal Death*. Springfield, Illinois: Charles C Thomas, 1974.

Kreps, J. M.: *Lifetime Association of Work and Income: Essays in the Economics of Aging*. Durham, North Carolina: Duke University Press, 1971.

Kübler-Ross, E.: *On Death and Dying*. New York: Macmillan, Inc., 1969.

Kübler-Ross, E.: *Questions and Answers on Death and Dying*. New York: Macmillan, Inc., 1974.

Kuhlen, R. G.: "Developmental changes in motivation during the adult years." *In* J. E. Birren (Ed.): *Relations of Development and Aging*. Springfield, Illinois: Charles C Thomas, 1964.

Kuhlen, R. G., and Johnson, G. H.: "Changes in goals with increasing adult age." *Journal of Consulting Psychology* 16(1):1–4, 1952.

Kuhn, M.: "Foreword" in Adler, J.: *The Retirement Book*. New York: William Morrow and Co., 1975.

Lack, S.: "Referral: Hospice." *In* R. A. Kalish (Ed.): *The Later Years: Social Applications of Gerontology*. Monterey, California: Brooks/Cole Publishing Company, 1977.

Landis, J. T., and Landis, M. G.: *Building a Successful Marriage* (4th Ed.). Englewood Cliffs, New Jersey: Prentice-Hall, 1963.

Landis, J. T., and Landis, M. G.: *Building A Successful Marriage* (5th Ed.). Englewood Cliffs, New Jersey, Prentice-Hall, 1968.

Landis, P. H.: *Making the Most of Marriage* (5th Ed.). Englewood Cliffs, New Jersey: Prentice-Hall, 1975.

Lawton, M. P.: "Psychology of aging." *In* W. C. Bier (Ed.): *Aging: Its Challenge to the Individual and Society*. New York: Fordham University Press, 1974.

Leaf, A.: "Getting old." *Scientific American* 229:45–52, 1973.

Leaf, A.: *Youth in Old Age*. New York: McGraw-Hill Publishing Company, 1975.

Lear, M. W.: "Is there a male menopause?" *New York Times Magazine* January 28, 1973.

Lehman, H. C.: *Age and Achievement*. Princeton, New Jersey: Princeton University Press, 1953.

LeMasters, E. E.: "Parenthood as a crisis." *Marriage and Family Living* 19:352–355, 1957.

LeMasters, E. E.: *Parents in Modern America: A Sociological Analysis.* (3rd ed.) Homewood, Illinois: The Dorsey Press, 1977.

Lenzer, A.: "Health care services." *In* R. A. Kalish (Ed.): *The Later Years: Social Applications of Gerontology.* Monterey, California: Brooks/Cole Publishing Company, 1977.

Lerner, R. M.: *Concepts and Theories of Human Development.* Reading, Massachusetts: Addison-Wesley Publishing Company, 1976.

Leslie, G. R.: *The Family in Social Context* (2nd Ed.). New York: Oxford University Press, 1973.

Leslie, G. R., and Leslie, E. M.: *Marriage in a Changing World.* New York: John Wiley and Sons, 1977.

Levinger, G.: "Sources of marital dissatisfaction among applicants for divorce." *American Journal of Orthopsychiatry* 36:803–807, 1966.

Levinson, D. J., Darrow, C. M., Klein, E. B., Levinson, M. H., and McKee, B.: "The psychosocial development of men in early adulthood and the mid-life transition." *In* D. F. Ricks, A. Thomas, and M. Roff (Eds.): *Life History Research in Psychopathology* (Vol. 3). Minneapolis: University of Minnesota Press, 1974.

Lipman, A.: "Role conceptions of couples in retirement." *In* C. Tibbitts and W. Donahue (Eds.): *Social and Psychological Aspects of Aging.* New York: Columbia University Press, 1962.

Lobsenz, M. M.: *Sex After Sixty-five.* Public Affairs Pamphlet No. 519, New York Public Affairs Committee, 1975.

Loeb, J., and Price, J. R.: "Mother and child personality characteristics." *Journal of Consulting Psychology* 30(2):112–117, April 1966.

Lopata, H. Z.: *Widowhood in an American City.* Cambridge, Massachusetts: Schenkman Publishing Company, 1970.

Lowenthal, M.: "Some potentialities of a life-cycle approach to the study of retirement." *In* F. M. Carp (Ed.): *Retirement.* New York: Behavioral Publications, 1972.

Lowrie, S. H.: "Early and late dating: some conditions associated with them." *Marriage and Family Living* 23:284–291, 1961.

Maddox, G. L.: "Disengagement theory: a critical evaluation." *The Gerontologist* 4:80–82, 103, 1964.

Maddox, G. L.: "Persistence of life style among the elderly: a longitudinal study of patterns of social activity in relation to life satisfaction." *In* B. L. Neugarten (Ed.): *Middle Age and Aging.* Chicago: University of Chicago Press, 1968.

Malm, M., and Jamison, O. G.: *Adolescence.* New York: McGraw-Hill, 1952.

Manion, U. V.: "Preretirement counseling: the need for a new approach." *The Personnel and Guidance Journal* 55(3), November 1976.

Marshall, W. A.: "The body." *In* R. R. Sears and S. S. Feldman (Eds.): *The Seven Ages of Man.* Los Altos, California: William Kaufman, Inc., 1973.

Maslow, A. H.: *The S-I Test: A Measure of Psychological Security-Insecurity.* Stanford, California: Stanford University Press, 1952.

Maslow, A. H.: *Motivation and Personality.* New York: Harper and Brothers, 1954.

Maslow, A. H.: *Toward a Psychology of Being* (2nd ed.). Princeton, New Jersey: Van Nostrand Reinhold, 1968.

Maslow, A. H.: *Motivation and Personality* (2nd ed.). New York: Harper and Row, 1970.

Maslow, A. H.: *The Farther Reaches of Human Nature.* New York: The Viking Press, 1971.

Masters, W. H., and Johnson, V. E.: *Human Sexual Response.* Boston: Little, Brown and Company, 1966.

Masters, W. H., and Johnson, V. E.: *Human Sexual Inadequacy.* Boston: Little, Brown and Company, 1970.

May, R.: *Love and Will.* New York: W. W. Norton, 1969.

McCandless, B. R., Roberts, R., and Starnes, T.: "Teachers' marks, achievement test scores, and aptitude relations with respect to social class, race, and sex." *Journal of Educational Psychology* 63:153–159, 1972.

McGinnis, T. C., and Finnegan, D. G.: *Open Family and Marriage, A Guide to Personal Growth.* St. Louis: C. V. Mosby Company, 1976.

McMahon, F. B.: *Psychology: A Hybrid Science* (3rd ed.). Englewood Cliffs, New Jersey: Prentice-Hall, 1977.

Mead, M.: *Culture and Commitment.* New York: Doubleday, 1970.

Middlebrook, P. N.: *Social Psychology and Modern Life.* New York: Alfred A. Knopf, 1974.

Mills, E. W.: "Career development in mid-life." *In* W. E. Bartlett (Ed.): *Evolving Religious Careers.* Washington, D. C., Center for Applied Research in the Apostolate, 1970, pp. 181–198.

Mischel, W.: *Introduction to Personality.* New York: Holt, Rinehart and Winston, 1971.

Mitford, J.: *The American Way of Death*. New York: Simon and Schuster, 1963.

Monahan, T. P.: "Does age at marriage matter in divorce?" *Social Forces* 32:81–87, 1963.

Mondale, W. S.: 2632 Federal Employees Preretirement Assistance Act of 1975. *Congressional Record*. Vol. 121, No. 164, pp. 519393–4, Nov. 6, 1975.

Montgomery, J. E.: *Social Characteristics of the Aged in a Small Pennsylvania Community*. State College, Pennsylvania: College of Home Economics Research Publication 233, The Pennsylvania State University, 1965.

Moore, A. J.: *The Young Adult Generation, A Perspective on the Future*. New York: Abingdon Press, 1969.

Mussen, P., Rosenzweig, M. R., et al.: *Psychology, An Introduction*. Lexington, Massachusetts: D. C. Heath and Company, 1973.

Myers, G. C., and Soldo, B. J.: "Older Americans: who are they?" *In* R. A. Kalish (Ed.): *The Later Years: Social Applications of Gerontology*. Monterey, California: Brooks/Cole Publishing Company, 1977.

Navran, L.: "Communication and adjustment in marriage." *Family Process* 6:173–184, 1967.

Neff, W. S.: *Work and Human Behavior*. New York: Atherton Press, 1968.

Neugarten, B. L.: "Adult personality: toward a psychology of the life cycle." *In* B. L. Neugarten (Ed.): *Middle Age and Aging*. Chicago: University of Chicago Press, 1968.

Neugarten, B. L.: "Grow old along with me! The best is yet to be." *Psychology Today* 5(7):45–48, 1971.

Neugarten, B. L.: *Personality in Middle and Late Life: Empirical Studies*. New York: Atherton Press, 1964.

Neugarten, B. L., and Gutmann, D. L.: "Age sex roles and personality in middle age: a thematic apperception study." *In* B. L. Neugarten (Ed.): *Personality in Middle and Later Life: Empirical Studies*. New York: Atherton Press, 1964.

Neugarten, B. L., and Moore, J. W.: "The changing age status system." *In* B. Neugarten (Ed.): *Middle Age and Aging*. Chicago: University of Chicago Press, 1968.

Neugarten, B. L., and Weinstein, K. K.: "The changing American grandparent." *In* B. L. Neugarten (Ed.): *Middle Age and Aging*. Chicago: University of Chicago Press, 1968, pp. 280–285.

Neugarten, B. L., Wood, V., Kraines, R. J., and Loomis, B.: "Women's attitudes toward the menopause." *Vita Humana* 6:140–151, 1963.

Neuman, B. M., and Neuman, P. R.: *Development Through Life: A Psychosocial Approach*. Homewood, Illinois: The Dorsey Press, 1975.

Nicholson, T., and Copeland, J. B.: "A right to keep working?" *Newsweek,* July 18, 1977, p. 79.

Nixon, R. E.: "Psychological normality in the years of youth." *Teachers College Record* 66:71–79, 1964.

Nye, F. I., and Berardo, F. M.: *The Family: Its Structure and Interaction*. New York: Macmillan, 1973.

O'Neill, N., and O'Neill, G.: *Open Marriage, A New Life Style for Couples*. New York: M. Evans and Company, 1972.

Orbach, H. L.: "Social and institutional aspects of industrial workers' retirement patterns." *In Occasional Papers in Gerontology, No. 4*. Ann Arbor, Michigan: University of Michigan—Wayne State University Institute of Gerontology, 1969, pp. 1–26.

Otto, H.: "The new marriage." *In* H. Otto (Ed.): *The Family in Search of a Future*. New York: Appleton-Century-Crofts, 1970.

Paige, K. E.: "Women learn to sing the menstrual blues." *Psychology Today* 7(4), September 1973.

Palmore, E.: "Differences in the retirement patterns of men and women." *Gerontologist* 5:4–8, 1965.

Palmore, E.: "Compulsory versus flexible retirement: issues and facts." *Gerontologist* 12(4):343–348, 1972.

Parkes, C. M.: *Bereavement: Studies of Grief in Adult Life*. New York: International Universities Press, 1972.

Parry, J.: "Abilities." *In* R. R. Sears and S. S. Feldman (Eds.): *The Seven Ages of Man*. Los Altos, California: William Kaufmann, Inc., 1973.

Pattison, E. M.: "Attitudes toward death." *In* E. M. Pattison (Ed.): *The Experience of Dying*. Englewood Cliffs, New Jersey: Prentice-Hall, 1977(a).

Pattison, E. M.: "The experience of dying." *In* E. M. Pattison (Ed.): *The Experience of Dying*. Englewood Cliffs, New Jersey: Prentice-Hall, 1977(b).

Peck, R. C.: "Psychological developments in the second half of life." *In* B. L. Neugarten (Ed.): *Middle Age and Aging*. Chicago: University of Chicago Press, 1968.

Perry, J., and Perry, E.: *Pairing and Parenthood: An Introduction to Marriage and the Family*. San Francisco: Canfield Press, 1977.

Peterson, J. A.: "Anticipation of things to come." *In* M. E. Lasswell and T. E. Lasswell (Eds.): *Love–Marriage–Family: A Developmental Approach.* Glenview, Illinois: Scott, Foresman and Company, 1973, pp. 524–531.

Pfeiffer, E. A., Verwoerdt, A., and Wang, H. S.: "Sexual behavior in aged men and women." *In* E. Palmore (Ed.): *Normal Aging.* Durham, North Carolina: Duke University Press, 1970, pp. 299–303.

Phillips, D.: *Statistics: A Guide to the Unknown.* New York: Holden-Day, 1972.

Pierson, E. C., and D'Antonio, W. V.: *Female and Male: Dimensions of Human Sexuality.* Philadelphia: J. B. Lippincott and Company, 1974.

Plutchik, R., Weiner, M., and Conte, H.: "Studies of body image, body worries, and body discomforts." *Journal of Gerontology* 26:244–350, 1971.

Post, F.: "Personality." *In* R. R. Sears and S. S. Feldman (Eds.): *The Seven Ages of Man.* Los Altos, California: William Kaufmann, Inc., 1973.

Powell, D. H., and Driscoll, R. F.: "Middle class professionals face unemployment." *Society,* January-February 1973.

Puner, M.: *The Good Long Life: What We Know About Growing Old.* New York: Universe Books, 1974.

Pyron, H. C., and Manion, U. V.: "The company, the individual, and the decision to retire." *Industrial Gerontology* 4:1–11, 1970.

Ramey, J. W.: "Emerging patterns of innovative behavior in marriage." *The Family Coordinator* 21(4):435–456, October 1972.

Rappaport, L.: "Adult development: Faster horses . . . and more money." *In The Personnel and Guidance Journal* 55(3):106–108, November 1976.

Rayner, E.: *Human Development.* London: George Allen and Unwin, Ltd., 1971.

Reed, H. B. C., Jr., and Reitan, R. M.: "Changes in psychological test performance associated with the normal aging process." *Journal of Gerontology* 18:271–274, 1963.

Reich, C.: *The Greening of America.* New York: Random House, 1970.

Reichard, S.: "Five patterns of adjustment to aging." *In* Reichard, S., Livson, F., and Peterson, P. G.: *Aging and Personality,* Part III. New York: John Wiley, 1962.

Reichard, S., Livson, F., and Peterson, P. G.: *Aging and Personality.* New York: John Wiley, 1962.

Reiss, I. L.: *Premarital Sexual Standards in America.* New York: The Free Press, 1960.

Report of the President's Council on Aging. Washington, D.C., U.S. Government Printing Office, 1961.

Riegel, K. F., and Riegel, R. M.: "Development, drop, and death." *Developmental Psychology* 6(2):306–319, 1972.

Riker, A. P., and Brisbane, H. E.: *Married Life.* Peoria, Illinois: Chas. A. Bennett Company, 1970.

Robbins, P. I., and Harvey, D. W.: "Avenues and directions for accomplishing mid-career change." *Vocational Guidance Quarterly* 25(4), June 1977.

Robins, A. J.: "Family relations of the aging in three-generation households." *In* C. Tibbitts and W. Donahue (Eds.): *Social and Psychological Aspects of Aging.* New York: Columbia University Press, 1962.

Roe, A.: *The Psychology of Occupations.* New York: John Wiley, 1956.

Rogers, D.: "The role of the father." *In* D. Rogers (Ed.): *Issues in Child Psychology.* Belmont, California: Brooks/Cole Publishing Company, 1969.

Rogers, K.: "The mid-career crisis." *The Saturday Review–Society,* February 1973, pp. 37–38.

Rollins, B. C., and Feldman, H.: "Marital satisfaction over the family life cycle." *Journal of Marriage and the Family* 32(1):20–28, 1970.

Rose, A. M.: "A current theoretical issue in social gerontology." *In* B. L. Neugarten (Ed.): *Middle Age and Aging.* Chicago: University of Chicago Press, 1968.

Rosencranz, H. A.: "Preretirement education." *In* H. A. Rosencranz (Ed.): *Pre-Retirement Education: A Manual for Conference Leaders.* Storrs, Connecticut: University of Connecticut Program in Gerontology, 1975.

Rosow, J. M. (Ed.): *The Worker and the Job: Coping with Change.* Englewood Cliffs, New Jersey: Prentice-Hall, 1974.

Rossi, A. S.: "Transition to parenthood." *Journal of Marriage and the Family* 30(1):26–39, February 1968.

Ruch, T. C., and Fulton, J. F.: *Medical Physiology and Biophysics* (18th Edition of *Howell's Textbook of Physiology*). Philadelphia: W. B. Saunders Company, 1960.

Sachs, H. L.: *Dynamic Personal Adjustment: An Introduction.* New York: Behavioral Publishing, 1975.

Saxton, L.: *The Individual, Marriage, and the Family.* Belmont, California: Wadsworth Publishing Compnay, 1968.

Schein, E. H.: "The first job dilemma." *In* J. DeCello (Ed.): *Readings in Educational Psychology Today.* Del Mar, California: CRM Books, 1970.

Schlesinger, B.: "Remarriage as a family reorganization for divorced persons—a Canadian study." *Journal of Comparative Family Studies*, Autumn 1970, pp. 101–118.

Schlossberg, N. K.: "Breaking out of the box: organized options for adults." *The Vocational Guidance Quarterly* 25(4):313–319, June 1977.

Selye, H.: *The Stress of Life*. New York: McGraw-Hill, 1956.

Shanas, E.: *Family Relationships of Older People*. New York: Health Information Foundation, 1961, p. 38.

Shanas, E., Townsend, P., Wedderburn, D., Friis, H., Milhoj, P., and Stehouwer, J. (Eds.): *Old People in Three Industrial Societies*. New York: Atherton Press, 1968.

Sheehy, G.: *Passages: Predictable Crises of Adult Life*. New York: E. P. Dutton and Company, 1976.

Sheidman, E.: *Death of Man*. Baltimore, Maryland: Penguin Books, 1974.

Sheidman, E. S.: "You and death." *Psychology Today* 5:43–45, June 1971.

Sheldon, W. H., Stevens, S. S., and Tucker, W. B.: *The Varieties of Human Physique*. New York: Harper Brothers, 1940.

Shepro, D., Belamarich, F., and Levy, C.: *Human Anatomy and Physiology*. New York: Holt, Rinehart and Winston, 1974.

Sherfey, M. J.: *The Nature and Evolution of Female Sexuality*. New York: Random House, 1972.

Shertzer, B., and Stone, S. C.: *Fundamentals of Guidance* (3rd Ed.). Boston: Houghton Mifflin, 1976.

Shock, N. W.: "The physiology of aging." *Scientific American* 206:100–110, January 1962.

Shope, D.: *Interpersonal Sexuality*. Philadelphia: W. B. Saunders Co., 1975.

Simpson, I. H.: "Problems of the aging in work and retirement." *In* R. R. Boyd and C. G. Oakes (Eds.): *Foundations of Practical Gerontology*. Columbia, South Carolina: University of South Carolina Press, 1969.

Smith, B. K.: *Aging in America*. Boston: The Beacon Press, 1973.

Smith, D. W., and Bierman, E. L.: *The Biologic Ages of Man, from Conception Through Old Age*. Philadelphia: W. B. Saunders Company, 1973.

Sorensen, C.: *Adolescent Sexuality in Contemporary America*. New York: World Publishing Company, 1973.

Spence, D., and Lonner, T.: The empty nest: a transition within motherhood. *Family Coordinator* 20:369–375, October 1971.

Spence, D. L.: "Differential use of time: its meaning in retirement." *In* H. A. Rosencranz (Ed.): *Preretirement Education: A Manual for Conference Leaders*. Storrs, Connecticut: University of Connecticut Program in Gerontology, 1975.

Steckle, L. C.: *Problems of Human Adjustment*. New York: Harper and Row, 1957.

Stein, S. B.: *About Death*. New York: Walker and Company, 1974.

Steinberg, R.: *Man and the Organization*. New York: Time-Life Books, 1975.

Stinnett, N., Carter, L. M., and Montgomery, J. E.: "Older persons' perceptions of their marriages." *Journal of Marriage and the Family* 34(4):665–670, November 1972.

Streib, G. F.: "Changing roles in the later years." *In* R. A. Kalish (Ed.): *The Later Years: Social Applications of Gerontology*. Monterey, California: Brooks/Cole Publishing Company, 1977.

Streib, G. F.: "Intergenerational relations: perspectives of the two generations on the older person." *Journal of Marriage and the Family* 27, November 1965.

Streib, G. F.: "Older people in a family context." *In* R. A. Kalish (Ed.): *The Later Years: Social Applications of Gerontology*. Monterey, California: Brooks/Cole Publishing Company, 1977.

Stroup, A. L.: *Marriage and Family, A Developmental Approach*. New York: Appleton-Century-Crofts, 1966.

Suelzle, M.: "Women in labor." *Trans-action* 8:50–58, November 1970.

Super, D. E.: "Vocational adjustment: implementing a self-concept." *Occupations* 30:88–92, 1951.

Sussman, M. B.: "Relationships of adult children with their parents in the United States." *In* E. Shanas and G. F. Streib (Eds.): *Social Structure and the Family: Generational Relations*. Englewood Cliffs, New Jersey: Prentice-Hall, 1965.

Swenson, C. H.: The Love Scale. Copyright May 1968.

Sykes, G. M.: *Social Problems in America*. Glenview, Illinois: Scott, Foresman and Company, 1971.

Taylor, C.: "The nurse and cultural barriers." *In* D. Hymovich and M. Barnard (Eds.): *Family Health Care*. New York: McGraw-Hill Book Company, 1973.

Taylor, R.: *Welcome to the Middle Years*. Washington, D.C.: Acropolis Books, Ltd., 1976.

Terman, L. M.: *Psychological Factors in Marital Happiness*. New York: McGraw-Hill Book Company, 1938.

Thomas, L. E., Mela, R. L., Robbins, P. I., and Harvey, D. W.: "Corporate dropouts: a preliminary typology." *The Vocational Guidance Quarterly* 24(3):220–228, March 1976.

Thompson, W. E., and Streib, G. F.: "Meaningful activity in a family context." *In* J. Eshleman (Ed.): *Perspectives in Marriage and the Family.* Boston: Allyn and Bacon, 1969.

Thorndike, R. L.: "Growth of intelligence during adolescence." *Journal of Genetic Psychology* 72:11–15, 1948.

Tiedeman, D. V.: "The self-constructionist alternative to today's develop or wither career crisis at mid-life." Paper presented at Symposium on Career Development and Crises at Mid-life, Convention, American Personnel and Guidance Association, April 11–14, 1976.

Timiras, P. S.: *Developmental Physiology and Aging.* New York: Macmillan, 1972.

Tolstoy, L.: "The death of Ivan Ilych." *In* L. Tolstoy: *Death of Ivan Ilych and Other Stories.* New York: New American Library, 1960. (Originally published in 1886.)

Troll, L. E.: "The family of later life: a decade review." *Journal of Marriage and the Family* 33:263–290, 1971.

Troll, L. E.: *Early and Middle Adulthood.* Monterey, California: Brooks/Cole Publishing Company, 1975.

Udry, J. R.: *The Social Context of Marriage.* Philadelphia: J. B. Lippincott and Company, 1966.

Udry, J. R.: *The Social Context of Marriage* (3rd ed.). Philadelphia: J. B. Lippincott and Company, 1974.

Uhr, L. M.: *Personality Changes in Marriage.* Ph.D. dissertation, University of Michigan, 1957.

Ullmann, C. A.: "Preretirement planning: does it prevent postretirement shock?" *Personnel and Guidance Journal* 55(3):115–118, November 1976.

U.S. Bureau of the Census: *Marital Status and Living Arrangements.* March, 1972, Current Reports, Series P-20, No. 242. Washington, D.C.: U.S. Government Printing Office.

Verwoerdt, A.: "Psychiatric aspects of aging." *In* R. R. Boyd and C. G. Oakes (Eds.): *Foundations of Practical Gerontology.* Columbia, South Carolina: University of South Carolina Press, 1973.

Verzár, F.: "Intrinsic and extrinsic factors of molecular aging." *Experimental Gerontology* 3:69–75, 1968.

Vincent, E. L., and Martin, P. C.: *Human Psychological Development.* New York: Ronald Press, 1961.

Vriend, T. J.: "The case for women." *Vocational Guidance Quarterly* 25(4):329–331, June 1977.

Walters, P., Jr.: "Promiscuity in adolescence." *American Journal of Orthopsychiatry,* 35:670–675, 1965.

Weigand, E.: *Use of Time by Full-Time and Part-Time Homemakers in Relation to Home Management.* Ithaca, New York: Cornell University Agricultural Experiment Station, 1954.

Weisman, A. D.: *On Dying and Denying: A Psychiatric Study of Terminality.* New York: Behavioral Publications, 1972.

Welford, A. T.: *Skill and Age: An Experimental Approach.* New York: Oxford University Press, 1951.

Welford, A. T., and Birren, J. E. (Eds.): *Behavior, Aging, and the Nervous System.* Springfield, Illinois: Charles C Thomas, 1965.

White, R. W.: *Lives in Progress, A Study of the Natural Growth of Personality* (2nd ed.). New York: Holt, Rinehart and Winston, 1966.

Whitworth, R.: "Nursing home care in the United States." United States Senate Subcommittee on Long Term Care, Report of May 19, 1975.

Williamson, R. C.: *Marriage and Family Relations.* New York: John Wiley and Sons, 1966.

Winch, R. F.: *Mate Selection.* New York: Harper and Brothers, 1958.

Wollman, M., Johnson, D. A., and Bottoms, T. E.: "Meeting career needs in two-year institutions." *The Personnel and Guidance Journal* 53(9), May 1975.

Young, A. M.: "Going back to school at 35." *Monthly Labor Review* 96(10):39–42, October 1973.

Young, P.: "For a zestier life . . . R_x sex over sixty." *The National Observer,* pp. 1, 18, February 1, 1975.

Zubek, J. P., and Solberg, P. A.: *Human Development.* New York: McGraw-Hill Book Company, 1954.

1970 Census of Population, Detailed Characteristics, United States Summary. Washington, D. C.: U. S. Government Printing Office, 1973, Table 219.

NAME INDEX

Adams, B. N., 184, 191
Adelson, J., 126
Aiken, L. R., 164, 168, 186, 188, 202, 203, 218, 227
Albee, G. W., 144
Allport, G. W., 27–33, 34t, 35, 38, 43, 85
Atchley, R. C., 202, 203, 204, 208–210, 212, 213, 214
Ausubel, D. B., 102

Bahr, H. M., 198
Baltes, P. B., 18, 19, 105, 164
Bardwick, J. M., 98
Barfield, R. E., 206
Baron, R. A., 235
Barrett, J. H., 156
Bart, P. B., 128
Bartell, G. D., 62
Bayley, N., 20, 21
Belamarich, F., 230
Belbin, R. M., 93
Belcher, D., 32, 33
Bell, R. R., 38, 40, 41, 46, 47, 53, 60, 73
Bender, M., 144
Benson, L., 69
Berardo, F. M., 39, 108, 109, 136, 184, 186, 193, 198, 229
Bierman, E. L., 100
Birren, J. E., 2, 5, 5t, 11, 12, 13, 18, 20, 93, 104, 173
Bischof, L. J., 2, 4, 17, 18, 20, 108, 164, 203, 206
Bjorksten, J., 11
Blau, Z. S., 176, 198
Blood, R. O., 49, 67, 69, 70, 72, 74, 131, 193
Bloom, B., 18
Bloom, K. L., 169
Bock, R. W., 229
Bond, K., 202
Botwinick, J., 104, 108, 163, 164, 165
Bourestom, N. C., 190
Bowlby, J., 232
Brammer, L. M., 87
Brayshaw, A. J., 131
Brim, O. G., Jr., 109, 144
Brisbane, H. E., 85
Bromley, D. B., 6, 6t, 13
Brotman, H. B., 188
Brown, T. E., 144, 145, 149
Buhler, C., 12, 113–115, 122
Burchinal, L. G., 55, 56
Burg, A., 94
Burgess, E. W., 53, 186, 193, 197

Burr, W. R., 41, 61, 62, 63, 66, 74
Butler, R. N., 156, 158, 164, 175, 186, 189, 190, 191, 205, 221, 222
Byrne, D., 225

Canestrari, R. E., Jr., 104
Carp, F. M., 174, 203
Carter, H., 138, 197
Carter, H. D., 88, 90
Cavan, R. S., 193
Chaskes, J. B., 41
Christenson, C., 188
Clayton, P. J., 231
Clayton, R. R., 46, 47, 49, 69, 73, 77, 137, 138, 150
Comfort, A., 10, 158
Corso, J. F., 163
Cowgill, D. O., 12
Cox, F., 33, 36, 56
Cumming, E., 173, 174

D'Antonio, W. V., 34, 36, 39, 43
Davis, J. L., 80
Davis, K., 132
De Beauvoir, S. D., 220
DeCarlo, T. J., 16
Deese, J., 3
Denfield, D., 62
Dennis, W., 103
Deutscher, I., 131
DiCaprio, N. S., 13, 33, 34t, 117
Dodson, F., 74
Dreyer, P. H., 54
Driscoll, R. F., 152
Duberman, L., 36, 50, 51, 57, 60, 66, 73, 74, 139
Dullea, G., 153
Duvall, E. M., 184, 186, 192, 198
Dyer, E. D., 66

Elkind, D., 18, 20, 22
Entine, A. D., 152, 202, 206
Epstein, C., 220
Epstein, J., 137
Epstein, L. A., 202
Erikson, E. H., 6, 7t, 13, 28, 29, 29t, 35, 49, 111, 122, 127, 169, 170, 180, 220

249

SUBJECT INDEX

Page numbers in *italics* indicate illustrations; page numbers followed by a "t" indicate tabular material.